PRELUDE TO POWER

Jack Richard Censer

# PRELUDE TO POWER

## THE PARISIAN RADICAL PRESS
## 1789-1791

THE JOHNS HOPKINS UNIVERSITY PRESS
Baltimore and London

This book has been brought
to publication with the generous assistance of the
Andrew W. Mellon Foundation.

Manufactured in the United States of America

The Johns Hopkins University Press, Baltimore, Maryland 21218
The Johns Hopkins University Press Ltd., London

Library of Congress Catalog Card Number 76-7968
ISBN 0-8018-1816-8

Library of Congress Cataloging in Publication data
will be found on the last printed page of this book.

TO MY PARENTS

# Contents

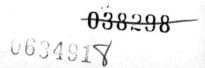

## FIGURES

## PLATES

## TABLES

# Preface

From 1789 to 1792 many revolutionary politicians, both aspiring and successful, published newspapers in order to disseminate their ideas and concerns. With little police interference and few professional standards to restrain these editors, they were able to concentrate in their newspapers upon those events, individuals, institutions, and ideas that interested them. Historians of the French press, from Hatin to Godechot, have therefore used these journals—correctly I believe—to examine the personalities of political journalists.

The press, however, can tell us much more. Studied collectively, the newspapers of the French Revolution illuminate the common concerns of a very important group of opinion makers and constitute the most important source of information for the public at that time. At the beginning of the Revolution, politicians shied away from structured parties, and journalists with established forums could dominate informed opinion. Public opinion was, likewise, dominated by the press. Lacking other regular sources of news and opinion, Frenchmen turned to newspapers. Those who could not read or could not afford to subscribe listened to street readers or joined reading societies, while their wealthier and better-educated neighbors purchased their own journals.

Although a complete survey of revolutionary newspapers could lead to important conclusions about publicists, politicians, and the public, no such survey could be undertaken by a single scholar. Over 2,000 revolutionary periodicals still exist, and any individual wishing to study the newspapers collectively must be content to examine a subgroup. Personal and academic interests dictated my choice of the Parisian radical press,

1789–91. These particular journalists, embattled outcasts, intrigued me. Inspired by the new revolutionary freedoms, they expressed themselves as they wished, although they were continually, if ineffectually, harassed by the local authorities. On the other hand, I was discouraged from studying provincial journalists because, generally, they were too diffuse geographically or politically to constitute a coherent group. The provincial journalists were also less interesting because so much of their material was borrowed unchanged from Parisian newspapers. Furthermore, I chose to conclude my monograph with the dissolution of the National Assembly in October 1791. With new elections, old enemies and friends of the radicals departed, and any examination of the radicals' interests would have to cope with this almost complete turnover of personnel. Consequently, logic, personal interests, and limitations of time and space demanded that this individual's study of a collective group of journalists be restricted to the Parisian radical press, 1789–91.

The message of the radical press, reflecting the interests of the journalists, focused primarily on the promulgation of an ideology. Events, individuals, and institutions were, of course, important, but they were reported in such a manner as to make them subordinate to ideas. A detailed content analysis makes it apparent that the events that were printed were those that symbolized the commitment of the radicals to their ideology. Indeed, the events that counted most for the radicals—those that accompanied and presumably caused some change in opinion—were a host of isolated occurrences of 1790. The insignificance of these events leads one to the conclusion that such occurrences were relatively unimportant in themselves and merely reflected the development of the ideological predispositions that sprang from the intellectual milieu of the publicists. Further, the radicals, in their descriptions of the men and institutions of the Revolution, drew heavily from the stereotypes provided by their ideology. In fact, the effect of such remarks was as much a reemphasis of their ideology as it was an accurate characterization of a certain group or individual.

Thus, this investigation should and does focus on the theoretical stance of the radicals. In brief, the radicals believed that a moral, egalitarian *peuple* had developed, who were opposed by a selfish and self-indulgent *aristocratie*. This *aristocratie* wished to preserve by any means, including violence, their old power and luxuries and to monopolize any new positions created by the Revolution.

To oppose the "aristocratic" menace to the social ideal of the *peuple*, the radicals suggested a literal adherence to popular sovereignty. The infallible *peuple*, already imbued with a morality of concern for their fellows, would ensure that government could do nothing contrary to their wish. Government would be left weak, with vigorous action reserved to the *peuple* themselves, who could be trusted never to abuse their power. Also, cultural life would be similarly organized, with the *peuple* fully able to express their opinions and with the *aristocratie* severely restricted. However, in the realm of economics, the radicals were more hesitant to redefine existing institutions. While they believed in equal fortunes, they could not bring themselves to advocate proposals (such as an end to free trade) that might actually destroy the fortunes of the *aristocratie*.

Thus, from 1789 to 1791, the Parisian radicals were obsessed with this ideology of popular sovereignty and paid far less attention to events, individuals, and institutions. This information makes a contribution in a number of areas. The radicals of 1789 to 1791 have been virtually neglected, and the description here should improve our understanding of their collective interests and concerns. For example, the primacy of ideology for these men belies the assertion that circumstances were the chief determinants of action in the Revolution. At least for these radicals, ideology governed throughout 1789, 1790, and 1791. And, insofar as events had any impact on the radicals, it was not those occurrences that have been customarily assigned importance (e.g., the flight to Varennes), but those of 1790, which coincided with radical shifts in opinion. Subsequent and more famous events came too late to have much impact on radical views.

Furthermore, the observations of this study reveal that Jacobin thought of 1792 and 1793 had definite origins dating from 1789. The similarity between radical and Robespierrist ideology proves that Jacobinism was not a hasty doctrine of the moment but the direct product of positions assumed since 1789. Those who would have Jacobinism a fragile construct, born of political necessity, must take note of the close relationship between these two ideologies.

It would be impossible to thank by name all those who assisted me directly or indirectly with this study. I have received both psychological support and intellectual sustenance from peers, parents, acquaintances, professors, and others. Particularly, the members of the Johns Hopkins History Seminar and the librarians of Cornell University have been helpful. Nonetheless, of all these people, a few have been especially gracious, and I wish to take this opportunity to mention them separately.

Jacques Godechot and W. J. Murray gave me much bibliographic assistance and provided reflective assessments of my work. Likewise, Orest Ranum and Steven Kaplan spent many long hours helping me shape my ideas into a usable pattern. Louis Galambos and Laura Morlock are responsible for any merit found in my content analysis of the radical press. Without their aid, I would have accumulated much data, but little of it would have conformed to the standards of statistical analysis.

William Harris labored through the manuscript repeatedly and gave needed encouragement. Thomas Kemnitz, Hugh Davis Graham, Jane Turner, and Matthew Crenson also read drafts of the book and offered many improvements, corrections, and useful suggestions. Henry Tom and Olga Kessel of The Johns Hopkins University Press gave needed encouragement and judicious prodding. Among my many colleagues at the College of Charleston who so patiently listened to my ideas were Peter McCandless, Kendra Faber, and Wendy Salinger. Also, I greatly appreciated the efforts of Helen Needham and Lisa Ferrett, who typed several drafts and painstakingly sought to render my handwriting legible. Financial assistance was provided by the College of Charleston Foundation.

Both my adviser Robert Forster and my colleague and close friend Lenard Berlanstein deserve special thanks. Both listened unfailingly to the original plans for this study; both read this manuscript; and, most important, both helped me cope with the personal, intellectual, and stylistic demands of historical research.

PRELUDE TO POWER

# 1
# Introduction:
# The Problem Defined

N LATE 1790 the political writer of the *Feuille du Jour* looked at revolutionary Paris and warned: "A king without a crown, an assembly whose power is not established, disobedient troops, finances hampered by lack of credit, a religious order without religious spirit, a monarchy without order, a thousand opinions which rage without any concern for the public—such is, in this moment our position."[1] Although this journalist overstated the disruptions plaguing Paris, his description accurately revealed that there was little calm in the city. Indeed, the years of the National Assembly (May 1789 to October 1791) were characterized by frenetic political activity in a number of spheres. The National Assembly, the courts, the municipality, the king —all exercised legitimate power. They did not, however, monopolize the political scene, for there were the clubs, the districts (later the sections),[2] the cafés, the impromptu lectures given throughout the city, and the press. Paris was flooded with—no, drowned in—newspapers between 1789 and 1791.[3] Within that political context, this book is a study of a particular group of these journals, linked by their political radicalism.

Before describing the aims of a study of the radical press, it is first requisite to define what is meant by radical or extreme left—two terms used interchangeably in this monograph. While the adjective *radical* has been variously employed in the course of European history—to describe republicans in 1830, anarchists in 1890, and communists in 1920—this term applies here only to that group of men who, in the revolutionary situation of 1789 to 1791, desired the most far-reaching changes in French government and society.[4] Surprisingly, there has been little systematic work done to define the locus of the political extreme in early revolutionary Paris. For example, when Professor Jacques Godechot wrote of "*la presse d'extrême-gauche,*" he failed to describe the general ideology or

1

persuasions of these journals.[5] Alphonse Aulard identified republicanism with radicalism, but he made no effort to substantiate this generalization.[6] Eric Thompson, in his book on popular sovereignty, defined "extreme-left" in the National Assembly, but he did not indicate whether the most radical representatives in the chamber accepted the extremist view of the Paris streets.[7] In fact, I would claim that the views of the leftist deputies were similar to, but hardly synonymous with, those of the most radical groups outside. For example, force and violence were frequently advocated in the street, while such talk was almost never heard in the National Assembly. In addition, Paris orators and publicists called for more drastic alterations in government, in the army, and in the courts than the delegates ever considered. Consequently, one must construct one's own working definition of "extreme" political behavior in the years from 1789 to 1791.

If there is no agreement about what a radical was, there is consensus among contemporaries and historians alike about who the radicals were and where they congregated. Certain cafés, certain districts, certain assemblymen, certain journalists were thought of, by both friend and foe, as centers for extreme politics. And from the first, it was the Cordelier district government, presided over by Georges Jacques Danton, that furnished the leadership and the direction for this movement.[8] Later, in May 1790, when Parisian local administration was reorganized into sections, the Cordelier district was divided and deactivated. To continue their drive, Danton and his followers founded the Cordelier Club to replace the dismantled district as the center for radical agitation. Later in 1790, the Cordeliers also gained power in the section created out of their past district and used this body, *la section du Théâtre Français*, as another base.

Moreover, the guiding principle of these Cordeliers in their district, their section, and their club was that the populace itself was the rightful possessor of sovereignty. While they accepted the necessity of rule by representatives, either in the National Assembly or in the municipality, they insisted upon their ultimate prerogative of self-government. From the inception of the district, there were continuous efforts to safeguard popular sovereignty against the encroachments of any representative body. In sending representatives to participate in the municipal government of Paris, the Cordeliers made it understood that they intended to control their own delegates and that they planned to continue to operate independently. For example, when the municipality failed to arrest Baron Besenval, an officer who led troops against the July Paris Revolution, the Cordeliers instructed their delegates to demand quick action and appealed by posters and leaflets to the other districts for support. The municipality objected that such imperious orders left little dignity to its members and that the districts had arrogated, without consultation, the right to placard announcements. Predictably, the Cordeliers adhered to their conception of popular sovereignty and replied that their ability to act required that they possess the right to communicate freely, and they defiantly added:

> It is incontestable that the different districts have the right to demand that their own representatives suggest to the Municipal Assembly to take up an object for consideration; this right is the same one which permits the Assembly to give orders to the Commander of the National Guard because, clearly, it is a different case when free citizens give instructions to their representatives than when a free citizen speaks to another individual.[9]

Since the Cordeliers envisioned themselves as the embodiment of popular sovereignty, they believed it to be their duty to challenge the local and national authorities whenever disagreement arose.

Nonetheless, the National Assembly, the National Guard, and the municipality began to work to limit the prerogatives of the citizenry. At first there had been no disagreement over popular sovereignty; in 1789 the members of the third estate had boldly held out against the other Orders, had renamed themselves the National Assembly, and had sustained what Abbé Sieyès had theorized, that the nation was sovereign.[10] Their position that sovereignty had, indeed, passed to the nation from the king was reconfirmed by the National Assembly in the Declaration of the Rights of Man and Citizen. The Assembly had declared in Article 3, "The principle of sovereignty rests essentially in the nation. No body and no individual may exercise authority which does not emanate from the nation expressly."[11] But no sooner had sovereignty theoretically passed to the nation than the nation's assembly, aided by the Paris Municipality and National Guard, began to regulate and actually to remove the exercise of this power by the populace. First came a distinction based on wealth between "active" and "passive" citizens. Those citizens whose taxes were less than three-days' average wages were disfranchised. The National Assembly also began to restrict political participation even by the "active" citizens. In mid-1790, the representatives reorganized the local Parisian political structure and reduced the autonomy of the districts. Through this action the Assembly intended to break apart old alliances and lessen the strength of the local Parisian politicians, whose power depended on the district machines.[12] The political activities of the populace were constrained further by Lafayette's National Guard, which worked by police action to make the city obedient to the legally constituted bodies. This effort, of course, was particularly directed at individuals who openly spoke or wrote in favor of spontaneous action or in opposition to passive acceptance of authority. From the point of view of the National Assembly, all of these efforts to reduce autonomous political strongholds were necessary. Paris was volatile, and the National Assembly's effectiveness and freedom were severely compromised by weakness of authority at its center.[13] J. M. Thompson would have us believe that this political struggle was reinforced by social differences between the wards and the government, and this hypothesis seems plausible.[14] Nevertheless, there is as yet little direct evidence to support this assertion.

Consequently, as the local and national delegates abandoned their belief in direct political participation, tension increased between the upstart Cordeliers and the authorities. Although content at first with polemics, the Cordeliers were increasingly willing to use force to assert their belief in popular sovereignty. By deploying their battalion of the National Guard, they prevented the municipality from enforcing "objectionable" laws within their district. In particular, they blocked all efforts at censorship. By mid-1790, the Cordeliers had expanded their opposition to include all of Paris. They organized numerous gatherings against the decisions of the National Assembly and the municipality. Justified by the belief that the acts of representatives were not final, the Cordeliers organized a demonstration against the National Assembly's suppression of an army mutiny at Nancy. Later, they assembled a crowd to prevent the National Guard from escorting the king to an Easter mass at Saint-Cloud. By the summer of 1791, their boldness and their appeal had grown so great that they were able to gather 10,000 people on the Champ de Mars to protest the king's reinstatement following his abortive escape from the capital.

Thus, it seems fair to define a radical as one who agreed with the National Assembly's initial commitment to popular sovereignty. When his representatives began to concentrate power in their own hands, this same radical persisted in his earlier habits and began to criticize those who deserted the defense of direct sovereignty. To be sure, this attitude toward popular sovereignty is not the sole characteristic of a radical; but one could hardly have been included at the Cordeliers without such an opinion. In fact, those who rigorously adhered to a belief in continuous participatory power for the nation were sure of an amiable welcome by radical circles. In chapters three, four, and five, other aspects of radical politics will be treated, but the remainder of this study is designed to add dimension and depth to this single, though crucial, characteristic of the members of the radical movement in Paris from 1789 to 1791.

A study of the journalists and the newspapers coming out of the radical movement yields much information about the extreme left. Radical newspapermen did not differ very much in attitudes and opinions from their fellow Cordeliers. These newspapermen generally saw themselves as politicians with a primary responsibility to influence the course of events and with little allegiance toward any abstract journalistic ethic. Consequently, the journalists shared the spirit, approach, practical politics, and perspective of the other radicals. Furthermore, for a number of reasons discussed below, the journals themselves were a faithful reflection of the hopes and plans of their authors.

The government, hampered by inadequate power and adhering to a policy that favored freedom of the press, did not and could not wish to contain the press. Prior to the beginning of the Estates-General, the few papers that had existed were prohibited from publishing any political news; but Mirabeau, claiming the right of a delegate to the Assembly to inform his constituents of the developments of events, was reluctantly permitted by the crown to publish his journal, *Etats-Généraux*. Although it was stipulated that Mirabeau and any others who might wish to communicate with their districts in this way must restrict themselves to a rigid account of the facts, the burgeoning number of papers, coupled with the general weakness of royal authority, made this dictum a dead letter. The National Assembly endeavored to fill the gap left by the royal administration. Their position on this issue was important enough to be included in the Declaration of the Rights of Man, wherein the delegates guaranteed complete freedom except where the law might declare abuses. Despite their legalization of the political press, the legislators wished to restrict journalists—especially radical ones—from slandering and vilifying opponents. In order to control the press, they enacted a series of libel laws. However, actions of the Parisian revolutionaries to protect the journalists usually prevented any prosecution and made even the decrees on libel ineffectual.[15]

Furthermore, the journalists wrote their honest opinions without a cynical desire to manipulate the public for their own ends. Indeed, Georges Lefebvre has posited that the revolutionaries were initially immune to hypocrisy.[16] This surge of ingenuousness carried idealism to new levels, and the radicals were, in general, more affected than anyone else. Regardless of their initial motives for joining the movement, they were captivated by this altruistic sentiment and, throughout this early period, were not at all jaundiced. They were, indeed, "true believers." Danton was a notable exception, as he had no sense of personal abnegation; but most others devoted themselves to the cause with no desire for personal gain. There is, of course, no direct proof of the radicals' sincerity, but their personal poverty, resistance to frequently offered bribes, and defiance of government suggest that they sought fulfillment in self-denial, not self-aggrandizement. Only later in the Revolution did the lure of power corrupt this honesty.

Additionally, the rudimentary technology of the press, which kept these individually owned papers rather small, contributed to the journalists' candor. Until 1815, the industrial revolution had caused no innovations in printing. Hand-operated wooden presses could produce only 3,000 sheets in a twenty-four-hour day. With these simple presses, a man with modest financial resources could afford to own or, at least, use a machine. Because a large amount of capital was not needed, the journalist could avoid associating himself with an organization that might restrict his self-expression.[17] Since the newspaperman was proprietor, he saw little reason to produce what was not of personal interest, and in revolutionary situations, what could concern one more than one's own opinons?

Finally, authors customarily expounded their own views without much commitment to the narration of impartial detail because their immediate ancestors, the pamphleteers, had written in such a fashion. Pamphlets had actually spawned the press, which emerged in 1789 as a result of the increased flow of news and an atmosphere of freedom.[18] Thus, for all these reasons, an investigation of these papers provides a clear insight into the mentality, both of the radical journalists and of the Cordeliers as a group.

More complete comprehension of the Parisian radicals will provide some answers to questions that have concerned historians. First, there is very little recent work on the political activity of the Parisians from 1789 to 1791. While a long bibliography could be compiled of the historical works in this area, most of these are old, consist largely of political narrative, and lack a social or psychological dimension.[19] Examples of the state of research on the early radicals are the two books available on the Cordelier Club. One is over eighty years old, the other over sixty, and both are primarily collections of the documents circulated by the Cordeliers.[20] There is George Rudé's work on radical activity from 1789 to 1791, but he leaps from *journée* to *journée* without describing the constant turbulence that was so important in the making of these grand days of the Revolution. Rudé tells us that the crowd, motivated by dearth, acted politically for the benefit of, and under the direction of, the middle-class leaders.[21] He fails, however, to explain how the economic demands of the *menu peuple* were converted into political ones. Perhaps the daily leadership given by the radicals provided the organization for this transformation. In any case, this study should begin to remedy the paucity of research on these early radicals.

In addition, an increased understanding of the extreme left should illuminate some aspects of the debate between Albert Soboul and Richard Cobb. Soboul's work on Year II describes various reasons for the failure of the *sans-culottes*.[22] Cobb has charged that Soboul's explanatory powers might be more usefully brought to bear on how the *sans-culottes* gained power in the first place. He claims that the strength of these *sectionnaires* was illusory and transitional at best.[23] An understanding of those radicals who tried, from 1789 to 1791, to empower the *menu peuple* should clarify our picture of these later *sans-culottes'* strengths and weaknesses.

Working on the other chronological end of this study, Robert Darnton has begun to chart the history of the radical revolutionaries prior to 1789. He has developed the notion that the most ardent after 1789 were found among the "grub-street" radicals in the 1780s. The members of Darnton's groups were united by their mutual rejection by the established intellectual community. Alienated and impoverished, they began to write political satire strongly tinged with pornographic allusions.[24] An analysis of the revolutionary production of some "grub-streeters" should confirm or qualify Darnton's findings. If there is little continuity between the writings of the prerevolutionary radical society and the adherents of Cordelier politics and policy, then the "grub-street" activities of the 1780s may represent only a temporary phenomenon rather than the formative influence Darnton suggests.

Because the Jacobins of 1792–93 were recruited in large part from the Cordeliers of the National Assembly period, one can also test Michael J. Sydenham's thesis that the differences between the so-called Girondins and the Jacobins were born out of pragmatic politics and lacked an ideological dimension.[25] A study in depth of the radicals from 1789 to 1791 should reveal whether Sydenham's description of the Jacobins of 1792–93 is accurate.

Moreover, while research into the press should tell us much about the journalists and their political allies, such historical effort goes beyond prosopography. I have argued that the radical papers were personal statements of the journalists. Yet the journals were more than that. Personal or not, the press as a whole was a significant determinant in how the public viewed the world. The written word was king in the early Revolution, and both the literate and the illiterate (who were accustomed to street readings) depended on it. If we know what an important segment of the press was saying, we can reasonably assume that at least part of the Parisian populace shared, and another larger part were influenced by, these views. Most important, one can begin to see one of the elements that entered into those considerations that sent many Parisians toward confrontation with the National Assembly and sent others toward a foreign sanctuary.[26]

Thus, the study of the press can reveal an essential element in the creation of mentalities. Unfortunately, most of the historians of the press have not approached the subject in a way that sheds light on this question. With a single exception,[27] the monographs on the Paris press have been limited either to a single newspaper or to a very short period of time.[28] By this approach, the historian can ascertain what a particular paper says, but he cannot hope to have a coherent view of the impact of the press as a whole. The inadequacy of this methodology is demonstrated by the treatment of the press in the most recent general text, *L'Histoire générale de la presse française*. This book combines all of the latest research in the field but must rely on studies of very limited scope. For the most part the author can only present individualized summaries of the format and contents of each of the important revolutionary newspapers, and he is unable to argue any generalized notion of the politics, rhetoric, or ideology of the whole press.[29] The direction here will be to show how a certain segment of the journals portrayed the Revolution, and, consequently, to move toward an understanding of how the press at large formed public mentality. The radical press is not the entire press, but it is a much larger segment of it than scholars have previously treated.

A collective study, moreover, leads to findings that are not usually available to the historian concerned with a single journal. With a close survey of a large number of papers, the common and the unique begin to separate. Rhetorical styles, particular issues, ideology take on new clarity and significance. What an author may have omitted is far more revealing if one can observe what was widely reported elsewhere. No doubt the individuality of each paper is lost to some degree in a collective study, but I contend that this is a small toll for the benefits to be derived.

In order to study the extreme-left press in Paris from 1789 to 1791, one must select periodicals whose positions conform to the definition of radical.[30] Regrettably, this is no easy task, for Paris, in the early Revolution, witnessed a spectacular expansion of the press. Indeed, there are today in French libraries more than 1,400 newspapers published in Paris from 1789 to 1799. Moreover, the bulk of the rapid growth in the number of newspapers occurred in Paris in the first two years of the Revolution. In the capital alone, under the regime of the National Assembly, there were 408 journals that established some periodicity. There were 107 other papers that were announced, perhaps published a single edition, and then closed operations. All these estimates are conservative ones, based solely on those journals that have been preserved. Assuredly, there were other newspapers, which, in the chaos of the Revolution, were not saved and have consequently been lost to the historian.[31]

Nevertheless, the papers that survived are sufficient to indicate an incredible explosion in newspaper publication. Of the 408 more substantial journals, 139 were dailies, 100 were published two or three times per week, 80 were weeklies, and 89 were produced less often than once per week. This last category of 89 actually contains two kinds of papers: established periodicals produced monthly or twice monthly and several weak journals, which were too poorly financed or organized to produce more than an occasional issue.

TABLE 1.1[32]
Parisian Newspapers from May 1789 to October 1791

| Duration (in months) | Number of Papers | Percentage of Total Number of Papers |
|---|---|---|
| Single issue | 107 | 21 |
| Less than 1 | 172 | 33 |
| 1–3 | 78 | 15 |
| 3–6 | 52 | 10 |
| 6–12 | 53 | 10 |
| 13–18 | 11 | 2 |
| 19–24 | 14 | 3 |
| Over 25 | 28 | 6 |
| Total | 515 | 100 |

It is true that the majority of these papers in the period from 1789 to 1791 enjoyed, at best, brief existence. Without including those 107 that appeared only a single time, 250 others perished within three months. Nonetheless, in Paris (a city of 600,000 people) there were still 52 papers that continued from four to six months, and 53 that lasted from seven to twelve months. Fifty-three other newspapers continued from at least one year to the entire twenty-nine-month period under consideration here.

To gain a more accurate understanding of the magnitude of the press explosion, one should check on a monthly basis the number of papers published in Paris. Figure 1.1 indicates by month how many papers were published in Paris and their frequency.

In general, the graph shows a steady increase in the number of papers published during 1789–91, and this corresponded to a steady proliferation of political groups and interests. Some nuances are, however, worthy of mention. The most rapid acceleration in newspaper production between 1789 and 1791 occurred after July 1789 and was, no doubt, the result of the increased politicization and freedom issuing from Bastille Day. The second sharp rise, during the first half of 1791, was, most probably, caused by the growing political activity in Paris. By early 1791, the differences between the revolutionaries and the king were explicit and hotly contested, and the increase in journals reflected both a rising popular interest in daily news and national politics and a growing number of people who wanted to publicize their own opinions. Finally, the relative decline of the press in the last three months of the National Assembly was surely related to the repression of various journals, of both pro- and counter-revolutionary persuasions, following the massacre at the Champ de Mars in July 1791. The authorities shut down some newspapers, while fear of repression made publishing unappealing for others. The freedom that all journalists had enjoyed was beginning to diminish.

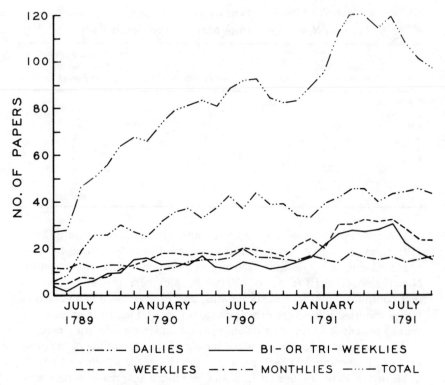

FIGURE 1.1.   Papers Published in Paris, 1789–91 (By Months)

SOURCE: See note 32 for a discussion of the sources of this graph.

NOTE: In order not to overstate the Parisian press explosion, I have not included in this graph those 107 journals published only once.

Probably contributing further to this decrease was a decline in public interest in the National Assembly as its affairs came to a close. Also, some journalists, who had been elected to the incoming Legislative Assembly, quit writing articles. But the most important fact indicated in figure 1.1 is the extraordinary number of papers available to Parisians.

It is difficult to imagine how 600,000 Parisians could have supported all these newspapers. Available, in the average month, were some 33 dailies, 12 papers published twice or three times each week, 19 weeklies, and 14 produced over longer intervals.[32] In mid-1791, this effusion reached a peak with the printing of 45 dailies, 27 bi- or tri-weeklies, 31 weeklies, and 17 papers of more sporadic production—120 journals in all. Even London, which was much larger than Paris (over 1,000,000 inhabitants in 1790) and which was noted for the size and tradition of its political press, had only 22 periodicals in publication in 1790.[33] What a welter of information besieged the Parisians and now besieges the historian!

To identify journals that supported the Cordeliers, one must sample from this enormous press. For two reasons, I reviewed only those papers that lasted longer than one year: one, this technique reduces the number of papers to be considered from 408 to 53; two, and most important, because these papers lasted longer, they are more amenable to analysis. It is obviously easier to discover subtle changes in perspective over a long period of time rather than a short one. Also, for the most part, those papers that endured longer have left the most information about themselves as newspapers. Where they were printed, who the editors were, and other essential data became public information over time. However, choosing a sample in this way leaves out a large number of papers and journalists and makes conclusions about the whole press more tentative. It is difficult to see, at least within one political tendency, how the points of view in those papers that failed or were disbanded would differ from those that endured. Perhaps those that lasted were blessed with a certain style, verve, or vigor that made their work sell, while others were not. Perhaps those that survived for a long period were supported by a source of independent wealth, which, as we shall see, was sometimes the case. But, perhaps too, those that lasted accurately judged the political temperament of a certain market for their journals. But among the radicals at least, the reporting in the long-lived journals probably did not differ significantly from that in the poorly established papers. The voluntary commitment of both the successful and the unsuccessful publicists to Cordelier beliefs and politics should ensure a general conformity in the content of their newspapers.

In order to select the papers for my sample, I carefully scrutinized all fifty-three papers lasting more than a year. I checked each journal for its treatment of radical interests and for its editors' membership in, or attendance at, the Cordeliers. Of the papers published from 1789 to 1791, none of those that lasted from thirteen to eighteen months or longer than two years could be classified as radical. There appeared, however, six radical journals that published, in the period in question, from eighteen to twenty-four months. These papers were the *Journal Universel,* the *Orateur du Peuple,* the *Mercure National,* the *Révolutions de France et de Brabant,* the *Révolutions de Paris,* and the *Ami du Peuple.*[34] The exact duration of their existence is indicated in figure 1.2. These journals and their journalists were linked both by a commitment to practical Cordelier politics and by a devotion to the Cordelier ideal of popular sovereignty. Surely they looked for allies beyond the Cordelier camp, but all expressed their admiration for Danton and his followers and defended that cause whenever necessary. All subscribed to a rigorous notion of popular

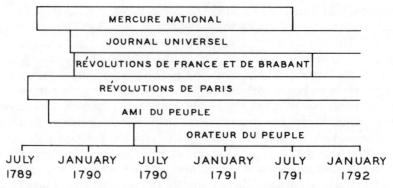

FIGURE 1.2.   Duration of Six Radical Newspapers, 1789–92

sovereignty and sought to defend it even against the prestigious National Assembly.

In addition, there can be no doubt that these six papers and their editors consciously recognized a common bond of interest. Although they often enlisted others in their behalf, they primarily relied on each other. Their calls for mutual aid are too numerous to cite here.[35] They must also have had frequent personal encounters at the Cordelier Club. Contemporaries likewise recognized the common cause of the journals, as this letter written to the *Ami du Peuple* attests:

> Explain to me then, my dear Marat, author of *Ami du Peuple* why Prud'homme editor of the *Révolutions de Paris,* Camille writer for the *Révolutions de France et de Brabant,* Audouin journalist for the *Journal Universel,* the *Mercure National,* and other papers do not give the greatest publicity to the violent attack that you have just made on the leader of the municipality, Bailly, and on the head of the Paris National Guard, Lafayette, these cowardly enemies of the Revolution. I must make an exception in favor of the *Orateur du Peuple* who has seconded you with all his force. . . . I desire that all the patriotic writers not neglect this occasion to aid the nation in revealing the turpitudes of its mortal enemies.[36]

Here Jean-Paul Marat's correspondent clearly envisioned a group of patriotic writers that he expected would work together on political issues. Finally, this is not to say that the radical journalists always selected the same allies or that they always agreed among themselves. But they were clearly associated by ideology, by political adherence to the Cordeliers, and by contemporary recognition of their commonality, and this justifies their consideration as a subject of this study.

In the following chapters, I shall endeavor to present the political positions and journalistic techniques of these six papers and to suggest the possible impact of these publications. I shall first describe in greater depth the individuals and the organizations that operated these journals.

# 2
# The Papers
# and the Journalists

EFORE INVESTIGATING the radical press as a whole, it is necessary to deal with the individuality of each journal. Biographies of the major contributors to each paper and summaries of the history of each journal provide a necessary background to an understanding of the entire group. Ideally, it would be useful to discuss the organization for financing and printing each paper, the format of each paper, and the special events that influenced the history of each paper. Unfortunately, not much information exists about the supporting fiscal structure of the periodicals. If any business records were kept, they have not survived, and investigations of the archives of Paris have produced very little. Consequently, for this information, the historian is dependent on contemporary observations and on the internal evidence to be found in the journals. With these goals and reservations in mind, what follows is a brief historical survey of each newspaper. Although the journalists shared a commitment to Cordelier ideology and politics, they differed greatly in the virulence of their charges; and for the sake of convenience, the six papers are arranged roughly from the mildest to the most vitriolic.

## MERCURE NATIONAL

The journal that other historians have labeled the *Mercure National* actually had a succession of titles that varied according to the whims of the editors and because of several mergers.[1] Originally called the *Journal d'Etat et du Citoyen*, the newspaper was initially issued on August 13, 1789, and was published every Thursday. It was composed of sixteen pages, whose dimensions were 4¾ by 8 inches. In October, because of popular demand for current news, the editors added a Sunday issue, but they reduced each issue to eight pages.[2] The price for subscribers was two livres, eight sous per month in Paris, and three livres in the provinces. It is not certain whether single issues of this journal could be purchased, as there is no reference to such a possibility. The editors obviously felt that there was a large and widespread market for their paper, for they contracted with seventeen distributors, two of which were located as far away as Switzerland and England.[3]

The *Journal d'Etat et du Citoyen* was printed in the establishment of N. H. Nyon, whose shop was located on the Left Bank, within the confines of the Cordelier district. The layout of the paper was neat and the spelling accurate—no small feat in 1789. While many articles had headlines, others were separated only by a bold line. Most articles were based on political speeches, and the debates of the National Assembly were treated in a separate, regular feature. These reports were punctuated, and sometimes dominated, by the editorial comment of Mademoiselle Louise Félicité Guinement de Kéralio, who was probably assisted in her efforts by her father, Louis Guinement de Kéralio. Other sections, which centered on foreign affairs and literary publications, were gradually added, and partisan comment did increase; but the original organization, which emphasized reporting over comment and impartiality over passion, was maintained. This emphasis on fact was amenable to the editors, who, while radical, wished more than most Cordeliers to avoid encouraging divisiveness.

Louise de Kéralio was the primary editor of this journal. Nothing is known of her financial relationship with Nyon or the amount of assistance she received from her father, but her central role is accepted.[4] Born on August 25, 1758, she received no formal schooling but was well educated by her father. Prior to the Revolution, she had already translated a number of books and had written a biography of Queen Elizabeth of England.[5] Detailed information is lacking, but it seems likely that her father was a minor noble. He was a chevalier de Saint-Louis and a professor of tactics in the Parisian *école militaire*. Like his daughter, Kéralio was interested in intellectual affairs, and he wrote on natural history. When the Revolution arrived, he had some reservations about the accompanying random violence. Nonetheless, he generally approved of the Revolution; he became a National Guard commander, later joined the army, and in December 1793 died on the northern frontier in defense of the Republic.[6]

In late December of 1789, the Kéralios changed the name and the organization of their periodical. The biweekly *Journal d'Etat et du Citoyen* became the weekly *Mercure National ou Journal d'Etat et du Citoyen*. The sixteen pages per week expanded to seventy-two (with slightly larger print size), and Nyon was replaced by L. Potier de Lille. The new price is unknown. At the same time, new collaborators, principally Nicolas-Jean Hugou de Bassville, Jean-Louis Carra, and François Robert were added to the staff.[7] Probably the arrival of the latter was responsible for the unexplained change in the periodical. Robert, born in 1763 in Belgium to a family in commerce, was well educated in an atmosphere where both Jansenist nonconformism and Enlightenment ideas were prevalent. He became an *avocat* at Givet in France and was very active in the early part of the Revolution. Sent to Paris to report on a local fraud in August 1789, Robert sensed that his greatest opportunities for success would be in the capital. He decided to remain in Paris and, purely by coincidence, moved into the same building as the Kéralios. Romantic and political bonds grew between the new tenant and Louise, and the *Journal d'Etat et du Citoyen* was recast, with Robert a major contributor. (In 1791, the romance would culminate in marriage.) In addition to his journalistic efforts, Robert played an active role in the Cordeliers and tried, through the tutelage of his club, to unify the popular societies of Paris. In July 1791, Robert was instrumental in organizing the protest at the Champ de Mars. With the temporary collapse of the popular societies and the Cordeliers after this debacle of July 1791, Robert negotiated with Jacques Pierre Brissot in the Legislative Assembly for an ambassadorial sinecure. In 1792, a political revival by the Cordeliers and rejection by Brissot sent Robert hurrying to Danton's side. Robert cooperated with the Dantonists in the ouster of the Girondins and allied himself closely with them, but he managed to escape their later fate. Instead of climbing the scaffold, he fell into political obscurity. He returned to private life, where he became a successful merchant and died in 1823 in Belgium.[8]

Another newcomer was Jean-Louis Carra. He authored only a few articles for the Kéralio paper, since he also worked with Louis-Sebastien Mercier on the *Annales Patriotiques*. Born in what is now known as the department of Ain in March 1742 and educated by the Jesuits, Carra had had a varied career, ranging from an illustrious, if brief, association with the Encyclopedists to a two-year prison term. In 1789 Carra was financially bankrupt, ideologically opposed to the Old Regime, and eager to embrace revolutionary ideas. He joined the Jacobin Club and participated actively in its politics. Also, he served in the Jacobin government and became influential in the formulation of foreign policy. Despite this dedication to the Jacobins, he had earlier accepted a post in a Girondin administration; Robespierre and Marat, distrusting his connections, had him executed in October 1793.[9]

Hugou de Bassville was only an occasional contributor to the *Mercure National*, and his other political activities in 1790 are still unknown. He must have had "connections" in the Old Regime, for he had become an abbot with a teaching position in Paris. In general, his life remains hidden in obscurity until 1792, when the Convention appointed him ambassador to Rome. There, in January 1793, he incited a riot by wearing the patriotic cockade and was killed in the crush.[10]

The Kéralios, Robert, Carra, and Hugou de Bassville continued publication of the *Mercure National ou Journal d'Etat et du Citoyen* until early September 1790, when, for no announced reason, they merged with another journal, *Révolutions de l'Europe*, edited by Alexandre Tournon. For two weeks, the paper was called *Révolutions de l'Europe et Mercure National Réunis*. By mid-September the dominance of Robert and the Kéralios was assured, and the paper was renamed *Mercure National et Révolutions de l'Europe*.[11] Its twice-weekly issues, now thirty-two pages long, carried the familiar features and editorialized reports. No price was listed. There was a succession of printers, whose work shows a sharp deterioration in quality from that of their predecessors. The occasional articles of Carra disappeared entirely, and Tournon, the new collaborator, contributed some news stories and editorials.[12]

Born in Arras in 1760, Tournon had come to Paris at a tender age. All that is known of his prerevolutionary activities is that he wrote books for the instruction of children. He was engaged in the early publication of the *Révolutions de Paris*, but in a squabble with the publisher, he quit and founded the journal later absorbed by the *Mercure National*. Tournon associated closely with Danton and in 1794 was executed with the other members of this political faction.[13]

The coalition with Tournon and Hugou de Bassville survived only until March 1791, when the newly wedded Roberts dissolved the moribund partnership,[14] and combined with another journalist, Pierre Lebrun-Tondu. Changes included a new printer, Lefort and Company, a slightly larger page (5 by 8 inches), and a listed price, approximately five livres per month. The paper was now entitled *Mercure National ou Journal Politique de l'Europe*, and a sixteen-page edition came out daily. It had minute type, comparable in size to that employed in modern classified advertisements. The Roberts did most of the writing,[15] and although Lebrun contributed some articles on foreign affairs, his role was primarily financial.

Born at Noyon in 1763, Lebrun received most of his education at Louis-le-Grand, where he lived on a scholarship provided by the king. Upon graduation, he entered the church as an abbot, but tiring of a sedentary existence, joined the army. Following this effort at an adventurous army career, Lebrun emigrated to Belgium, where he established a successful journal that specialized in foreign affairs. In 1790 he closed down his paper and gravitated to Paris, where he eventually joined the Roberts in March 1791. The three operated their periodical together until

July 5, 1791, when the partnership dissolved because Robert's financial resources were completely exhausted and the incoming revenue proved insufficient.[16] Lebrun established a new paper, but his journal differed politically with the *Mercure National* and represented a sharp break with that journal. Lebrun moved away from the political views of the Corde-liers and finally associated himself with the Girondins, whose fate he shared at the guillotine in December 1793.[17]

There are some gaps in our knowledge of the *Mercure National*—little is known of the financial backing of the paper, for example, but Robert's lack of funds in 1791 and the frequent mergers point to the editors themselves as important sources of money. These maneuvers also suggest fiscal weakness, and one suspects that the *Mercure National* did not have a great circulation. It is evident, however, that the *Mercure* was well printed and elegantly written, by contemporary standards. Further, the tone of criticism, although not the ideas themselves, was subdued. The polish and restraint of the *Mercure National* possibly was related to the relatively refined backgrounds of its journalists. Insofar as we know, they were generally individuals who, raised in fairly stable families and well versed in the literature of the Enlightenment, embraced the Revolution, not because of previous bitter defeats, but because of their intellectual predispositions and a certain degree of calculation. They lacked the impatience, the fervor, and the militancy of the frustrated. They sup-ported the Revolution with some restraint, could compromise more easily, and, indeed, were not as strident as their fellows.

## *JOURNAL UNIVERSEL*

The longest-lived of the six papers discussed here was the *Journal Universel*. Begun on November 23, 1789, it was published daily, without exception, up to 30 Germinal of the Year III. Two abortive resumptions carried the paper to 14 Prairial of the same year and to a total run of 1,993 issues.[18] Each day with exceptional regularity for a revolutionary journal, Pierre-Jean Audouin, apparently working alone, turned out this eight-page periodical. The print was large and the pages small (5 by 8¼ inches). Nonetheless, the consistency of production is the astonishing characteris-tic here. In mid-1790 Audouin had the size of print and the margins sharply reduced, and he practically doubled his production of words. In all five and one-half years of publication, he used only two printers, Veuve Herissant, whose shop was located on Rue Notre-Dame, and D. J. Gelé on the Rue du Fouare. Audouin maintained his own office on the Rue du Petit-Bourbon, near St. Sulpice. Herissant's establishment was on the Île-de-la-Cité, but the other two locations were very near the Cordelier's meeting place. The newspaper was marketed from Audouin's own office and from various bookshops, at the price of nine livres per quarter in Paris and for slightly more in the provinces. Again, it seems that single issues were not available.

Initially, Audouin planned the *Journal Universel* to be a series of featured sections that would contain new reports every day. He concentrated on news from the National Assembly, the districts, the municipality, the provinces, and foreign countries, with a miscellaneous section to include letters, the arts, and other subjects. These features were well defined by a bold heading, and they were anticipated by headlines grouped together on the first page. Over time, this organization broke down. Only the National Assembly report remained intact, while other interests were no longer covered systematically. The format changed as well, with many news items contained in a single paragraph or separated only by an extended hyphen.

Audouin's prose was, to say the least, straightforward, simplistic, and dull.[19] One wonders how the *Journal Universel* enjoyed such a long existence. Most of the articles were a recitation of the facts, with editorial comment injected at odd and unpredictable intervals. Audouin gave extended opinions in relatively few cases, and he, like the writers of the *Mercure National*, stated his views in a subdued tone. His opinions were those of the Cordeliers, but he lacked passion. He leveled the same charges against Lafayette as his fellow radicals did, but he did so with a respectful, even apologetic tone. Permeating the *Journal Universel* was a desire to support every move of the Cordeliers, yet without admitting the drastic differences between the radicals and their opposition. His articles exhibited a certain tolerance for the deficiencies of Cordelier foes; in fact, Audouin took public pride in his temperance.[20]

Audouin's background does not explain his moderation, although it gives good clues to his motivations for supporting the radical movement. He was born in Paris to parents of modest circumstances on December 24, 1764, and nothing is known of his prerevolutionary life except the following police report, discovered by Robert Darnton: "Audouin: calls himself a lawyer, writes *nouvelles à la main*, peddler of forbidden books; he is connected with Prudhomme, Manuel, and other disreputable authors and bookpeddlers. He does all kinds of work; he will be a spy when one wants."[21] In short, Audouin fits clearly into Darnton's "grubstreet" society, and the Revolution must have appeared as a golden opportunity to him. He began the *Journal Universel*, was active in the National Guard, and was popular enough in Paris to be asked by the "conquerors of the Bastille" to become an honorary member of their prestigious group.[22] He continued to agitate with the Paris radicals throughout 1791 and 1792, and he was important in organizing the Commune's efforts on August 10. Although he abandoned some of the moderation of his journal in this period, he was hardly the most virulent of the journalists. His political activities were rewarded in September 1792, when he was elected to the Convention. The customary balance in his positions—that is, radical notions coupled with calm rhetoric—served him well at this time. He was active in Jacobin affairs and did not run afoul of Robespierre; and he was also sufficiently subdued to survive the Thermidorian Reaction. This devotion to his principles without abuse for his opponents characterized Audouin and brought him through both the Terror and the Thermidorian Reaction to a seat in the Council of Five Hundred. Under the Directory, he continued to maintain balance, condemning royalism while favoring some measure of amnesty for *émigrés*. His term in the council expired in May 1798, but he continued to serve in a number of government posts. Under Napoleon, Audouin's opportunities were severely restricted, and in 1808 he died in obscurity in Bayonne.[23]

It is difficult to explain, but not to describe, Audouin's approach. He always backed the radicals, but he avoided inflammatory attacks on their enemies. His position of minimizing differences could hardly be called opportunistic. While his caution saved his head in Thermidor, it also cost him his opportunity for an important share of political power. As a final and tangential note, the circulation for his journal must have been substantial, since Audouin, without personal wealth, was able to publish continuously for over four years.

## *RÉVOLUTIONS DE FRANCE ET DE BRABANT*

Sold in a gray folder with a print affixed to the outside, the *Révolutions de France et de Brabant* was published weekly and customarily contained 48 pages (4½ by 7⅞ inches) of fairly large print. After the collapse of the revolution in Brabant, the title was abbreviated to *Révolutions de France*. The periodical also had another unwieldy and seldom-used title, *Révolutions de France et des royaumes qui, demandant une Assemblée Nationale et aborant la cocarde, meritront une place dans les fastes de la liberté*. Its price per quarter was six livres, fifteen sous, in Paris and seven livres in the provinces. Published from November 28, 1789, to July 25, 1791, the journal had a succession of printers. Evidently, these printers played a far more significant role here than in other radical newspapers. For example, the second printer, Garnery, believed the paper to be rightfully his possession, as he independently continued to publish the paper when Lucie-Camille-Simplice Desmoulins, the original journalist, temporarily put down the pen. The importance of the printers in producing the *Révolutions de France et de Brabant* is further demonstrated by the existence of a contract between Desmoulins and Jean-Jacques Laffrey, the successor to Garnery. In this contract, Laffrey promised Desmoulins and his new (and short-term) collaborator, Stanislas Fréron, also editor of the *Orateur du Peuple*, 11,000 livres annually to write the journal.[24] This arrangement, where the printer took the risks and guaranteed the journalists a very substantial income, was undoubtedly based on Desmoulin's popularity, his vivid prose, and his newspaper's high circulation, estimated at 3,000 copies per week.[25]

The printers, for their part, did a creditable job. The *Révolutions de France et de Brabant* came out regularly, had few technical errors, a uniform print size, and even a cumulative table of contents. Articles were clearly separated, although there were no headlines. The journal originally had three sections, one on France, one on Brabant and other nations in revolution, and a miscellaneous section for reviews, letters to the editor, and the like. However, these sections were soon abandoned, and there was no logical order to the articles. This disorganization among topics also spread to individual articles. These deficiencies were not the fault of the printers, but were caused by Desmoulins's own lack of focus. To be sure, he gave the news, but these reports served only as a springboard for personal reflections. He often wrote long articles, permitting his imagination to wander from topic to topic. Yet in Desmoulins's hands, this uncertain direction and irregular format became a strength, not a weakness. His imagination could not be bound by the typical journalistic structure and format. Desmoulins employed sarcasm, irony, analogies, and classical references—all to great effect. There is in these sheets an airy, light, enjoyable flavor laced with bitter humor that proved as devastating to opponents as the serious critiques of Audouin and Robert, and even the shrill warnings of Fréron and Marat. In short, the *Révolutions de France et de Brabant* exhibited an irrepressible gaiety that characterizes this paper and distinguishes Desmoulins, its editor, from his contemporaries.[26]

Lucie-Camille-Simplice Desmoulins, born at Guise on March 2, 1760, was the son of a wealthy and influential officeholder in the bailliage court. From a very tender age to adulthood Camille Desmoulins evidenced two persistent and pronounced traits—a turbulent and troubled personality and a tendency to find solace in escapism. This latter tendency was nurtured by his education at Louis-le-Grand, where classical training and Enlightenment ideas fused to supply Desmoulins with an image of a better existence, of some future utopia. After leaving Louis-le-Grand in 1779, he qualified as an *avocat* at the *Parlement* of Paris. Unfortunately, he and other lawyers agreed that he was temperamentally and physically unsuited for such work. He was too impulsive and undirected for the legal profession and he stuttered. Rejected and dejected, he drifted aimlessly in the late 1780s and hoped for something new.

Desmoulins did not have too long to wait. The Revolution brought new opportunities. He rejoiced over the calling of the Estates-General, but it was in July 1789, that his own chance arrived. Indeed, it was Desmoulins who, speaking from a café table in the Palais-Royal, roused the crowds that surged through Paris from July twelfth through the fourteenth. Solidifying his reputation was the coincidental publication of his *La France Libre*, which assailed monarchs and monarchy. His popularity assured, Desmoulins had little difficulty in finding a printer willing to support his venture in journalism, *Les Révolutions de France et de Brabant.* In this periodical, Desmoulins allied himself with the political positions taken by the Cordeliers, who, more than any other group, sought the utopia of Desmoulins's dreams. While his attacks were tempered with humor, they were nonetheless incisive and equal in effect to the more sober prose of other editors. The queen, under personal attack by Desmoulins, thought him her most formidable enemy.[27] The authorities also did not think him humorous, and like others, Desmoulins was plagued by governmental hostility. Finally, in order to avoid the feared reaction following the massacre at the Champ de Mars, Desmoulins discontinued publishing his journal. Desmoulins had repeatedly complained of the rigors of newspaper work and even though public authorities failed to act, he decided to abandon the project entirely.[28]

The end of the *Révolutions de France et de Brabant* signaled the beginning of Desmoulins's decline. His lack of seriousness and his sardonic humor, which had made his prose so readable and so devastating, rendered him unacceptable for responsible positions in any of the revolutionary governments. Robespierre, who understood his old classmate and had occasionally protected him, thought Desmoulins a spoiled child and surely unfit to exercise authority. The ex-publicist did occupy some minor posts and was a member of the Convention, but he was assigned no significant duties on committees or on missions. His pen, however, could still give him access to power, and when, allied with the Dantonists, he began a new paper attacking the Terror, he posed a dangerous threat to the Jacobin government. Robespierre, despite earlier personal sympathies, saw only recklessness and treason in Desmoulins's appeals. He sent Desmoulins, along with the Dantonists, to the guillotine on April 5, 1794.[29] Unsuccessful and dissatisfied before the Revolution, Desmoulins had joined the ranks of the Cordeliers to achieve his ideals. He died without fulfilling his dreams.

## RÉVOLUTIONS DE PARIS

The *Révolutions de Paris* was assuredly the most widely read paper in Paris and throughout France. According to Camille Desmoulins, it had 200,000 subscribers. While this figure may have been exaggerated, the number of counterfeit editions, reports of clients in Corsica, and the envy and praise of other journalists suggest the great importance of the *Révolutions de Paris*.[30] That there was a high circulation is further supported by the financial success of the editor, Louis-Marie Prudhomme (1752-1830). Prior to the Revolution, he operated a small bindery and bookshop in Paris from which he distributed pamphlets propagating the most advanced political ideas. He suffered for his subversive publishing from much police harassment and served several brief terms in prison. When the Revolution erupted, he decided to publish a newspaper. Since his activities in the 1780s had not been lucrative, he had to contract with printers to publish his journal, but after barely five months of production, he was able to afford his own press, which he established on the same square as the paternal Cordeliers. At first Prudhomme had been allied with the neighboring quarter, St.-Augustine, but his move brought him under the protection of the Cordeliers. Guillement ran the print shop, while Vitry marketed the journal. Prudhomme continued to publish into the Year II, when the Robespierrist strictures on freedom moved him to an early and voluntary retirement.[31]

The reasons for the success of the *Révolutions de Paris* are easy to discover. The paper was arranged in a pleasing way that must have increased circulation. Initially it was organized like a diary, and each article was a record of the events of one day in the past week. Gradually, however, regular features, such as the National Assembly reports, memoirs of the Bastille, and foreign dispatches, began to emerge. Although there was no indication of the contents from the cover, all the articles were clearly separated by bold lines and sported headlines that indicated the subject. Regularly distributed each week, the periodical was uniform in size (48 pages, 4½ by 7 inches) and evenly and accurately printed.[32] Also, attractive and interesting engravings occasionally enhanced this journal.

Adding still further to the popularity of Prudhomme's newspaper was its factual content. No journal gave as much information as the *Révolutions de Paris*. Léonard Gallois asserted that the paper, while it maintained revolutionary principles and achieved great popularity, provided accounts sufficiently detailed for historical research.[33] Moreover, this wide variety of news was reported in a style that must have added to the success of the journal. The reports, factually exhaustive, also included perceptive critiques. The arguments were soundly constructed and, while

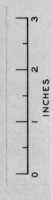

PLATE 1. *Révolutions de Paris*, September 26, 1789. Many journals used small type in order to include as much information as possible.

PLATE 2. *Révolutions de Paris*, October 10, 1789. The prints in this journal were produced irregularly and were found only occasionally by 1791.

designed to arouse support, did so by appealing to reason and conscience rather than by evoking crude societal prejudices and purely emotional impulses. The *Révolutions de Paris* attacked the same enemies as did the most virulent journals, but rather than ruthlessly denouncing or sarcastically assaulting an opponent, its journalists generally marshaled an overwhelming factual case, supported by what they considered to be universally accepted principles. The articles, though not always exciting, were not bland; these factually supported arguments had their own emotional force.

It is difficult to determine who actually composed the pages of the *Révolutions de Paris*, since all the writers were anonymous. But if Prudhomme did not personally write the articles, he certainly influenced their style. True, there were many collaborators—Tournon, Loustallot, Fabre d'Eglantine, Chaumette, and Maréchal among others—but all of these were transients. Some stayed for a few issues, some for a year, some a little longer, but all moved on, while the *Révolutions de Paris* remained the same. The similarity in the prose of the *Révolutions de Paris* in 1789 and in 1793 indicates that no matter who wrote, Prudhomme determined the parameters in opinion, content, and diction. Nonetheless, knowledge of these contributors is important in increasing our understanding of the people who were involved in the radical press.[34]

Prudhomme's initial collaborator in 1789 was the same Tournon who joined the Roberts in 1790. Tournon, however, severed his contacts after only a single issue.[35] Replacing him as the chief journalist was Elisée Loustallot, who remained with the paper through sixty-four issues until his untimely death in 1790. It was in this period that the *Révolutions de Paris* climbed out of obscurity, and perhaps it was this success that encouraged Prudhomme to sustain the perspective and prose of Loustallot. It is more likely that through his experience Prudhomme knew what he wanted and would never have considered any other political positions or journalistic style.

Loustallot was born in 1771 to a family of *avocats*, was educated at Bordeaux, and entered journalism before the Revolution after an abortive law career in Paris. He may have been associated with Prudhomme prior to the Revolution. Contemporaries perceived Loustallot as the spirit of the popular *Révolutions de Paris*, and his death was felt to be a sharp blow to the Revolutionary cause.[36] As I have noted, however, the journal maintained its verve under Prudhomme's guidance by his able selection of new collaborators.

Succeeding Loustallot were Maréchal, Chaumette, Fabre d'Eglantine, and possibly other lesser figures. Although Pierre-Sylvain Maréchal, the famous Babeuviste, was accepted as an *avocat* at the *Parlement* of Paris, he had chosen a literary life. Prior to the Revolution, he was best known for his outspoken atheism. A lifelong iconoclast, Maréchal naturally turned to the Cordeliers, who agreed most with his hostility to existing authority. Thus, before joining Prudhomme in 1790, he had begun to contribute to other radical journals. He wrote extensively in the *Révolutions de Paris* and he remained on the staff for at least a year and a half.[37]

Playing a lesser role in the publication of this journal was Anaxagoras Chaumette. He was born in 1763 at Nivers. Though intelligent, he was probably mischievous or politically rebellious, as he was expelled from school. He studied, and then indifferently practiced, medicine in his native town. He did not go to Paris until 1790, when he hastily abandoned his original goal of concentrating on medicine and became very involved in politics—apparently he had found in politics a *métier* worthy of strong commitment—and joined the *Révolutions de Paris* staff. Active with the Commune and the *sans-culottes* from 1792 through 1794, Chaumette was seen as a challenge to Robespierre's power and was executed in the Year II.[38]

Philippe Fabre d'Eglantine (1750–94) epitomized in most ways the members of "grub-street" society. Although he was a university professor for some time, he found this career unrewarding and turned to the theater. He acted, he wrote, he romanced—all with very little success. The Revolution was a new opportunity, and Aulard has claimed that Fabre d'Eglantine's *Le Philinte de Molière,* written in 1790, captured perfectly the political spirit of the Cordeliers. The play enjoyed an overwhelming success. Fabre d'Eglantine played a minor role in the production of the *Révolutions de Paris,* and he devoted his main efforts to supporting Danton. He was the latter's closest associate and, not surprisingly, died with him in 1794 on the guillotine.[39]

Indeed, the *Révolutions de Paris,* directed by Prudhomme to a political and financial triumph, was actually written by men who had no professional standing in 1789. They were intelligent, but, because of failure, ideological convictions, or lack of interest, they had made no mark in the liberal professions. With the exception of Chaumette, they had all, prior to the Revolution, turned to literature or journalism as an outlet for their considerable skills. Their revolutionary production contrasts the Old Regime with the revolutionary regime in an obvious way, as the latter opened opportunities unforeseen but a few months before.

## AMI DU PEUPLE

Of the journals and journalists under consideration here, the *Ami du Peuple* and its editor, Jean-Paul Marat, are probably the best known. Begun in relative anonymity, the *Ami du Peuple* achieved fame and notoriety during the Revolution. The *Ami du Peuple* started publication on September 2, 1789, under the name *Le Publiciste Parisien, Journal Politique, Libre et Impartial*, but by the sixth issue, the phrase *Ami du Peuple* was prefixed to the title. Contemporaries gradually came to know the paper solely by the added expression, *Ami du Peuple*. This paper was first printed by the same establishment that initially produced the *Journal Universel*. After a short period of working with the widow of Herissant and some experimentation with other printers, the editor, Jean-Paul Marat, indicated that he was assuming responsibility for the printing and established a shop called L'Imprimerie de Marat on the Rue de l'Ancienne Comédie,[40] a location very near the meeting place of both the Cordelier district and the club. However, at certain periods he used other Left Bank and Ile-de-la-Cité printers.[41] Marat also gained control of the marketing of his periodical. He originally had contracted with Dufour of the Cordelier district to sell and distribute his journal, but by the spring of 1790, Marat assumed that function himself. According to Marat, Dufour had been the recipient of three-fourths of the receipts, while Marat's share had been consumed by expenses.[42] Needless to say, Marat was anxious to end this situation. The income must have been substantial, since Marat charged the high price of twelve livres for a three-month subscription, and was able, without other means of support, to live adequately and to publish a journal until his assassination in the summer of 1793.

The *Ami du Peuple* was scheduled to be a daily journal of eight pages (5 by 8½ inches in size), but this schedule was not often fulfilled. Intermittently, there would appear two, four, or even eight extra pages. There were other periods when Marat's radical opinions brought him under attack and forced a temporary cancellation of the paper. There was, in fact, always a degree of uncertainty of production; in many weeks only six of the announced seven issues were produced. Such unreliability also characterized the printing of the paper. Spelling and grammatical errors were legion, the quality and even the color of the newsprint varied, and the size of the print changed between pages. Furthermore, although the front page contained a series of headlines, Marat was forced on several occasions to explain apologetically that there was no room for the corresponding article. In many instances, neither an article nor an apology appeared. This disorder was compounded because different topics were usually not separated, although occasionally thin lines were used to divide coverage. In sum, the subscriber to the *Ami du Peuple* would not have been at all surprised to find, delivered to his door, a sixteen-page journal, printed several days late, littered with mistakes, and published on pastel blue paper.

Despite its haphazard arrangement, the *Ami du Peuple* was written with a certain vigor that surpassed its competitors. Irony, wit, and devastating criticism filled each issue. There is, in these old pages, a flavor of sinister exaggeration that captivates the modern reader like the hyperbole of Edgar Allen Poe. Coexisting uneasily with Marat's constant vituperation were serious and perceptive critiques of individuals, institutions, and legislation of the day. Marat often hammered out complex refutations and proposals in the *Ami du Peuple*. In short, the prose was a mixture of vigorous writing and incisive criticism, and the latter usually capsized under the flood of enthusiasm. The aggressiveness of the *Ami du Peuple* made Marat the most assertive defender of the radical cause from 1789 to 1791. The reasons why he championed the Cordelier positions are not difficult to discover.

Jean-Paul Marat was born in Boudry, Neuchâtel (Switzerland) on May 24, 1743. He was raised in moderate circumstances; his father was both a language teacher and a cloth designer. Through his own efforts Marat was well-educated, and he attempted to climb the social ladder as best he could. His endeavors took him to England, where he received a medical degree that was of somewhat questionable value. Nonetheless, he developed a fairly successful practice in London. As an avocation, he began to write political tracts. While some historians have claimed that Marat had developed a revolutionary political philosophy during his stay in London, his American biographer, Louis Gottschalk, has insisted, I believe correctly, that Marat's political conceptions were diffuse before 1789. Some of Marat's ideas did presage the Revolution, while others were common values of the Old Regime.[43] For unknown reasons, Marat quit London for Paris in 1777 and took a position in the entourage of the Comte d'Artois. During this period he built a creditable reputation as a physician until his resignation in 1783.

The next six years were dominated by medical research and personal failure. The more work he did, the more recognition he received in salon society, and the more he was frustrated by the failure of his theories to be accepted by the *Académie des Sciences*. Marat had submitted his theories on electricity to the *Académie*, and a panel led by Voltaire had held them to be unsubstantiated. This frustration was exacerbated by Marat's own psychological make-up. He was acutely paranoid, and he imagined that those scientists who were skeptical of his work were really malicious schemers, and representatives of a sick society.[44] His rejection, personal disappointments, and the resulting fundamental distrust of Old Regime society, exemplified by the *Académie*, led Marat to the radicals. With the Revolution under way, this same paranoia exaggerated the image and dimensions of his new enemies, the *"aristocratie,"* and led him to oppose in the most extreme manner those who would challenge the validity of the radical position.[45]

Initially Marat had a minor role in the political history of the Revolution. He was voted an elector to choose national assemblymen from Paris and may have played some small part in the Paris Revolution of July 1789. But soon, the caustic attacks of the *Ami du Peuple* against the Châtelet (and ultimately against all public officials) won him the attention of both the extreme left and the Parisian authorities. His character assassinations caused the Paris Municipality to warn Marat that such ardor would not be tolerated. In January 1790, his continued assaults on public officials and institutions brought recriminations and legal action against him. The Cordeliers had also noticed Marat and offered him their protection. They were able to deter the National Guard troops sent by the municipality to apprehend Marat, and the journalist made good his escape from Paris, fleeing to London. Three months later he returned under the safeguard of the Cordeliers, and resumed his scurrilous attacks. The municipality and later the Legislative Assembly repeatedly tried to arrest Marat, but all attempts failed. Through the *Ami du Peuple*, Marat continued from 1790 to 1792 to assail all his enemies. Because of official hostility, he had to work clandestinely and had to restrict his political role to the publication of his journal. However, after August 10, with the Feuillants defeated and with the radicals greatly strengthened, Marat emerged from the confines of the Cordeliers to play a part in the Convention. He was elected as a delegate to the Convention, and there his characteristic diatribes inflamed the differences between his supporters, the Mountain, and his opposition, the Girondins. Marat was one of the leaders of the assault on the Girondins, and he did all he could to smear them as traitors. After the triumph of his party in May 1793, Marat maintained his pursuit of all those groups and factions whom he conceived to be counterrevolutionaries. His activities were, however, considerably reduced by an eruption of a chronic skin disease that was complicated by a lung disorder. By midsummer his illness had become so grave that he was forced to remain continuously immersed in water. Despite this affliction, he continued to pursue both real and imagined enemies through his journal. It was in his bathtub that Charlotte Corday found Marat and stabbed him to death on July 13, 1793.[46]

Marat's personal popularity and the long existence and many imitations of his newspaper attest to the popularity and circulation of the *Ami du Peuple*. Perhaps, the journal was successful because Marat's paranoia struck a corresponding chord in the French people. The terror and panic exemplified in the Great Fear reveal a sort of national susceptibility to this neurosis. Such speculation must go unsubstantiated here, but the triumphs of Marat, and the radicals as well may be partially founded on a widely experienced paranoia.

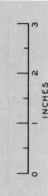

L'ORATEUR
DU PEUPLE;
PAR MARTEL.

Qu'aux accens de ma voix la France se réveille; Rois, soyez attentifs; peuples, prêtez l'oreille.

N°. XXXI.

*L'Orateur du Peuple aux juges du tribunal des Minimes, devant prononcer aujourd'hui dans la cause du brave Santerre contre Desmotiès et la Fayette.*

*Bataillons de jureurs commandés pour investir le tribunal.*

*Arrestations de citoyens dans le jardin de Luxembourg.*

*Décret qui condamne à être pendu tout traître à la patrie, ou prenant les armes contr'elle.*

*Nouvelles de Givet.*

Juges nommés par le peuple, voici le moment de justifier sa confiance, voici le mot...
Tome VI. Hh

( 248 )

l'heureuse découverte des moyens de combattre avec un succès assuré, la plus affligeante et la plus redoutable des maladies.

Il n'est point de pères et mères barbares et dénaturés au point de refuser aux gages innocens de leur tendresse, les secours que réclamoit depuis si long-tems l'humanité souffrante.

L'application de ces nouveaux moyens curatifs, fondés sur l'expérience, devant être à raison des circonstances particulières qui se rencontrent dans chaque individu rachitique, il est de toute nécessité que ce médecin soit préalablement bien informé de l'origine et des progrès de la maladie.

Les malades demeurans à Paris, sont priés de le consulter; ceux qui vivent éloignés de la capitale, doivent indispensablement lui faire parvenir un rapport exact et circonstancié de l'état passé et présent de leur maladie, et surtout ne pas lui laisser ignorer s'il a été question d'éruption répercutée.

On aura soin d'affranchir les lettres.

Sa demeure est rue des Moulins, n°. 10, butte S. Roch, au rez de-chaussée. On pourra l'aller consulter tous les matins, depuis 9 heures jusqu'à midi, & tous les soirs, depuis six heures jusqu'à neuf.

A PARIS, de l'Imprimerie Patriotique, cour du Commerce.

PLATE 3. *Orateur du Peuple*, 1791 (exact date not known). The print size of this journal was larger than that of the other radical papers.

## ORATEUR DU PEUPLE

Last of the six papers to begin production, the *Orateur du Peuple* was initially issued on May 22, 1790. The journal was planned to have a daily eight-page edition, whose dimensions were 4¼ by 7¼ inches, and whose cost was 36 livres annually. The print of the journal was large and uniform from page to page. Headlines, listed on the front, reliably announced the subjects within. But the different editions of the paper were not dated, and even in the text, dates were deliberately omitted. Further, like the *Ami du Peuple*, the *Orateur du Peuple* was peppered with spelling and grammatical errors; articles were not separated from each other except by an occasional new paragraph; and, finally, the paper was not published as regularly as announced.[47] In sum, the similarities with the *Ami du Peuple*, coupled with the lack of a date on each issue, made the *Orateur du Peuple* appear more as a hastily produced pamphlet than as a conscientiously published newspaper.

The content of the articles reinforces this impression that the *Orateur du Peuple* is more a pamphlet than a newspaper. There was comparatively little interest taken in the events of the day. To be sure, there was some analysis of specific actions, but the tendency was to harangue the public on a succession of general topics—the aristocrats, wars, patriots, and the like. Indeed, dominating this journal was a monotonous obsession with the schemes of the counterrevolutionaries and with the failure of the "patriots" to crush the opposition.

The tenor of these warnings contributes further to the impression that the *Orateur du Peuple* was much like a pamphlet. There were very few impartial accounts. Its journalist, Stanislas Fréron, knew little reserve, and his repeated denunciations were issued with extraordinary vigor and with a dramatic flair far removed from any mundane news reporting. Indeed, every event, regardless of its gravity, was greeted by Fréron with the same ferocious histrionic reaction. He assailed his enemies with a vengeance that today bores the reader by its constant repetition. But, during the early 1790s, Fréron's dramatic, if not very news-oriented, appeals were popular, as the long existence of the paper (May 1790 to November 1792) and his personal popularity clearly show.

Stanislas Fréron was born on the Left Bank of Paris in 1754. Of the men considered here, his background was the most prestigious and financially secure. His father, Elie Fréron, was the editor of the *Année Littéraire*, which for quite some time yielded a very substantial income. While the funds from his father's journal provided Fréron with a fine boyhood home and a good education (eight years at Louis-le-Grand), the paper was also the source of many problems. The *Année Littéraire* was objectionable to both *philosophes* and government alike, and these two groups found ample opportunity to attack, abuse, and even arrest the elder Fréron. The young boy, of course, sided with his father. After the death of Elie in 1780, Stanislas took over the journal and continued his struggle with the intellectual and governmental establishments. Embattled on all sides, he was even attacked by his stepmother for his editorial policy. Through court action, she eventually (in 1783) gained control of the paper by paying him only a small pension. All these problems were intensified for the young man by his unstable personality, which saw success as pure bliss and failure as final doom. Fréron, assaulted all his early life by influential segments of society and then stripped of his inheritance, fell into deep despair. Understandably, his misfortunes led him to a life of debauchery and idleness. The Revolution and the radical cause surely appeared as welcome opportunities for personal vindication over past enemies.

Fréron was an active participant in the storming of the Bastille, but street violence was not to be the preferred role of the past editor of the *Année Littéraire*. He wanted to return to journalism, but earlier he had agreed with his stepmother, in exchange for an increase in his pension, not to publish a competitive journal. At first, he was content with writing anonymous articles, but his penury and his desire to assert his own personal policy encouraged him to establish a new periodical. To avoid the penalties for violating a contract, Fréron searched for someone to be nominal head of the paper. Promising fame and money, Fréron persuaded an unwitting acquaintance, Marcel Enfantin, to pose as the editor and to deal with printers and clientele. At first there was difficulty in finding a printer, for the acid pen of Fréron was too dangerous or too objectionable for most. At wit's end, he enlisted his brother-in-law, Jean François La Poype, who successfully engaged a Monsieur Laurens, whose shop was a few blocks from the Cordeliers.[48] Fréron, once his popularity was ensured, abandoned all secrecy. He easily secured a printer and, like many other journalists, frequently changed from one to another. His longest agreement, between 1790 and 1791, was with Madame Colombe, who printed his journal along with the *Ami du Peuple* for about a year.[49]

The *Orateur du Peuple* soon attracted the attention of both friend and foe. Fréron was encouraged by Marat and came to regard the *Ami du Peuple* as his model. Also, he signed a contract with Camille Desmoulins to write one-half of the *Révolutions de France et de Brabant*.[50] Eventually, Fréron moved his residence to the *quartier* of the Cordeliers. Like his compatriots, Fréron disturbed the authorities in both the National Assembly and the municipality. His encounters with the law were too numerous to be cited here, but Fréron's troubled relationship with the government can be shown by his decision to flee Paris after the Champ de Mars incident. Experience had taught him that he would be a target for arrest. The anticipated repression never materialized, and Fréron briefly returned to his periodical before abandoning it to a friend, Labenette, at the beginning of the Legislative Assembly.

The political alliances established between 1789 and 1791 led Fréron to participate first in the insurrections of the summer of 1792, and, later, to assist as a member of the Convention in the implementation of the Terror. His role *en mission* was a particularly brutal one, and at Toulon he was responsible for a major massacre. These experiences and the execution of his close friends, Danton and Desmoulins, soured Fréron on Robespierre's government. Beginning with Robespierre, his disaffection spread to the entire Jacobin movement, and finally Fréron embraced, and then led, the reactionary *jeunesse dorée* in October 1795. His subsequent political career is difficult to trace, but during the Directory and after the turn of the century, he clearly became more moderate. As an agent of the Directory and an associate of the Bonapartes, he reversed his previous extremism and worked to reduce divisions in France. Nonetheless, this political turncoat paid dearly for his shifts in ideology. Fréron found himself abandoned by both old and new colleagues as he aged and his personal power waned. He died in disgrace and obscurity in Saint-Domingue in 1802.[51] Disgruntled and disconsolate before 1789, Fréron had enjoyed great success during the Revolution. The end must have been a bitter one.

Any conclusions about the general characteristics of the newspapers —their format, their financing, their content, their editors, and their rhetorical style—must at first glance stress their differences. Some of their characteristics may be reduced to tabular form and are summarized in table 2.1. From this table one can see that there was divergence in the formats of the journals. Also, some were dailies, others weeklies—the *Mercure National* existed at different times as a daily and as a weekly. Marat and Fréron were virulent in their attacks; Audouin and Robert wrote in a subdued manner. Kéralio was a minor noble and a career soldier; Carra spent time in jail. But these differences, though important, were not as significant as the similarities of the six newspapers and their journalists.

In appearance, the journals were not very different. They all had about the same dimensions, and all published approximately the same number of sheets—50 to 70—per week. Differences in print size were responsible for some minor variations in the quantity of news. While some of the papers had more separation between topics than others, these divisions were rudimentary. Headlines, columns, and tables of contents were sparingly and somewhat irregularly employed. Each issue was unlike the last in that regular feature articles were few. Finally, all these papers were

TABLE 2.1

A Profile of the Six Newspapers

| Principal Title | Frequency of Appearance, per Week | Cost per Mo. in Paris | Average Number of Pages per Week | Size of Pages, in Inches | General Rhetorical Tone | Principal Editors | Occupational Training | Occupation in 1785 |
|---|---|---|---|---|---|---|---|---|
| Journal d'Etat et du Citoyen | 1 (later 2) | 2 Livres 8 Sous | 16 | 4¾ × 8 | Restrained | Louise de Kéralio<br>Louis de Kéralio | Writer<br>Military | Writer<br>Professor |
| Mercure National ou Journal d'Etat et du Citoyen | 1 | Unknown | 72 | 4¾ × 8 | | Louise de Kéralio<br>Louis de Kéralio<br>François Robert<br>Jean-Louis Carra<br>Hugou de Bassville | Writer<br>Military<br>Lawyer<br>Writer<br>Abbot,<br>Teacher | Writer<br>Professor<br>Lawyer<br>Unknown<br>Abbot,<br>Teacher |
| Mercure National et Révolutions de l'Europe | 2 | Unknown | 64 | 4¾ × 8 | | Louise de Kéralio<br>Louis de Kéralio<br>François Robert<br>Hugou de Bassville<br>Alexandre Tournon | Writer<br>Military<br>Lawyer<br>Abbot,<br>Teacher<br>Writer | Writer<br>Professor<br>Lawyer<br>Abbot,<br>Teacher<br>Writer |
| Mercure National ou Journal Politique de l'Europe | 7 | 5 Livres | 102 | 5 × 8 | | Louise Kéralio Robert<br>François Robert<br>Pierre Lebrun-Tondu | Writer<br>Lawyer<br>Journalist | Writer<br>Lawyer<br>Journalist |
| Journal Universel | 7 | 3 Livres | 56 | 5 × 8¼ | Dull, straight-forward | Pierre-Jean Andouin | Unknown | Writer |
| Révolutions de France et de Brabant | 1 | 2 Livres 5 Sous | 48 | 4½ × 7⅞ | Spirited, assertive | Camille Desmoulins | Lawyer | Unemployed |
| Révolutions de Paris | 1 | 3 Livres | 48 (later 56) | 4½ × 7 | Reasoned, aggressive | Louis-Marie Prudhomme<br>Alexandre Tournon<br>Elisée Loustallot<br>Pierre-Sylvain Maréchal<br>Anaxagoras Chaumette<br>Fabre d'Eglantine | Unknown<br>Writer<br>Lawyer<br>Lawyer<br>Doctor<br>Professor | Bookdealer, printer<br>Writer<br>Journalist<br>Writer<br>Doctor<br>Playwright |
| Ami du Peuple | 7 | 4 Livres | 56 | 5 × 8½ | Vitriolic, powerful | Jean-Paul Marat | Doctor | Scientist |
| Orateur du Peuple | 7 | 3 Livres | 56 | 4¼ × 7¼ | Vitriolic, repetitive | Stanislas Fréron | Journalist | Unemployed |

expensive, about 36 livres per annum. This seemingly exorbitant price, about one-fifth of the yearly income of most artisans, is less significant when one considers that most of the audience were not home subscribers, but listeners at public readings, where many shared the expense.

Unfortunately, our knowledge of the financial structures of these journals is limited; but the available information indicates considerable variance among journals. Robert and his associates probably relied chiefly on their own fortunes; Desmoulins contracted with a printer. Nonetheless, commonly, efforts were made to establish regular financial and marketing arrangements. Journalists contracted for extended periods with the same printer; they seemed to have taken some measures to ensure effective marketing of their journals. Prudhomme probably purchased his own presses, not only to achieve maximum profits but also to have a reliable business organization. For the most part, these formal structures were crude; still they represented a remarkable improvement over those of the pamphleteers.

Further, all the journalists reported news; all editorialized extravagantly by modern standards. All could write dispassionate prose; they were all capable of using emotion to attack opponents and lionize allies. The balance between news and opinion, between calm and bombast, varied from paper to paper; but none lacked any of these qualities.

Finally, the journalists shared some important characteristics in their backgrounds. All were well-educated and most were members of some liberal profession. Moreover, there was nothing in their pasts that would have encouraged them to act against the Revolution of 1789. None had wealth or position that was seriously jeopardized by the liquidation of the Old Regime. Further, they had been influenced by Enlightenment thought and wished to transform their hopes for human improvement into reality. Many had found the Revolution attractive because, like the men of "grub-street," they had felt either real or imagined rejection by the establishment. They were anxious to vindicate themselves. Indeed, with the exception of the contributors to the *Mercure National,* all these editors had experienced setbacks in their chosen careers. These factors help explain why these men joined the radicals, but they are certainly not conclusive. Individual personality traits, an especially severe career setback, or a combination of these and other unnamed factors also played a part in forming these radicals. Marat was activated by a need for martyrdom; Desmoulins by a special penchant for utopian idealism. Surely chance events of 1789 to 1791 were important in determining the philosophies of these individuals. In fact, the educational and early career frustrations of these journalists cannot alone explain their precise political position.

Nonetheless, we cannot discount their biographical experiences in our search for those things that moved these men to radical politics and to support for popular sovereignty. It is significant that they all were highly educated in the tradition of the Enlightenment, that none had a stake in Old Regime society, and that most were frustrated in their careers. The repetition of these common points in their backgrounds underlines these factors as very important ones in explaining their involvement with the Cordeliers.

# 3

# The Ideology
# of Popular Sovereignty

EGARDLESS of what motivated Marat, Desmoulins, and their comrades, all of these journalists shared the desire to publish newspapers that would persuade the public of the truth of radical opinions. Of course, they occasionally exaggerated facts to substantiate their point of view, but generally they reported to others what they believed themselves. If their reporting seems incredible or contradictory to twentieth-century eyes, it was that they themselves were credulous and tossed about by the wave of the Revolution. Further, these views were shared by a loose coalition, based first on the Cordelier district and, later, on the club of the same name. In sum, they reported the world as they saw it. With this in mind, an examination of the substance of the journals is in order.

What did these newspapers report and how did they express their point of view? These questions are inseparable, for the organization, style, and language of the papers were as deliberate and revealing as the factual substance. Current thought in communications and linguistics supports the thesis that even if the journalists made no conscious organization of material, they unconsciously manipulated the make-up of their papers to emphasize certain points.[1] The men of the radical press were, moreover, quite aware of the interrelationships among the content of an article, its style, and its physical location within the newspaper. They made use of italics, headlines, caricatures, and different print sizes, to hammer home one or another point.[2] Hence, we may reduce our two questions to one: What did the radical press say openly through its reporting and more subtly through its style and innuendo?

Admittedly, our selection of papers has to some degree predetermined the results of this query. The radicals centered their reports upon the activities and ideas that were of concern to the Cordeliers. Thus, it should not be surprising that the discussion of the content of the radical press in the next three chapters is, in many ways, only an amplification of the basic principle of popular sovereignty, as outlined in chapter 1.

Nevertheless, the political persuasion of the newspapermen did not determine all of their reporting. Most of their opinions were directly related to a belief in Cordelier thought and action; but exactly how such opinions were expressed cannot be predicted solely from a knowledge of the central doctrine. For many vital interests, such as political economy, a commitment to the radical platform implied little or nothing. There were also a number of events, apparently unrelated to the political platform of the radicals, that were reported in the heat of the moment. The vicissitudes and confusion in Parisian politics of the 1790s made it even more difficult for the journalists to maintain any consistent "line" or philosophy. Consequently, to interpret the radical press, one must try to explain their deviations from, as well as agreement with, the principles and actions of the Cordeliers.

As a first step in answering the question, What did the radical press say?, let us examine the assumptions of the radical journalists as revealed in their articles. By assumptions, I mean only the opinions and attitudes that these men consistently held about their society from 1789 to 1791. I wish specifically to exclude their presuppositions about the physical and biological world, items that are interesting but that are too peripheral to be considered here. Because newspaper columns usually refer implicitly to the general notions of their writers, there exists the pitfall that the historian will create, instead of reconstitute, the basic assumptions of the radicals. In order to consider as many elements of radical thought as possible, some must be treated more briefly than others. With these cautions in mind, what follows is an attempt to describe the unformulated social ideology of the Cordelier publicists, which remained relatively constant in these six papers.

The most important principle of radical ideology, and the one most obvious to the eighteenth-century reader, was the doctrine of popular sovereignty. The devotion to this principle rested, moreover, on a rather peculiar view of society. The men of the extreme left divided the population of revolutionary France into two very distinct groups. One group, invariably referred to as the *peuple*, favored the Revolution. If left alone, the *peuple* were intrinsically "good." Exactly who the *peuple* were and what was "good" in the opinion of the radicals will be described below, but the radicals did have a clear and distinct notion of a segment of society, the *peuple*, whose values and actions were always laudable to any "reasonable" observer. Moreover, when the radicals wrote, they identified their own sentiments with those of the *peuple*. On the other hand, there existed a second group, the *aristocrates*, who were the very opposite of the *peuple*. All that was despicable to the radicals was associated with these *aristocrates*. Moreover, it was this notion of society, a society sharply rent by two opposing and mutually alienated groups, that spawned and reinforced the radicals' incessant reiteration of their belief in popular sovereignty. The radicals believed that in order to limit the power of the *aristocrates* effectively, it was necessary to reserve power—that is, sovereignty—to the *peuple*.

## THE *PEUPLE*

Whom did the radicals have in mind when they appealed to or praised the *peuple*? They were far more vague about the identity of the *peuple* than of the *aristocrates*, their enemies. Prudhomme, in recommending candidates for office in France, gave the specific suggestion to avoid magistrates, judges, nobles, the *anoblis*, the *bourgeoisie* with large "feudal" holdings, "fiscal agents," *avocats*, doctors, *procureurs*, pensioned intellectuals, and ecclesiastics. Instead, he was in favor of *laboureurs, artisans,* or *cultivateurs* for office.[3]

There were occasions when the radical journalists were somewhat more precise about those social groups to be included in the *peuple*. Such an instance was an appeal by Prudhomme to organize the sale of the *assignats* for the benefit of the *peuple*. He demanded that these fiscal plans be formulated to aid not the *agents de change*, but rather, "the *peuple*, the *marchand*, the *artisan*, the *ouvrier*, the *rentier*, and the *bourgeoisie*. . . ."[4] In another situation, the *Mercure National* praised the honest "race" of *laboureurs, artisans*, and *commerçants*.[5] Marat, while disparaging the National Assembly, insisted that only action by the "*cultivateurs*, the *petits marchands*, the *artisans*, and the *ouvriers*, the *manouvriers*, and the *prolétaires*" could form a free nation.[6]

True, these terms are not as precise as a modern social historian might wish, since the journalists never paused to explain exactly what they meant by such labels as *bourgeoisie, marchand,* or *cultivateurs*. These words and others could describe individuals of widely varying social status. For example, Parisians sometimes equated *bourgeoisie* with the recognized residents of the city. At other times, they employed a broader social usage of the term, thinking of those men who, without noble titles, lived as nobles, that is, without work. Moreover, as an adjective, *bourgeois* indicated a modest, proper life style.[7] *Cultivateur* was only somewhat more precise than *bourgeois*. The dictionary of the *Académie* defined *cultivateur* vaguely as "one who cultivates the earth."[8] True, this term referred only to those who personally worked the land, but this group was hardly homogeneous. *Manouvriers, fermiers*, and *métayers* all tilled the soil, but while the *manouvriers* barely subsisted on a meager wage, the *fermier* could possibly be secure and might entertain some thoughts of a better life for his offspring.[9] One could expand these examples of imprecise expressions employed by the radicals to describe the *peuple*, but it should be evident that the journalists had no exact notion of this group.

Nonetheless, it is clear that the radicals used the term *peuple* to cover a wide spectrum of French society. *Rentiers, marchands*, even Marat's *petits marchands* were considerably removed, both socially and economically, from *manouvriers*, and especially *prolétaires*. For example, compare the *rentiers* with the *prolétaires*. Although excluded from noble privileges or style of living, *rentiers* may have had substantial wealth invested in land and in government bonds, which paid regular annuities. Such individuals might not need to work, and, if they did, not at any manual occupation. At the other extreme of this broad spectrum were the *prolétaires*, who had no certain income and who could only hope for periodic, poorly paid, and backbreaking urban labor. They were on the very lowest rung of the social ladder and were often classed with the indigents. Creating further uncertainty was Marat's habit of identifying the *peuple* as the *pauvre bourgeoisie*.[10] Indeed, the *pauvres* were those who did not have sufficient food or shelter; and, by any definition, the *bourgeoisie* were respected residents of the city. Consequently, Marat, in considering the *peuple*, seemed to include all from the poorest members of society to those whose shops or securities provided them with an assured income. In sum, the *peuple*, for the radical journalists, meant the vast majority of French society.

Despite this tendency to see the *peuple* as a broad spectrum of French society, the radicals did make several conscious and obvious omissions from their ranks, including the *officiers*, the wealthier commercial and landed groups, the nobility, and the upper clergy. The *gens de lettres* were neither specifically included or omitted, as the journalists rarely dealt with them as a group. Thus, while the radicals usually thought of the *peuple* as a collection of a wide variety of social and occupational groups, they excluded most of those who did not have to work and all those who customarily enjoyed luxuries, prestige, and Old Regime offices. Conversely, the radicals included all those whose income and positions were at best modest.

If the *peuple*, the favorite of the radicals, included a collection of very different social types, one segment of this wide group was preferred. The journalists occasionally gave a special role to the well-to-do artisans and shopkeepers. For example, the *Révolutions de Paris* recommended that it should be those who found themselves between the rich and the poor, who might best lead in a mediated settlement of the just demands of the impoverished.[11] Consider this passage from Prudhomme's paper in the spring of 1791:

> The *petite bourgeoisie* held the middle ground between the nobles, the rich, and the *peuple*; it is a very large group and is composed of the lower clergy, retail merchants, master workmen, *artisans aisés*, clerks, and many *gens de lettres*, especially in these last days. The Revolution owes much to the *petite bourgeoisie*; it has contributed most efficaciously to the controlling of the hoards of *brigands* that the ministry has released on us about the capital, which is pregnant with liberty; one-third of the National Guard are of the *petite bourgeoisie*. It has always worked on the side of the *peuple*, which has not always rendered it justice.[12]

Evident here was not only specific praise for the shopkeepers, well-to-do artisans, and those from similar occupational groups, but also a recognition of some tension between the *peuple* and such men. This journalist actually separated the *petite bourgeoisie* from the *peuple*, though he indicated that their political interests were the same. Although all the journalists accepted the *petite bourgeoisie* as a distinct segment of the *peuple*, only Prudhomme suggested that there was some hostility between them. During the Terror, such distinctions would become important, but the early Revolution witnessed little of this.[13]

If the men of the six radical newspapers favored the *petite bourgeoisie*, they shared some misgivings about the most wretched members of the *peuple*. To be sure, there was usually praise for those who subsisted with little support. Desmoulins insisted that the generous actions of some Versailles *ouvriers* proved that all of the poor, even the most indigent, desired only patriotism and virtue.[14] Audouin seconded the remarks of Desmoulins.[15] The *Révolutions de Paris* of Prudhomme also lauded the "honorable *indigens*," while exhorting them to reject the seductions of the *aristocrates*.[16] Although labeling the *indigens* "honorable," Prudhomme's writer revealed a nagging suspicion toward those who could not support themselves. He feared those with nothing to lose might be corrupted, and his anxiety found some echo in other journals. Marat too pleaded with the *indigens* not to abandon their patriotism and sell out to the *aristocrates*.[17] The journalists were not primarily champions of the unemployed; they considered them too susceptible to corruption.

For the most part, however, praise for the wealthier members of the *peuple* and scorn for their opposites was rare. Generally the radical journalists treated all the *peuple* with the same overwhelming compassion. They emphasized inclusion over exclusion. They preferred a wide to a narrow spectrum of society in their definition of the *peuple*. In sum, they had defined *peuple* in a way to include most of France, and they generally rejected raising internal barriers to wall off groups from each other. The radicals wanted to see the *peuple* unified against the *aristocratie*, and they believed exclusion and internal distinctions to be unimportant, if not destructive to their cause. By 1793, the *sans-culottes* would not be so tolerant in their views and would exclude those *marchands* and *rentiers* who were generally included by the Cordeliers from 1789 to 1791.

If for the sake of unity, the radicals wished to make an imprecise determination of the membership of the *peuple*, they had exceedingly clear expectations for the behavior of this major part of society. The Cordeliers believed that the *peuple*, because of their intelligence and "morality" (or "virtue"), desired and deserved liberty. For the radicals, both judgment and high morals were absolutely necessary before a group could achieve liberty.

Where did this morality, requisite for liberty, originate? According to the journalists, the life style of the *peuple*—indeed, the "adversities" they faced—had given the *peuple* no opportunity for vice.[18] Fate alone had favored this segment of society and kept it from the cesspool of aristocratic life, where luxury, debauchery, and narrow self-interest ran amuck. With these temptations absent, the *peuple* had been able to develop their own "superior" moral life. Thus, the morality of the *peuple* had been a fortunate historical accident, a happy development that must be closely guarded.

What characterized the morality of the *peuple* according to the radical journalists? The central tenet of their virtue was a commitment to universal brotherhood. Repeatedly, the journalists praised how the *peuple* referred to one another as *frères* and *soeurs*. In the journalists' eyes, the collective effort to construct the festive site for the first Bastille Day was a prime example of the brotherhood of the French *peuple*. Torrential rains and other problems had caused work delays, and thousands of Parisians contributed their time freely to complete the planned stadium. The importance of this scene to radical ideology was revealed by Desmoulins, who was particularly moved by the cooperation of the *peuple*. He wrote:

> A young man takes off his coat, puts down two watches, takes a shovel, and goes to work elsewhere. But your two watches? Oh, surely one does not distrust his brothers—and this depository of sand and pebbles is as inviolate as a deputy of the National Assembly.[19]

Brotherhood, seen here as communal labor for the welfare of society, was the cornerstone of the morality developed by the *peuple*.

In the minds of the journalists, one of the ramifications of this collective concern was the desire of the *peuple* to see all arbitrary distinctions vanish. Both corporate and noble privileges had to end.[20] They admired talent in an individual but did not want anyone to receive special privilege. It was reward enough to serve more ably than one's comrades. In an appeal to the first and second estates following the abolition of nobility, the *Mercure National* exclaimed:

> Hurry then to adopt the Holy Decrees of the French legislators; no longer conserve more outrageous distinctions between some citizens and other citizens; forget about the existence of the three orders; all men in nature form the same class; hurry then to join and identify yourself with the mother country.[21]

In advocating the fellowship of man and the consequent elimination of distinctions, this journalist assumed that he spoke for the *peuple*. In this way, he attested to his belief, and that of other radicals, that the *peuple* were inflamed with the desire to destroy privilege.

Furthermore, for the Cordeliers, this brotherly affection, the core of the morality of the *peuple*, manifested itself in the tolerance of the *peuple* even for their enemies. Desmoulins noted that despite the attacks and the oppression of the *aristocratie*, the only demand of the *peuple* was that they be recognized as equal to all men.[22] In the *Mercure National* a journalist insisted that the *peuple* must watch their enemies, yet with the compassion that the best of their former oppressors had shown.[23] The *Révolutions de Paris* echoed this sentiment in advocating leniency of the *peuple* for the *aristocratie*.[24] But to be brothers was not only to be tolerant; it was to exact just punishment as well.

Marat was confident that the *peuple* were capable of determining justice.[25] Fair punishment was not reserved solely for the *aristocrates*; the *peuple* were, also, desirous and capable of exacting equal retribution from their own number.[26] Tolerance was praiseworthy, to be sure, but even the National Assembly must be dealt with firmly.[27] The *peuple* reserved the right to judge all their institutions—so thought the radicals.

Brotherly concern dictated more than tolerance, justice, and an end to distinctions. The *peuple* had, in Cordelier opinion, a sound moral commitment to work in a "useful" occupation. Often when referring to the *peuple*, radicals spoke of them as the group, *la plus utile*, in society. In a slightly different style, the Roberts labeled the *peuple* as the most capable and most talented in France.[28] Why their work was the most useful was left unexamined by the radicals; they seemed to assume that because the *peuple* usually worked hard, what they did was useful. Even workers in the luxury trades and domestics in noble homes were not condemned for their occupations.

In addition, the Cordelier writers posited that the concern of the *peuple* for their comrades included a desire for some parity of incomes. Indeed, the radicals postulated that since there was only a limited amount of wealth in the nation, no "true" member of the *peuple* could conceivably want to have so much that he would reduce another member of society below the level of subsistence. They wished no absolute equality; they wished no *loi agraire*, where the land was divided equally among all, but they did wish to limit fortunes so that all would be provided with necessities. The *Mercure National* recommended that the *peuple* not confiscate the properties of the wealthy, but teach them the proper use of money. Demonstrate to the rich, stated the journalist of the *Mercure*, that, rather than thinking only of expanding their fortunes, they must, like you, employ at a decent wage those who serve and defend them.[29] Indeed, when the *peuple* demonstrated their concern for the impoverished, the radical press quickly pointed out their "superior" morality. As noted above, Desmoulins believed that all, even the indigents, would give up bread to make certain that everyone had sufficient provisions.[30] Examples abound where radicals excitedly pointed to the generous efforts of the *peuple* to aid their fellows.[31]

Further, all "true" members of the *peuple*, imbued with brotherhood, abhorred wealth because of its "inevitable" consequences—luxuries, self-indulgence, and consequent callous disregard for the remainder of society. The radicals thought that the monied classes, mired in selfish indulgence, could never have concern for their fellows. They could think of no situation where riches did not lead to luxury and libidinous pleasure, and they repeatedly showed how the *peuple* scorned such luxury. When a crowd sacked the home of the duc de Castries because he had wounded the popular assemblyman Charles Lameth in a duel, the journalists proudly announced that no personal property was taken, that the *peuple* were only exacting a just political retribution, and that they disdained the furnishings and jewels of the mansion.[32] Marat insisted that now a new, more rigid morality had replaced the soft living and hypocritical generosity of past centuries.[33] Prudhomme explicitly recalled the remarks of Rousseau that in a free state there could be no pleasures of luxury.[34]

But it was not just wealth and luxury that the *peuple* avoided. They also disdained their accompanying evils. Marat believed he spoke for the *peuple* when he cried:

> Paris is the home of all the vices, and its inhabitants claim to be free! No, No, they flatter themselves: in order to be free, one needs enlightenment, courage, virtue. Some men here—ignorant, frivolous, cowardly, groveling, yielded to dissipation, softness, pleasures, gambling, even debauchery—are slaves . . . .

He called on the *peuple* to continue to rally against such an existence.[35] Indeed, according to radical opinion, the *peuple* recognized that the attendant ills of luxury were incompatible with brotherhood, and they formulated a new morality where gambling and debauchery of all kinds were excluded.

Audouin, in his *Journal Universel*, surely believed that he represented his constituency, the *peuple*, in advocating laws against gambling.[36] Prudhomme, with the same assumption that he stood for the *peuple*, attacked the government lottery as an "immoral, detestable game, which destroyed both love of work and order in society."[37] Debauchery was equally attacked. The *Mercure National* told of two imaginary countries. While one survived because the dauphin was trained to be sober and temperate, the other fell because sexual morality deteriorated, and because priests and young men frequented prostitutes. The children of these encounters, raised without families, without attention, were easily corrupted and were employed to help bring about the downfall of the state.[38]

For the open debauchery of the Old Regime, the radicals and consequently the *peuple* substituted the family.[39] For example, in an article arguing that the domestics of the *aristocrates* could be purged of the evils of their masters, Louise Robert glorified the family:

> Why would the peace which constantly reigns in a closely-knit family, why would the complaisance, the concern of a virtuous woman for her dear and respected husband, why would the confidence and love of a husband, why would the kisses of children not make in the soul of these one-time domestics—an impression as deep as the picture of the dissipation spawned by luxury and immorality.[40]

For the *peuple*, there was family life, not debauchery.

Further, the radicals believed that a rigid morality required a miniscule political role for women. The scandalous behaviour of Madame de Pompadour, Marie-Antoinette, and other *courtisanes* were fresh examples to reinforce their opinion that women acted politically through sexual attraction. This "fact of life" taught the radicals that women in public were always debauched; if licentiousness were to end, so must a public role for women.[41] According to these antifeminist newspapermen, the women of the *peuple* desired only to live in the home and care for their children and husbands. They were content to educate their sons to be good patriots, to raise their daughters to be loyal wives, and to work to free their husbands for political duties. True, in emergencies, they might rush to aid the men in the streets or at meetings; but their place was primarily in the home.[42] Even Madame Robert, the editor of the *Mercure National*, whose own life was so politically oriented, subscribed to this notion.[43] In short, in embracing brotherhood and rejecting selfish indulgence, the *peuple* adhered to a rigid sexual standard, emphasized the family, and insisted that their women remain at home.

To conclude, the morality ascribed to the *peuple* was the moral paradigm of the journalists. Thus for a definition of radical virtue, one has only to consider the morality of the *peuple*. There one will find a heterogeneous collection of individuals linked by mutual concern—by brotherhood. This altruism toward one another, made possible by the absence of aristocratic mores and values, called for legal equality, tolerance and justice, a certain degree of economic equality, and a rejection of luxury and its related vices. This was no morality of self-indulgence; it was a stern, almost ascetic morality, and certainly impossible to realize entirely. It was in direct contrast with the radical view of aristocratic life, as we shall see later. Probably it developed as a direct reaction against aristocratic life.

This morality was central to the political role of the *peuple*. Audouin warned the delegates of the National Assembly:

> Morality! Morals! Without them, there is no liberty. If you have no morals, you cannot have liberty, and you will soon strip it from others. Because if you abandon yourself to luxury, to excessive gambling, to enormous expenses, you will necessarily open your soul to corruption.[44]

Prudhomme echoed Audouin's testament of faith in morality by affirming that as long as the *peuple* were virtuous, they could not be led astray by an aristocratic appeal.[45] A contributor to the *Mercure National* cautioned that morality had to be maintained or the Old Regime would regain its position in France.[46] Thus, morality was essential; it provided immunity from further aristocratic appeals, and it nurtured the desire for freedom.

Nonetheless, morality by itself would not lead to liberty. For some time, the *peuple* had been virtuous; yet they had not been free. Only the "philosophic" advances of the last century had placed liberty within their grasp, and Marat announced that the time of *philosophie* had now arrived.[47] A journalist of the *Révolutions de Paris* rhetorically asked if the *aristocrates* would have a chance against the *peuple*, "already instructed by the torch of wise *philosophie*."[48] Audouin added that since *philosophie* had finally been received in France, nothing would be able to resist its force.[49] In agreement was Fréron, who remarked that *philosophie* had penetrated into all the nations of Europe.[50]

But what did the journalists mean when they said *philosophie* had arrived? In general, they were saying that the *peuple* had learned to reason about politics. And what was this "reason" attributed to the *peuple*? The Cordeliers were not so naive as to assume that the *peuple* possessed great analytical skills. The newspapermen did not expect that untutored men could analyze and dissect metaphysical systems or understand Lockean psychology. Prudhomme hinted that the reasoning of the *peuple* was instinctual.[51] Camille Desmoulins succinctly stated the radical notion in a comment on a former executioner who sought public office in the new regime: "It is this instinct, or rather the voice of nature, which makes the *peuple* regard the activities of Samson [the office seeker] as sinister."[52]

Thus, reason for the *peuple* was an instinct, or a certain comprehension of "nature." In sum, through *philosophie* the *peuple* had learned to understand nature and follow its dictates.

The Cordelier newspapers left unexplained how the *peuple* had learned to reason. Apparently, the radicals never clearly examined this process. Nevertheless, by associating reason with the triumph of *philosophie* they at least indicated a connection between the *lumières* of the century and the sudden intellectual development of the *peuple*. They seemed to assume that Montesquieu, Voltaire, the Encyclopedists, Rousseau, and other lesser lights encouraged and fostered the innate wisdom of the workmen; but they left unclear how illiterates and semiliterates had imbibed the critical abilities of the *philosophes*. The historian must resist the tantalizing possibility that the publicists believed themselves to be the carriers of such ideas, since the newspapers never once suggested this possibility.

Nonetheless, the *peuple* could know nature and consequently could reason, and the journalists never tired of expressing their confidence in the *peuple*. Desmoulins exclaimed, "The good sense of the *manouvrier* and the *journalier* surprises me every day more and more; each day the Faubourg Saint-Antoine grows in wisdom."[53] This sentiment was widely reiterated throughout the radical press. Prudhomme noted:

> I have seen an Englishman, once so disdainful in a circle of frivolous and idle Frenchmen. I have seen him stupefied these days with astonishment in meeting a cluster of citizens, poorly dressed, but rich in luminous and profound ideas. I have seen the more subtle efforts of the *aristocratie* upset by the instinct of the assembled *peuple* which is coarse but just and penetrating. From the moment that the *peuple* opened their eyes at the first glimmer of liberty, nothing has deceived them; the names, the titles, all the social considerations, which formerly held them in a stupid respect, have ceased to impose anything on them; they no longer believe in talismans. This *peuple* is not at all a ferocious beast, which as soon as it felt itself unleashed, threw itself on its enemies; it is rather a *peuple* which, after a long denial of justice, first manifested an only too just impatience and today reasons all its actions.[54]

Louise Robert echoed this general sentiment when she asserted that it was the ability of the *peuple* to educate themselves that had saved them from aristocratic manipulation.[55] On occasion, Marat went so far as to claim that the only rational segment of society was the *peuple*,[56] but this was not a widely held belief among the radicals. The *aristocratie* could reason; they simply chose corruption. Nonetheless, when Cordelier journalists claimed that theirs was the century of *philosophie*, their usual intention was to underline the ability of the *peuple* to know nature—to reason.

To understand nature was to know a great deal. A knowledge of nature was worth more than a knowledge of law.[57] Further, witness all the benefits of such reason described above—"luminous and profound ideas," "wisdom," and, most important, "freedom." Morality could make one desire the "good," yet without reason one would not know what to establish. But with reason as guide, one knew one wanted freedom. The historian may search in vain for a logical relationship between reason —this instinctive understanding of nature—and the wish for freedom; but in the minds of the publicists the two were inextricably linked. All reasonable men wanted freedom.[58] Thus, the *Révolutions de Paris* justified greater freedom for Paris than for the provincial districts, because the *peuple* of the capital were more reasonable.[59] The *Mercure National* also claimed that, had the provinces been more reasonable, the French would have been free a century earlier.[60]

Moreover, when the journalists wrote of the desire of this reasonable *peuple* for freedom, they were not primarily concerned with individual liberties. They were thinking more of the liberty of the *peuple* as a group to determine their destiny. They recognized only a negligible difference between personal and societal needs. The brotherhood of the *peuple* and universal ability to comprehend the dictates of nature ensured that the needs of individuals would not differ greatly from the needs of the *peuple* as a collectivity. There was no distinction between freedom of the *peuple* and freedom of the individual.[61]

Consequently, a moral *peuple*, taught to reason by an age of *philosophie*, desired freedom and made a revolution. The desire for freedom evinced by the *peuple* was then a mandate for a new and better society.[62] Yet the radicals never articulated the details of this new society of the virtuous, moral, wise, and freedom-loving *peuple*. They did not express utopian expectations; they resigned themselves to a continuing struggle between the *peuple* and their enemies, the *aristocratie*.

## THE *ARISTOCRATIE*

Among the *aristocratie*, so detested and feared by the Cordeliers, were all those who were not included in the *peuple*. In broad terms, these were the *riches*, the first two orders, the nonnoble *officiers*, and the *brigands*. More specifically, the journalists leveled their blasts at the *avocats* and the legal profession, the nobility of all genres, the nonparish clergy, and the financiers and grain dealers. Moreover, although the components of the *aristocratie* were better defined than those of the *peuple*, both categories retained an amorphous quality. For example, the radicals did not explain why they linked nobles with successful businessmen; they also failed to differentiate between wealthy and impoverished nobles or between *banquiers* and *négociants*. Only the legal profession was seen in all its diversity. Probably the journalists believed that everyone could identify the enemy, the ghoulish *aristocratie*, and consequently, they saw no necessity for refined definition. Also they made only gross distinctions, because they knew no others. In general, the publicists saw the world of the *aristocratie* from a distance that precluded precise understanding. Possibly they recognized fine divisions within the legal profession because of their own experiences that must have included some contact with the law.

The journalists spared no vitriol or rancor in their charges against the *aristocratie*. One need only witness their treatment of the nobility. While all the second estate was bombarded, the nobility at court was among the most open to attack. Marat charged that the court nobility had instructed the ministers to corrupt both the officers of the army and certain delegates of the National Assembly in order to instigate a war and return to the Old Regime.[63] Nor was it uncommon for radical journalists to blame all the errors of the National Assembly on the representatives of the nobility.[64] Of all the nobles, the army *officiers* were the most vilified. Fréron asserted that the safety of France required the abolition of "this aristocratic race of colonels, captains, lieutenants who owed their commissions either to connections or to whores of the court."[65] The *Mercure National* and the *Ami du Peuple* added that these *officiers* machinated constantly against the interests of the *peuple*.[66]

The attacks on the *aristocratie* were intended to include much of the clergy as well. The parish clergy were not considered members of the *aristocratie*, and, although they revolted against the Civil Constitution, they were usually seen as dupes of bishops and monks.[67] On the other hand, the regular clergy and the church hierarchy were seen as idle parasites, oppressing the *peuple*. Desmoulins assailed the hypocrisy of these clerics who suppressed the political rights of the *peuple* in the name of the *prolétaire* Jesus Christ.[68] Additionally, the journalists unfailingly laid local revolts to the inspiration of the nonparish clergy. It was commonly accepted that the bloodletting in the papal province of Avignon was caused by the avarice of the Vatican hierarchy. The Vatican, bishops, and monks were all castigated by the radical press.

The *riches* were also included among the *aristocratie*. Audouin warned the Belgians, then in rebellion, to fear the wealthy as their most dangerous opponents.[69] In considering the *riches*, the radicals were most often thinking of the *financiers*. The journalists blasted these men for their "treasonous" manipulation of the money market.[70] Prudhomme charged that "*financiers*, bankers, and speculators, the scum of the *aristocrates*, will second Maury[71] with all their force in order to overturn the *assignats* from the start and in order to thwart everything which would withdraw the public treasury from their dominance."[72] The radical journalists feared still others among the *gens riches*—the large landholders, the *négociants*, and the dealers in grain. Of the three groups, the Cordelier newspapermen were most concerned about the grain dealers, who, it was believed, made their money, not by legitimate trade, but by monopolizing the supply to keep grain scarce and prices high. Marat blamed the shortage of grain on these traders, not on low production or poor transportation.[73] The *Mercure National* charged that the core of the "aristocratic plot" was control of the sale of grain.[74] In sum, the wealthy were a dangerous part of the *aristocratie*, and the corrupt speculators in grain and coin usually stood as representatives for the *riches*. The *riches* not only had too much money; they earned it through enterprises that contemporaries believed immoral.

The legal profession was likewise seen as part of the *aristocratie*. Their crime was to have helped the nobles, the clergy, and the *riches* strip away the possessions and the security of the *peuple*.[75] At one time or another, each element of the legal profession from the Paris *Parlement* to the lowest *huissier* was attacked.[76] All the men of the law were despised, but the *avocats* were the most scorned.[77] Prudhomme asserted that the advocates were the most vicious and aristocratic individuals in all France.[78] Also attacked were the *procureurs,* labeled by Marat the very worst men to elect to office, because they made their profession by creating lies, perjurers, and family discord.[79] The robe nobility suffered like their inferiors; the *Parlements* were assaulted by Fréron as the rallying points for the *aristocratie*.[80] The radicals excoriated all the men of the law. Perhaps they did so because of their own personal disappointments as lawyers; perhaps they did so because of the conservative political role played by most lawyers before and during the Revolution;[81] or perhaps they did so because they shared the popular prejudice against lawyers as fomenters of discord.

Finally, the privileged, the rich, and the lawyers were joined by the *brigands*, whose social background was that of the *peuple*, but whose political affiliation was with the *aristocratie*. In the minds of the radicals, these *brigands* were at best nondescript fellows worth little mention, and they were rarely the subject of editorial discussion. Their obscurity is itself important because it suggests that the journalists, and probably most urban revolutionaries, saw the aristocratic threat differently from the rural population. In 1789, the inhabitants of the countryside identified the *aristocratie* primarily with marauding *brigands*.[82] For the radicals, the term *brigand*, scarcely used, was always linked to political conspiracy, not to robbery and pillage.

While the radicals did not outline the *aristocratie* with the precision of a modern social historian, they were indeed more definite there than in their vague conception of the *peuple*. They specifically had included all the nonparish clergy, the wealthy, particularly the monopolists and the speculators, the men of the law, and the *brigands*. From our point of view, the *aristocratie* was more clearly defined than the *peuple*; yet it still lacked coherence. This *aristocratie* was a very loose coalition. It would be difficult to imagine that the court nobles and the provincial barristers had much in common; but, in the minds of the journalists, such men shared a common interest, a common goal. Deprived by their way of life of the morality and *philosophie* of the *peuple*, they were incapable of approving of the Revolution, and were, in fact, working furiously to overturn it.

It will surprise no one that for the journalists the *aristocratie* completely lacked the morality of the *peuple*. Brotherhood had motivated the *peuple* to destroy artificial differences among men, reduce economic disparity, and eradicate corrupting indulgence in luxury and vice. By contrast, the members of the *aristocratie* were often referred to as "egotists," as individuals completely opposed to the brotherhood of the *peuple*.[83] Their narrow self-concern, their focus only on their own needs rather than on those of society, led them to defend privileges, to engage in self-indulgence and vice, and to lust for wealth beyond their needs. They opposed a society of limited needs and mutual aid.

In the opinion of the radicals, *aristocrates* did not want civil equality; rather, they thought only of preserving their own privileged positions. The *Révolutions de Paris* charged that there were many *aristocrates* who wished to recover the artificial distinctions of the Old Regime. The *parlementaires* had joined this counterrevolution because they saw themselves stripped of their titles as legislators, defenders of the *peuple*, and advisers to kings. Adding their voices to this struggle were the judges, who feared the end of judicial tyranny, and the financiers, who resisted the suppression of their quasi-public positions. All these opposed political equality in favor of a system where their titles alone advanced them over merit, talent, and even justice.[84] Marat asked his readers how could one expect such men, so accustomed to their privileged and exalted positions, to accept political equality?[85]

Moreover, according to the journalists, the pervasive egotism of the *aristocrates* led to vice. While the *peuple* feared luxury and its evils, the *aristocratie* satiated themselves without pangs of conscience. Desmoulins and Prudhomme accused the *aristocrates* of being preoccupied with luxury.[86] The reader of this book may recall anew the blistering attack of the *Mercure National* on a society dominated by *aristocrates*. The journalist complained that in such a society "the deprivation of morals is general; a number of altars are raised to the God of luxury. Priests and prostitutes openly parade together."[87] The *Journal Universel* equated the domination of the *aristocratie* with the domination of luxury.[88]

While the moral *peuple* were concerned about social welfare, the egotistical *aristocratie* was not. Without the moral compunctions of the *peuple*, *aristocrates* could seek money without restraint. Indeed, all the journalists believed that beyond luxury and power, money was a crucial, if not principal, desire of the *aristocrates*.[89] With wealth these debased men could easily provide themselves with the luxuries and sinecures they might need. Gold could underwrite egotism. For instance, the radicals asserted that the clergy attacked the Revolution to preserve their wealth, with which they might continue their debased existence. The *Révolutions de Paris* announced:

> If the clergy regretted less its grandeur and its past riches; if it did not wish, no matter what the price, to foment a civil war, it would no longer resist the legal will of the nation. One would not see most of the bishops of France, agreed with the curés,[90] crying that the Catholic religion is lost, because it is stripped of the means to display an insolent luxury.[91]

The radicals also believed that wealth could be used to buy political power. Fréron complained bitterly about the exclusion of the *peuple* by the new electoral process and stated "the *aristocratie* of the wealthy replaces all the orders and four new orders are raised on the debris of the old ones: the order of the *patards* [pence], the order of the *ecu* [3 livres], the *pistole* [10 livres], and the order of the *marc* [about 50 livres]." Of course, the highest of the new orders was that of the rich.[92] Audouin as well saw the *aristocratie* as primarily a ruling group of the most wealthy.[93] For the journalists then, the struggle for money was a struggle for power.

The *peuple* thus faced an opposition whose primary goal was to acquire wealth, whether to enjoy *éclat* and luxury or to gain and hold political power. Both sorts of *aristocratie* appear in the radical press. The first notion belonged especially to the "grub-street" radicals of the 1780s: their *aristocrates* were decadent, weakened by their lust for luxury and vice.[94] The second notion was new and illustrates some differences between Old Regime and revolutionary mentalities; for in radical eyes these later *aristocrates* wanted to use their money for political ends.[95] The decadent parasites of the 1780s were partially replaced by dangerous, fearsome political antagonists.

Why did the *aristocratie* desire wealth, luxury, and power? Why did they want exclusive public positions? Why were they egotistical? In the first place, the radicals insisted that the background of the *aristocratie*, their lifetime acquaintance with power, vice, and wealth, had addicted them to self-indulgence. Do you, Marat asked his readers, expect men from the *aristocratie* to accept willingly political equality?[96] In other words, their environment was an inescapable trap of egotism.

Yet, the attraction of the aristocratic life style was based on more than the effects of a milieu and education. In fact, the radicals believed that the appeal of the *aristocratie* struck a resonant cord in the nature of man. All men were egotistical; all men wanted debauchery; all men wanted power; all men wanted money. This natural bent of men was powerful, because man was too weak, too stupid, too naive to extricate himself from these needs.

Consider the contrast between this human nature and that "nature" which endowed the *peuple* with "reason" and the knowledge of freedom. Obviously, these two concepts of nature are in conflict; yet the radicals believed in both. They were not the first to believe that "nature," in the sense of prescriptive law, taught understanding and moral imperatives, while the physical nature of man led to stupidity, domination, and sensual pleasure.[97] The radicals were not tortured by the apparent contradiction; they made no explicit attempt to resolve it. Perhaps it escaped their notice; perhaps they assumed that it required no explanation. In any case, they accepted consciously or unwittingly the existence of two natures: one, a universal, prescriptive, harmonious nature, which spoke for freedom; and the second, the nature of man, which sought egotism and self-indulgence.

Furthermore, there can be no doubt that the radicals believed in the existence of this second nature, the nature of man, which focused on egotism, vice, domination, wealth, and stupidity. Each paper asserted this point. Marat complained that the French were not made for liberty, for they were by nature vain, presumptuous, lazy; they were too often slaves to pleasure, leisure, and fortune to struggle for freedom.[98] Elsewhere he stated that "the love of power is natural to the human heart and the rarest of virtue is necessary not to abuse authority."[99] Agreeing with Marat was Prudhomme, who labeled all men "imbeciles."[100] The latter also believed men to be so driven by their lust for wealth that they would gladly sell their votes and play games of chance, no matter what the risks, to increase their fortunes.[101]

In the *Mercure National,* the journalists complained that wealth had procured the compliance of almost everyone. They decried the frivolity of the French, whose impulsiveness had not diminished at all.[102] Audouin, even while affirming his belief in the eventual triumph of freedom and *philosophie*, stated that men were still ignorant, egotistical, hedonistic, jealous, and ambitious.[103] Desmoulins also condemned man for his enslavement to luxuries and his supine acceptance of authority.[104] The *Orateur du Peuple* attacked man as basically a "stupid beast."[105] These statements ring unmistakably of the pessimism of Augustinian despair.

Thus, according to the radicals, the desperate search by the *aristocratie* for gold, influence, and vice was fueled by certain common characteristics in human nature. As men were congenitally avaricious, domineering, and vice-infested, it was to be expected that those who could indulge themselves would not hesitate to do so. However, an accident of history, the chance merger of environmental adversity and *philosophie*, had produced the morality and judgment of the *peuple*. This morality and reason were at best fragile and were simultaneously threatened from within by man's own nature and from without by the maneuvers of the desperate *aristocratie*.

It would be difficult to list all the different counterrevolutionary techniques ascribed to the *aristocratie*. They were guilty of committing every imaginable crime; they were ingenious enough to have concocted the most imaginative plots; they were industrious enough to have worked daily to overturn the *peuple*. The radicals insisted that all such endeavors were plotted secretly, were masked with pledges of loyalty to the Revolution, and were widespread efforts whose parts were intricately coordinated.

While the *peuple* decided and debated openly, the *aristocratie*, so stated the Cordeliers, machinated endlessly behind closed doors. The journalists constantly compared the closed meetings of the royalist and moderate clubs with the open assemblies of the *sociétés populaires*. Especially dangerous was the Austrian Committee, which, led by the queen herself, plotted against the Revolution in clandestine meetings. Desmoulins summed up radical sentiment when he wrote, "Those who wish to create evil look for shadows . . . ."[106]

The radicals also affirmed that the *aristocratie* disguised their plots from the *peuple* by declaring that all was well, that there existed no plan to subvert the Revolution. Indeed, the *Révolutions de Paris* accused the *aristocratie* of pretended acceptance of the Revolution in order to retain power. The *aristocratie*, wrote Marat, was trying to lull the *peuple* to sleep with slogans of peace and union.[107] Audouin stated that the counterrevolutionaries based their plans on first weakening their opposition.[108] Fréron even insisted that those who called for moderation, for calm and security, were worse than *aristocrates*; he asserted, "In working to plunge the *peuple* into a blind security, these moderates really work to lead it to slavery."[109]

The *aristocratie* also weakened resistance to their plots by undermining the ability of the *peuple* to find adequate food and shelter. The radicals charged that the rich avoided spending hard coin in order to ensure the impoverishment of the Parisians.[110] Not only gold but bread was denied the *peuple* to soften their will. The *Orateur du Peuple* insinuated that the ministers starved Paris to destroy the unity of the *peuple*.[111] More

specifically, Marat charged "Some new *compagnies de farine* are formed.
. . . Their agents arouse the *peuple* by reducing it to despair."[112] Prudhomme, as well, bluntly asserted that part of the planning by the
*aristocratie* included physically weakening the revolutionaries.[113]

With their maneuvers masked and their opposition undermined, the
*aristocratie* constructed the most intricate plots. The editors of the
*Révolutions de Paris* reported the details of one such plan that they
believed was currently unfolding. Jean Frédéric La Tour du Pin, the
minister of war, was to spread rumors that would cause dissension among
the troops and render them ineffective. Another unnamed minister had
already retarded the issuance of those decrees of the Constitution that
would bring the revolutionary government support. Further, the ministers had stripped the borders of heavy fortifications and had gained
control over the commanders of these frontier posts. After these tasks
were completed, the ministers were to urge other nations to marshal their
troops at the frontier of France. Simultaneously, the *garde-des-sceaux*
was to refrain from promulgating the decree destroying the *Parlements* in
the hope that these bodies might be useful as well. César-Henri Luzerne,
minister of the navy, was continuously working to stimulate disorder
among the sailors. Coordinating all these efforts for counterrevolution
was Guignard Saint-Priest, Minister of the Interior. On his shoulders lay
the responsibility for abducting the king in order to push this uneasy
situation into military collapse and bring about a resurrection of the
*aristocratie*.[114]

This plot, and it is simplified here, was no more complex than another
described in the *Orateur du Peuple*. Fréron warned of a scheme to
overturn the Revolution by subversion from within and without. There
would be no point in describing the conspiracy in detail, but an excerpt
should reveal the intricacy ascribed to the "aristocratic plots."

> . . . among the minor princes of Germany, the Maréchal de Broglie, who
> was put to flight by the chamber pots of Paris, was charged to foment their
> fervor at Vienna; it is the grand-visir Mohammed-Breteuil, black tyrant,
> soul of the Austrian league, whose punishment ought to be forced to swal-
> low all the *lettres de cachet* that he has expedited; at Madrid, Sartine,
> and La Vauguyon, whose cancer I discovered; at London . . . Calonne; in
> Switzerland le Noir . . .[115] there are these parricides who, together, each at
> his post, concoct with foreigners a plan for the destruction of his native
> land. A correspondence binds together this band of conspirators. The plan
> is set; they are burning to accomplish it. They desire the Capital over-
> whelmed in gulfs of blood and fire, the National Assembly disbanded, and
> despotism raising its hideous head.[116]

Despite the satiric remarks in this passage, Fréron clearly revealed his
conception of a plot composed of numerous intrigues all coordinated by a

master plan. Moreover, in the rest of this article, he stated that these *aristocrates*, conniving outside France, were aided by internal forces including ministers, priests, military officers, and others.

One could easily multiply the accounts of the conspiracies reported by the journals, but the pattern is now explicit. In the radical mind, the *aristocratie*, working secretly and deviously, extended long tentacles with agents protruding everywhere, ready to precipitate a counterrevolution. Within this framework, the *aristocratie* devised countless schemes to reach their goal. Although no complete enumeration can be made, their alleged plans fall into three general groups—attacks on morality and *philosophie*, subversion, and open assaults.

According to the radical publicists, the *aristocratie* tried to win converts to their side by undermining the morality of the *peuple*. With their money, life style, and appeal to a certain facet of human nature, the counterrevolutionaries might lure others into their trap. Marat claimed, for example, that they used the bait of gold to snare officials. Social distinctions as well were employed in the National Guard to encourage the civilian soldiers to feel separate from and superior to their neighbors.[117] The *Mercure National* asserted that the attraction of money had corrupted the majority of the National Assembly.[118] From the *Orateur du Peuple* came the remark that egotism had poisoned many Frenchmen and had made them willing subscribers to the *aristocratie*.[119] By distributing their money and their vices, the *aristocratie* was able to attract a certain following, weaning men from the moral purity of the *peuple*.

The *aristocratie* also employed prejudice and ignorance to destroy the newly acquired *philosophie* of the *peuple*. Audouin noted that the clergy disseminated superstition to spawn discord.[120] Prudhomme also pointed to the strenuous efforts of the *aristocratie* to silence the press and to facilitate the spread of ignorance.[121] In short, the radical journalists accused the *aristocratie* of trying to destroy the ability of the *peuple* to comprehend the dictates of nature—to know liberty.

In addition, the *aristocratie* sought to preserve their way of life by taking over the political structure of the Revolution. The Cordeliers claimed that the goal of the *aristocratie* was to usurp from the *peuple* the very government they had erected. Marat noted that, covered with the mantle of goodwill, the *aristocratie* planned to achieve the counterrevolution by monopolizing all the positions of authority:

> It is by filling the administrative bodies and the courts with their agents, by calling to positions only the supporters of the Old Regime, by assuring themselves all the public *functionnaires*, by corrupting all the "unfortunates," by seducing an army of spies, . . . by luring the *peuple*, and by winning it with caresses, promises, and gifts, that the *aristocratie* seeks to chain the *peuple* and to operate a counterrevolution.[122]

Other publicists warned of the same possibility.[123]

But if debasing the morality and degenerating the intelligence of the *peuple* proved unsuccessful and if insinuating themselves into office failed, then the *aristocrates* were willing to assault the Revolution directly. As before, they trumpeted their loyalty while plotting secretly and ubiquitously; yet now their plans, at least so the Cordeliers believed, called for a violent assault on the *peuple* and on the Revolution. Although scores of violent plots were projected, they usually included a similar set of circumstances. The radicals often repeated that the *aristocratie* planned to abduct the king,[124] start a civil war, or have foreign monarchs attack. Finally, all of these plots climaxed with a bloody slaughter of the *peuple*.

Habitually, the newspapermen warned that the aristocratic assault would begin with the abduction of the king. We have already seen that one journalist believed that it was the responsibility of Guignard Saint-Priest to spirit away the king to ignite a civil war. Fréron worried about the same problem and urged the king to try to resist the ploys of the ministers.[125]

The radicals also expected that the *aristocratie* would try to start a civil war in order to destroy the Revolution. Referring to an armed altercation between the citizens and the authorities, Desmoulins stated that such confrontations were all part of an aristocratic plan to shatter the *peuple*.[126] Marat also charged:

> In desperation over a new order of affairs which removes from the *aristocratie* the disastrous privilege to pillage and oppress the *peuple*, the enemies of the Revolution do not cease agitating to push the *peuple* to the disorders of anarchy, to divide it, to make it feel the evils of civil war, to disgust it with the responsibilities of new-born liberty, to bring it back to servitude, and to plunge it again into the abyss.[127]

Here Marat claimed that the *aristocratie* hoped to use the threat and the dislocations of civil war to disturb the *peuple* so that they would give up the Revolution; usually the ultimate motive of the *aristocratie* in inspiring internecine strife was to decimate the ranks of the *peuple*.[128]

Another counterrevolutionary strategy was an appeal to foreign powers to attack and overthrow the new regime. The *Mercure National* affirmed that the enemies of the *peuple* desired war.[129] Desmoulins warned that the *aristocratie* of Europe had massed against the French.[130] Marat explicitly stated that the aim of the ministers, whom the radicals completely identified with the counterrevolution, was to involve the *peuple* in a foreign war to divert their interest from the Constitution and from the fulfillment of their political goals.[131] Once again Marat pointed to aristocratic maneuvers and found them designed merely to distract, not destroy, the populace; but more often he and the other journalists thought that the direct assaults of the *aristocratie* would climax in devastating violence.

An excerpt from the *Ami du Peuple* will adequately demonstrate Marat's belief in the violent goals of the *aristocratie*. Haranguing his readers on the grave dangers faced by the Revolution, Marat speculated about a time when the king, in order to effect the counterrevolution, would arrest all those who had toiled for the new regime.[132] If they all surrendered without a struggle, Louis would place them in prison where they would languish until death. Moreover, the patriotic writers were to suffer the much more horrible fate of public torture. Marat then predicted:

> But if these patriots had offered resistance, all the citizens taken armed would be put to the sword without pity, their houses pillaged, their wives and daughters abandoned to the brutality of soldiers; and the leaders of these patriots will be put on the scaffold; they will only experience the most horrible punishments and France will be inundated with blood.[133]

Marat was not alone in his belief that the *aristocratie* would welcome a violent conclusion to their plans. The *Mercure National* added that an invasion by foreign troops would result in an incredible catastrophe with "women butchered, infants cut to pieces, old men mutilated, everywhere the cry of death, our cadavers dragged in mud, tortures everywhere, sons ripped from the arms of their mothers, fathers torn apart right before their sons' eyes, ripped to bits, the waters covered with blood, nature destroyed, humanity expiring, and the globe dishonored forever."[134] Such examples could be easily multiplied, but one more should suffice to illuminate the violence attributed to the aristocratic attack. Prudhomme (or more probably Loustallot) forecast: "If the aristocratic party triumphs over us, without indictment, without judgment, without cause, they will massacre all those who have distinguished themselves by vigorous actions and by pure sentiments . . . ."[135]

Thus, the views of the radicals presupposed an *aristocratie* that was no less than the most ghoulish ogre of a childhood fantasy. The *aristocrate* was an irresponsible egotist, who invariably looked only after his own welfare. Increasingly, his goal was wealth and power. Although what he did was inherent in human nature, by radical standards of morality, it was base and vile. This human nature contrasted in every way with the "new" nature of the *peuple*, so glorified by the journalists. The *aristocrate*, moreover, sought through secret plans to maintain his power and was ultimately willing to resort to the crudest villainies imaginable. While it is impossible for the historian to accept as fact this ubiquitous and horrible *aristocrate*, the existence of this spectre was unquestioned by the radicals. Theirs was a state of mind where paranoia and fanaticism ruled. The actual threats of nobles and clergy in the 1790s, combined with the personal anxieties of the publicists, make more understandable this exaggerated description of the *aristocratie*.

The radicals conceived of a world composed of two opposing and powerful groups—the *peuple* and the *aristocratie*. The journalists wavered constantly on the question of which one of these implacable opponents would triumph. This was a cataclysmic drama played out in the minds of the radicals. At times they felt certain that the freedom, morality, and the sanity of the *peuple* would endure; at other times, they despaired of it.[136] They constantly marveled at the weapons and the resourcefulness of the *aristocratie*. In the end, they probably believed the *peuple* would conquer and would not collapse from inner decay or from frontal assault. Nonetheless, we can be certain whom the radicals hoped would win. They believed in the morality and reason of the *peuple*; they revered the Revolution of the *peuple* and what it represented in French society and even in human nature; they detested the *aristocratie*; they feared the appeals and the power of the *aristocratie*; and they wanted to design a world that would favor the virtuous and restrain the immoral.

## THE POLITICAL, ECONOMIC, AND CULTURAL IDEAL OF THE *PEUPLE* AND THE *ARISTOCRATIE*

The ideal political world, envisioned by the radicals to satisfy the *peuple* and to enable them to keep the *aristocrates* in check, was constructed on a belief in popular sovereignty. Baldly stated, a commitment to popular sovereignty tells us very little, for all revolutionaries insisted on, and many moderate counterrevolutionaries conceded, the principle of popular sovereignty—that is, that sovereignty had passed from the king to the society as a whole. However, if considered as more than a transfer of the locus of power, popular sovereignty connoted very different ideas to different groups. It would be interesting to outline all the varied perceptions of this term, but such a task would result in a volume in itself.[137]

Nonetheless, as an example, one can examine how this term was defined in the Constitution of 1791. In composing the document, the legislators of the National Assembly reaffirmed their allegiance to the popular sovereignty that they had expressed in the Declaration of the Rights of Man. However, they did much to redefine and limit their initial promise that "all sovereignty rests essentially in the nation. No body and no individual may exercise authority which does not emanate from the nation expressly." First, the delegates determined that this "nation" was made up of only a portion of all Frenchmen. Legal qualifications curtailed the number who could vote (the "active citizens") and the number who could hold governmental posts. In the election of the Estates-General in 1789, almost all adult males could have voted and could have been elected, but the National Assembly chose to eliminate forty percent of the electorate. Further, less than one percent could hold office. The legislators even reduced the political activities of the "active" citizens by transfering administrative responsibilities from local control to the central authorities and by limiting the rights of petition. Also, constituencies had fewer opportunities for direct control over their representatives, as the latter were declared politically inviolable, subject neither to remonstrance nor recall. Finally, by instituting an indirect electoral procedure the National Assembly eliminated most connections between a delegate and his district.

The National Assembly's concept of popular sovereignty can further be illustrated by an examination of the procedures for constitutional amendment. There, after granting the theoretical right that the nation could alter its Constitution, the delegates proceeded to set up restrictions that would make changes virtually impossible. They specifically forbade the next two Assemblies (1791–95) from considering any alterations in the Constitution. Then, once change was possible, three successive legislatures had to pass a bill recommending an amendment, and a fourth, with 249 supplemental delegates, had to ratify this change. Thus, eight years would be required for all amendments, and it would be 1803 before the Constitution could be rewritten in any way.[138] For the members of the National Assembly, then, popular sovereignty meant the passage of sovereignty from the king to a reduced portion of the populace, which could exercise a restricted number of powers. But such was not the popular sovereignty of the radicals, who espoused a literal interpretation of this doctrine. They believed that almost everyone should be involved in the actual administration of power.

The radicals, like the delegates, gave formal adherence to popular sovereignty. The Cordeliers stated that law and the institutions of the state must be founded on and controlled by the desires of the citizen. An example of this belief in popular sovereignty appeared in the *Mercure National*, where the journalist wrote:

> The law must only be the expression of the common will, and must not have in sight anything other than the general interest; all decisions which do not have this character are not laws at all, but they are acts of tyranny.[139]

Audouin similarly noted that the citizens, who constitute the nation, have the right to make the civil, military, ecclesiastical, criminal—indeed, all of the laws.[140] In the *Révolutions de France et de Brabant*, Desmoulins rejected the claim of Leopold II that he could rule Brabant by the right of inheritance. Nations, Desmoulins wrote in disputing this claim, are not property: they may select their own rulers because "sovereignty resides in the citizenry, and they never delegate their power except by mandate . . . which is revocable at will, because the will of the populace is the supreme law."[141] Marat went so far as to affirm that regional units smaller than nations could decide their own political destiny. He stated that the provinces of France could determine whatever fate they desired, an interesting view for a future advocate of Robespierrist centralization.[142]

These theoretical affirmations of popular sovereignty differed little from those given by political moderates. However, the moderates could see no inconsistency in their principles when they advocated a sovereign parliament to interpret the will of the nation. Nor did adherence to the general notion of popular sovereignty prevent many from opposing either suffrage or elected office for the poor and propertyless. But the radicals interpreted popular sovereignty literally. Citizens were not simply theoretically sovereign; each and every one could and should share in the daily exercise of power. The goal of the radical campaign was to make this a reality.

The Cordelier publicists insisted that all, not just a portion of society, should participate equally in the formal political process. While the new Constitution was being hammered out and the National Assembly was eliminating about forty percent of the adult male population from the vote and over ninety-nine percent from holding office,[143] the radicals were calling for the eligibility of all adult males to vote and to hold office. To be sure, they did not wish to admit the *aristocratie*. However, so basic was their belief in universal male suffrage that the radical newspapers usually did not find it necessary to exclude specifically any portion of the adult male population. The *peuple* were synonymous with this population. The journals spoke constantly of the right of universal suffrage because, in the actual political arena, they were more concerned about including the poorest segments of society rather than removing any group.

Repeatedly the journalists railed against the pecuniary restrictions imposed on suffrage by the National Assembly.[144] In a typical statement Desmoulins wrote:

> If in place of forming a subterranean government, where a small number move the hidden controls and know the game, we would build a machine, encased in glass and very simply made, one run by hand *where everyone turns the wheel*, there would be no hiding places for rogues.[145]

There were rare occasions when antipathy for *aristocrates* or uneasiness over the reliability of the *indigens* provoked the radicals to oppose total inclusion in the electorate. For example, after claiming that all should have the right to vote, Marat proceeded to rule out a vote for transients, vagabonds, the venal, and the corrupt; clearly, this was an attack on the very poor and the very rich.[146] The radicals, however, usually advocated expanding political participation to everyone.

Not only did the Cordeliers desire that each individual participate in the formal government by voting and officeholding; they also wanted all to play a vigorous part in the informal political process. The *peuple* could "reason" best about their own moral and political needs; they comprehended best what the radicals called the *salut du peuple*.[147] This understanding, based on morality and reason, gave the *peuple* the right and the responsibility to rule the political order.

The *peuple* must do more than elect officials; they must also monitor both their representatives and the *aristocratie*. For these tasks, they required the right to assemble.[148] Prudhomme asserted that the privilege of assembly was the basis of any society and that those who obstructed it ought to die for their actions.[149] These conclaves of the *peuple* should be vigilant and watch for any efforts towards counterrevolution.[150] While surveillance was crucial, the *peuple* were not to limit themselves to passive outrage. Each journalist urged them to employ both nonviolent and violent means of resistance or repression against the counterrevolutionaries—the *aristocratie*.

The *Mercure National* echoed the general appeal for watchfulness over the opponents of the Revolution.[151] If mere surveillance failed to limit the *aristocratie*, these journalists urged a more active stand. They favored public denunciations,[152] and they saluted the sacking of the mansion of the duc de Castries as an excellent example of the *peuple* in action.[153] When the National Assembly did not respond to the demand for easy amendment of the Constitution, a journalist of the *Mercure National* advised his readers to institute, on their own initiative, a new constituent body empowered to alter the Constitution at frequent intervals.[154] The *Mercure National* also approved the more violent methods of the *peuple* when these were necessary to secure the Revolution, and it repeatedly sanctioned the glory of July Fourteenth as a model for political involvement.[155] Its positive attitude toward popular action was best phrased by Louise Robert:

> Let us assemble together, let the forty-eight sections reunite, let us form a coalition which will be imposing by the calm and moderation which will reign among us; let us be armed only with our rights and the firm resolution to maintain it. Let us address first the Department of Paris; if that does not suffice, then address the National Assembly with the Declaration of Rights and its own decrees in hand. Let us ask redress of our complaints—the recall of the mayor, who is either an imbecile or a prevaricator. That is to say, let us indicate to our representatives the general wish of the city of Paris on this subject . . . is that they decree according to the Rights of Man and

their own decrees sanctioned by the French *peuple*. But if our goal is not reached, then again *salus populi suprema lex esto*. You have called for insurrection, Lafayette. . . . Take care that this right is not used against you and your comrades.[156]

Madame Robert's threat of violence could have hardly been more clearly stated.

Audouin felt much the same as the editors of the *Mercure National*. He called on the citizenry to unite to struggle against dangers.[157] Like his comrades, he praised the attack on the house of the duc de Castries[158] and favored public denunciations of suspected traitors of the Revolution.[159] He also suggested the creation of patriotic societies as rallying points for the *peuple*.[160] In reporting the slaying of a grain monopolist by an aroused crowd, Audouin warned that all the counterrevolutionaries might justifiably meet the same end.[161] In an even more explicit suggestion of violence, he defended a plan to recruit a group of men, to be titled tyrannicides, whose mission would be to assassinate the kings of Europe should they try to attack France.[162]

Camille Desmoulins also encouraged the *peuple* to defend actively, even violently, their interests. Praise went to those whose efforts could alert the *peuple*. An aroused citizenry was, in the thinking of Desmoulins, desirable and capable of performing many tasks.[163] He suggested further that, if there were sufficient need, the *peuple* should seize the corn grown in their own locale.[164] Often he exhorted the citizens to censure, to denounce, those whose actions, while not illegal, were not ethical by revolutionary standards.[165] The *peuple* might shout down an enemy from the gallery of the National Assembly or circulate petitions against him.[166] Should such tactics fail, there was always violence. Indeed, Desmoulins had acquired his early reputation by urging the lynchings of several *aristocrates*. Consequently, it was no surprise to read in the *Révolutions de France et de Brabant* of the retribution promised those who had limited the suffrage of the "active citizens." Desmoulins, like the other radicals, believed that most, if not all, of the *peuple* were deprived of the vote; he insisted that since the legislators had refused so many entrance to political society, that those rejected, the *peuple*, could rightfully remove the legislators from society. He wrote to the National Assembly that "since you kill us in a civil way, we will kill you physically . . . when the legislators oppress the larger number of the citizens I know of no other law than vengeance."[167] Although this appeal to violence and others like it may seem somewhat rhetorical, the consistent support of street violence gave substance to these threats.

Perhaps the most ingenious designers of political activities for the *peuple* were Prudhomme and his assistants. As a means for controlling the theaters these journalists called on the *peuple* to boycott "aristocratic" productions.[168] Also, they suggested that each village establish patriotic meetings, where local officials would be assessed and judged.[169] These journalists also implored the *peuple* to use petitions, denunciations, and, if necessary, violence in order to achieve their ends.[170] They backed the establishment of the tyrannicides[171] and repeatedly praised the storming of the Bastille.[172] Despairing of peaceful efforts to control the "aristocratic" poison the editors cried, "We know only one means of discouraging them and their hirelings from committing illegal executions. Blow out the brains of all carriers of illegitimate orders."[173]

The appeal for popular action, especially violent action, reached an apogee in the pages of the *Ami du Peuple*. Marat to be sure, advocated many of the same peaceful means as his fellow journalists. He backed the use of petitions and public denunciations,[174] and he repeatedly called for confederations among the *peuple* for mutual support.[175] But, among the journalists of the radical press, Marat was the most likely to turn to force for a political solution. A major incident was caused by the publication of his pamphlet *C'est en fait de nous* in July 1790, in which Marat, after a list of shrill charges, demanded 800 heads. Many members of the National Assembly were outraged by Marat's call to violence and tried seriously, for the first time in the Revolution, to limit the freedom of the press. But even prior to this confrontation, Marat had suggested that the citizens slay their ministers on the altar of liberty in order to wash away ministerial crimes with blood. Following the horrified reaction of the delegates to *C'est en fait de nous*, Marat continued, even exacerbated, with little apology, his vituperation. By September 1790, Marat was demanding 10,000 heads to save the Revolution. In December, Marat insisted that a general insurrection with popular executions was necessary. Specifically, he demanded that the king, the queen, and the dauphin be arrested as hostages, and that Lafayette, the ministers and ex-ministers, the mayor, the Paris Municipality, the royalists in the National Assembly, and all the other counterrevolutionaries should be executed. Five thousand or 6,000 heads were necessary, but if these proved insufficient, wrote Marat, let 20,000 be given up for the Revolution.[176] And this was in 1790, not 1792 or 1793.

Like his close comrade Marat, Fréron prodded the *peuple* to relentless activity. Fréron especially urged public vigilance.[177] He called for public denunciations and printed them in his paper.[178] He also advised the Parisians to go to the National Assembly, sit in the galleries, and use their presence and voices to pressure the delegates to comply with their demands.[179] Like his mentor, Fréron had a penchant for violence. When the Constitutional Committee and the Commerce Committee suggested that debtors be imprisoned, the journalist replied that "if some blood of the representatives is necessary to keep an impoverished man free, then I announce to my comrades that this blood must flow."[180] On other occasions, Fréron recalled the glories of the armed *peuple* in their attack on the Bastille, and he promised the National Assembly another insurrection if the demands of the *peuple* were not met.[181] This threat marked Fréron's clear belief that violence was an important method for the *peuple* to exercise their own sovereignty.

Thus, the meaning of popular sovereignty to the radical publicists was substantially different from the notion of many of their contemporaries. The Cordeliers envisioned an entire *peuple* actively striving to exercise power. When they wrote that sovereignty rested with the *peuple*, they believed that it could be actually exercised by all the *peuple*. They supported all kinds of political participation, ranging from voting for representatives to violent insurrection.

Nonetheless, the journalists did not mean that the *peuple* would exercise their control continuously—only that they had the right to do so. Although it might be desirable for the *peuple* to monopolize legislation and administration, this was impracticable in a country as large as France. There must be a government, but one so organized that it could never acquire sufficient power to obstruct or to pervert the activities of the *peuple*.[182] The radicals assumed, as a matter of course, that popular sovereignty could not coexist easily with government. The exact source of their skepticism of the constituted authority is difficult to determine. However, one can suppose that experience taught them that governments, though theoretically founded on behalf of society, came to act for their own self-preservation and could not be expected, even when such action was called for, to bend before their populace. The journalists also feared government because they were convinced that politicians who had acquired power and prestige were more easily seduced by *aristocratie*. The *peuple*, however, as long as they lived and acted within the local community, would not lose their morality and good judgment.[183] In sum, the radical journalists believed that a government would usurp power that by right belonged to the *peuple*; consequently they proposed a government whose powers were few and easily controlled by the *peuple*.[184]

The radicals agreed that there should be a legislature but sought to limit its powers. They asserted that the deputies could at any time be recalled individually, or as a body, by their constituents.[185] Similarly, any law was subject to the veto of the *peuple*.[186] There were still other proposals designed to reduce the independence of the legislative body. The *Mercure National* insisted that all deliberation be open and public so that the *peuple* could monitor the proceedings.[187] Marat was very concerned about the presence of the *peuple* at the debates, since he desired that they exert direct moral and vocal pressures. He also complained about the meeting hall of the National Assembly (the Manège), which allowed so few spectators. There should be at least 2,000 seats for the *peuple* in the gallery. The Manège troubled Marat for yet another reason; he feared that its one narrow door could permit a few soldiers to protect the National Assembly against the *peuple*, thwarting their salutary role as watchdog.[188] From such proposals, it is clear that the radicals wanted the legislators to be no more than simple executors of the will of the *peuple*.

This pattern of suspicion and limitation was repeated in various forms for other parts of the government, including the judicial branch. The journalists were determined that the judges would be executors and not makers of the law. The radicals wanted strict procedures for arrest and trial so that jurists would be unable to impose arbitrary justice.[189] Further, the publicists denied the jurists the right to interpret law,[190] while they insisted on wide powers for juries, who were to rule in civil as well as criminal cases.[191] If the jury failed to dominate the judge, then the courtroom gallery was empowered to "supervise" court procedures.[192] In the *Révolutions de Paris*, Loustallot insisted that justice was only "societal" and indicated his support for increasing powers for both jury and audience.[193] Indicative of the attitude of the journalists was their position on capital punishment. The courts could no longer impose the extreme measure; the *peuple* should if they saw fit.[194] The instinct of the newspapers was to cripple the legislative and judicial powers of the formal governmental structure at the same time that they encouraged the *peuple* to initiate policy, propose law, and act as final judges.

When the radicals turned to the executive branch of the government, they asked two questions: Who should hold this authority and how independent should he be? Surprisingly perhaps, the radicals sometimes gave hesitant and provisional approval to the monarchy, but often they attacked kings and kingship with little reservation. Among many examples of their strong animosity were the remarks of Desmoulins.[195] Complaining about the investigation of the royal flight to Varennes in June 1791, Desmoulins wrote that he was not perturbed over the perfidy of the monarch and the queen, for they only did what he expected.

> That a king be corrupt, a monopolist, a swindler, ferocious, a counterfeiter, a perjurer, a traitor is no surprise. It is his nature to devour the substance of his *peuple* and to be man-eating, and I can no more hate him than a wolf who attacks us. As the tiger does when he sucks the blood of a voyager, the animal-king only follows his instinct when he sucks the blood of his *peuple*.[196]

Similar animosity led all the journalists at one time or another to question the usefulness of monarchy, and both Desmoulins and Robert suggested a republic as early as November 1789.[197]

However, the journalists were not invariably hostile to the monarchy; they admitted that, despite the iniquitous instincts of monarchy, it might be best to retain a king for the present. Indeed, all but the *Mercure* and the *Révolutions de France et de Brabant* sounded this latter note more often than they showed their distaste for the monarchy. And every journalist stated that as long as the monarchy could coexist with the new regime, it should be preserved.[198] There were even a few occasions when Prudhomme trusted, surely without much confidence in either, the monarch more than the National Assembly.[199] Even when the radicals did speak of a republic, they never explained how it should operate. Apparently a republic was a new and daring idea for the radicals of 1791. Few *philosophes* or current politicians had advocated such, and there was little support or precedent for such an idea. Thus, even after the flight to Varennes, the journalists usually wrote of removing Louis XVI, not the monarchy.[200]

In any case, it appears that the Cordeliers' position on monarchy as a viable institution remained ambivalent throughout this entire period. They despised kings while proposing no alternative. What was certain was that if there were to be a monarch, he, like the rest of government, would only be the executor for the *peuple*. Generally, the radicals referred to the king as the first officer of the nation. He was to be an important but passive agent. He was to be controlled not only by the vigilance of the *peuple*, but also by formal restrictions.[201] The authority of the king was not to extend to the judiciary or the military.[202] Marat took the extreme position that if the monarchy should be retained at all, the powers of the monarch should be limited to managing foreign affairs and commanding troops on the frontiers.[203] No doubt influenced by their distrust of monarchy, the radicals consigned the executive branch even less initiative than the judiciary or legislature.

Finally, the Cordeliers wished to deprive the armed forces of its potential to restrict or control the *peuple*. Basically they proposed two separate solutions, one for the standing armed forces, and one for the militia, the National Guard. To be sure, the radicals feared, with good reason, the army and the navy. The publicists correctly believed that these regular troops had been generally obedient in enforcing the edicts of the Old Regime; nonetheless, the radicals found hope, as the lower ranks, particularly after the opening of the Estates-General had increasingly mutinied against their noble officers. Indeed, the journalists announced their faith that the regular troops were allied with the *peuple*.[204] The Cordeliers endeavored to control the military by reducing its independence and by taking control from the Old Regime officers. The army, like all government components, was also to be small and clearly subordinated to the *peuple*.[205] The radicals appealed to local residents to watch closely the maneuvers of those troops stationed nearby. However, in the minds of the journalists, the most effective restraint on the standing military was to be provided by the common troops. Imbued with the morality and judgment of the *peuple*, the soldiers in the ranks could ensure the loyalty of the army and navy. The publicists insisted that the regular troops be empowered to elect their own officers. The radicals further argued that the troops were not, in essence, obedient, but deliberative, and encouraged the soldiers, like the *peuple*, to consider each order of their officers and to veto any which might hinder the Revolution. Further, the troops were to be tried for any breach of discipline by a civil, not a military tribunal.[206] By such methods, the Cordeliers relied on the lower ranks, in alliance with the *peuple*, to guarantee that the armed forces would not act against the Revolution.

The radicals suggested other means to ensure that the militia would have even less independence than the standing forces. Although most Parisians might have agreed in principle that the militia should be a civilian force that prepared for emergencies and included everyone, the actual National Guard headed by Lafayette in 1791 was hardly that. The general picked a staff that served at his discretion; he maintained certain companies on a paid basis. More important, recruits had to pay for their own uniforms and equipment, which excluded the poor from the guard. The radicals urged the abolition of these arrangements, demanding a spontaneously formed force of "minutemen," armed citizenry, brought together to repel any attack. No one would be excluded; no one would gain permanent powers as a result of a crisis.[207] The National Guard of the radicals would be little more than the *peuple* armed. Its organization would be dictated by the conditions of the moment. Indeed, the radicals wished to dismantle the militia more thoroughly than any other segment of government. Their ideal would have meant the destruction of the National Guard as Parisians knew it from 1789 to 1791.

Thus, the radicals wished to deny the government any independence.[208] Although their ideal government could still act, and act vigorously in certain cases, it could do so only under the direct supervision of the *peuple*. Further, this government often lacked authority as well as initiative. This emasculation of the government, coupled with wide-ranging powers for the *peuple*, defined the radical notion of popular sovereignty. When these publicists referred to popular sovereignty, they desired something different from the representative government that the National Assembly had decreed. The radicals wanted the *peuple* to have continuous active participation in all branches of government and the power of veto over the activities of all constituted bodies—legislative, judiciary, executive, and their military subordinates, the army, navy, and National Guard.

Before concluding our explanation of the ideas of the radicals, let us turn briefly to their cultural and economic ideals. As always, their goal was to satisfy their beloved *peuple* and deny the aspirations of the diabolical *aristocratie*.

To understand the economic position of the radicals, one must recall that the publicists believed that wealth was responsible in large measure for the evils of the *aristocratie*; consequently, one would expect them to urge destruction of great fortunes. And in fact, the radicals wished to reduce the wealth of the *aristocratie*. All the journalists inveighed against unequal treatment of children in the division of the family fortune, and one publisher demanded the abolition of wills.[209] They also urged a type of progressive taxation, unheard of in the Old Regime. The most far-reaching proposal was authored by Marat, who suggested the following scale of taxes in proportion to revenue:

| Tax (percentage) | Income in Livres | |
|---|---|---|
| | Single | Family |
| 2 | Above 1,200 | 2,400 |
| 3 | 1,500 | 2,500 |
| 4 | 1,800 | 3,000 |
| 5 | 2,100 | 4,000 |
| 6 | 2,400 | 5,000 |
| 7 | 2,700 | 6,000 |
| 8 | 3,000 | 7,000 |
| 9 | 4,000 | 8,000 |
| 10 | 5,000 | 10,000 |
| 25 | 15,000 | 25,000 |

Indubitably, this proposal would go very far, from the eighteenth-century point of view, to reduce the economic differences within French society. While most artisans and cultivators would go completely untaxed and most members of middle-income families (2,500–25,000 livres) would pay approximately what they had before 1789, the rich—important nobles and very successful businessmen—would pay a very high rate. Consider the case of a hypothetical court noble, who in 1789 paid perhaps six percent of his income in taxes, and who, under Marat's proposal, would have to give up one-quarter of his income, already reduced by the decrees of August 4. Although he would still retain his prerevolutionary landed estate, this high rate combined with the equal division of inheritances would certainly have reduced his fortune over time.[210] But this proposal, though interesting, was unique. More typical were suggestions that called for every citizen to pay the same tax rate and excluded only the very poor who were absolutely unable to pay.[211] Obviously, the last proposal would reduce fortunes somewhat, but was mild if compared with the proposition of the *Ami du Peuple.*

Despite these efforts to reduce the fortunes of the wealthy, and despite a theoretical hostility to wealth, the radicals rejected outright any sweeping suggestions to narrow disparities in income and wealth. They wanted the nation to reimburse all bond holders, including the *fermiers-généraux,* for their loans before the Revolution.[212] Also they insisted that property was privately owned and inviolable and could not be disposed of except at the discretion of the owner.[213] When the radicals advocated seizure, they were careful to give political justifications. They counseled that the *émigrés* should lose their estates, not because they were rich, but because sequestering their lands might induce them to cease their machinations against the new government.[214] Also, the radicals occasionally suggested the implementation of the *loi agraire*[215] to rectify political, not economic, behavior.[216] In short, the Cordeliers did not conceive of attacking fortunes by canceling the public debts or by direct confiscation of the property of the wealthy.

The radical journalists did make some economic concessions to the *peuple.* Theoretically, they had held the position that the wealth of the *aristocratie* should be redistributed to assure necessities to all. In practice, their proposed income tax offered some relief for the impoverished segments of society. Further, the radicals called on the rich for adequate wages for their employees and for greater spending to save the economy so that the poor might earn enough to avoid starvation. Prudhomme went farther and insisted that a society, to be productive, must provide the minimum subsistence for all.[217] But the radicals hedged even on these very small commitments. The journalists frowned on the loosely structured *ateliers de charité* and suggested that their laborers be marshaled as forced labor.[218] They also discouraged workingmen's associations designed to bargain for higher wages.[219] Finally, they used moral persuasion to encourage the rich to share their money,[220] but they stopped short of sponsoring any legal or extra-legal maneuvers to force them to share it. The Ventôse decrees of 1794, which called for free distribution of the suspects' lands to indigents, went far beyond their economic proposals.

The radicals theoretically wished to reduce the largest fortunes and to improve the lot of the poor, but they would not extend strong and comprehensive recommendations to alter economic conditions. In politics, they were willing to use violence to attain their ideal ends; in economics, they restrained themselves. They had conflicting ideals that caused them to delay in the latter area. Their commitment to free trade and private ownership was too great for them to approve forcible redistribution of property. To these traditional reasons given by Soboul and others for this economic conservatism, one could add that the radicals did not want to be accused of bringing about the Revolution for material gain. They wanted to change things without the taint of working for their own economic benefit. They abused the *aristocratie* for their avarice and feared any association with their greed. Also, the radicals did not want to alienate, by a policy of expropriation, potential allies in the all-important political sphere.[221] Perhaps they imagined that they could reduce aristocratic opposition by avoiding a confrontation over wealth.

When the radicals contemplated their cultural ideal, they sought to shape a system that corresponded to their opinion about the antagonism between the *peuple* and the *aristocratie*. In working to satisfy the former and restrict the latter, the journalists proposed that the *peuple* be sovereign and the *aristocratie* powerless. There was, however, some support given to universal freedom of conscience for all including even the *aristocratie*.[222] The newspapermen opposed any press law or governmental restriction of public expression.[223] Proposals for free expression, however, were the exception, not the rule.

In general, the radicals wanted to see strong efforts by the *peuple* themselves to raise aloft their true banners of morality, sanity, and freedom. The publicists suggested that the visual arts, books, schools, and newspapers should reflect the new revolutionary ideals. For instance, the *Révolutions de Paris* demanded that literature conform to the new revolutionary principles in order to reverse the influence of past royal patronage.[224] A journalist at the *Mercure National* suggested that the French language itself should reflect the revolution in men's minds:

> In spite of its imperfections, our language will soon be one of the most noble, the richest, the most sonorous, and the most expressive of the living languages, if we wish to study it, purify it at the fire of liberty, and render it finally dignified for a *peuple roi*.[225]

To the journalists, the new theater, the revitalized language, the entire revolutionary cultural production would not be passive indicators of their victory, but rather powerful weapons in the struggle against the ideas of the *aristocratie*. Desmoulins insisted that the journals alone, carrying the ideals of the *peuple*, would easily topple the remaining Old Regime governments.[226] Even the *aristocratie* was aware of the impact of this revolutionary literary production and feared it would easily overwhelm them.[227]

To supplement this effusion of revolutionary ideals, the radicals eagerly endorsed popular elimination of any aristocratic cultural expression. To be sure, the journalists distrusted and opposed any governmental interference with theaters or newspapers, but they agreed with Audouin that "the public, the public, there is the great judge, the impartial judge, the incorruptible judge of productions of all types."[228] The radicals probably preferred a popular boycott of "aristocratic" art, but they also advocated violent demonstrations at the theater and the smashing of newspaper presses to censure the art and literature of the *aristocratie*.[229] Thus, the radicals proposed a cultural ideal that closely resembled their political ideal. It gave the *peuple* absolute sovereignty and refused the *aristocratie* any place at all. The freedom of the radicals was the freedom to rule.

The radical journalists had a Manichaean view of society. On the one side, they saw the *peuple*—moral, reasonable, freedom-loving, and capable of governing themselves. On the other, they saw the demonic *aristocratie*, egotistical, debauched, and avaricious, who, through every possible means including violence, assaulted the *peuple* and their Revolution. The radicals believed in the reality of this polarization and constructed a political, economic, and cultural ideal to conform to, and influence, the outcome of the struggle. Thus, they chose to develop a societal structure that might reserve sovereignty to the *peuple*. Such a structure must give impetus, and not obstruction, to popular action. Because of their commitment to private property, the journalists were restrained in the economic sphere, but elsewhere they gave the *peuple* full power. It was indeed the radical image of royal power—absolute despotism—that the journalists were trying to capture for the *peuple*. "*Tel est notre plaisir*," said one radical newspaperman in justifying the action of the *peuple*.[230] No absolute monarch could have desired more.

# 4

# The Range of Reporting:
# The Treatment of Events
# in the Radical Press

GAIN WE MUST TURN to the question, What did the radical press say? Keeping in mind their general attitudes, let us look at their daily reporting of the political world. In this chapter, the radical press's treatment of events[1] will be discussed, and in the next chapter, their treatment of certain institutions and individuals will be similarly analyzed.

In reading the articles of the journalists of the extreme left, one is constantly impressed by their emphasis on specific events. The journalists seldom wrote selections unless inspired by a particular occurrence.[2] It must be apparent why daily happenings loomed large to the journalists, who, like most individuals, lived in an event-oriented world, where they hoped, feared, ate, and slept within the rubric of a succession of occurrences. So much happened in revolutionary France that it must have been difficult to find time for detached reflection. Consequently one must recognize and try to comprehend a mentality that perceived the world divided into distinct daily events and, nevertheless, simultaneously and consistently returned to the same ideology of popular sovereignty.

To determine how the radicals dealt with events required both the selection of a sample and a quantitative approach.[3] The thousands of events reported from 1789 to 1791 in the Cordelier newspapers cannot be summarized or understood without some selectivity; therefore, I chose to study the reporting in ten particular weeks—July 13 to September 20, 1790. Even with the use of this sample, there were approximately 1,000 articles concerned with 600 events; and if a researcher is to link these, he must be prepared to establish categories in which to class and tabulate his findings. For every article, then, I determined if a specific event had spawned that article, and if so, what institution, group, or individual had attracted the attention of the newspaperman. I labeled this institution the "source" of the story and placed it in one of the following categories.

"Sources"*
Formal governmental bodies
  National Assembly (6)
  Miscellaneous legal bodies: departments,
    municipalities, courts, National Guard
    general staff (7)
  Ministers and their subordinates (8)
  Monarch (9)
Informal political groups
  Prorevolutionary groups
  Clubs, sections, districts (10)
  Popular action, national and international (11)
  Counterrevolutionary groups
  Former privileged groups (12)
  New groups privileged by position or wealth (13)
  Middle groups (14)
  Brigands (15)
Foreign governments (16)
Books, plays, art forms, pamphlets (17)
Miscellaneous (18)

I was also interested in what type of action the "source" had taken, and I placed this action in its most appropriate category.

"Types" of activity
Political activity
  General politics—the establishment of a new political
    structure (19)
  Direct and participatory politics
    Considerations in legitimate political sphere on
    civil liberties and regulation of force in
    the state (state interference in freedom) (20)
  Spontaneous political action: plots,
    riots, meetings (21)
  Fiscal affairs (22)
  Economics of dearth (23)

---

*NOTE: The numbers in parentheses found here and in the following list refer to numbers used in the appendixes and will assist the reader to link the text with the supplementary material.

Arts (24)
Social services (25)
Foreign affairs (26)
Ecclesiastical affairs (27)
Affairs of the cultivators (28)
Miscellaneous (29)

In classing the reported events by their "sources" and by their activities, one can understand what sorts of occurrences interested the radicals. The logical hypothesis is that the publicists would be most devoted to items that related to popular sovereignty. But to understand clearly the importance of events to the radicals, one must take a microscopic look and examine how individual events were treated. With such a goal in mind, I found out how many newspapers followed each occurrence and how much space the journals devoted to it. This second approach should indicate conclusively whether the Cordelier journalists were more concerned with their ideology than they were with reporting single events. In summary, to evaluate the publicists' interest in events, I ascertained what "types" of activities received coverage, what institutions were involved, and the amount of time and newspaper space granted to particular occurrences.

To restate the case, we must begin with the reminder that the journalists returned with startling consistency to concrete and visible allies and enemies and also to certain abstract notions about society. At the same time, we should recall the consistent use of events in the radical press. The journalists constantly referred to the daily or weekly happenings throughout Europe, and, particularly, in Paris. Indeed, ninety-two percent of all the articles were based on the occurrence of some event; and these articles comprised ninety-three percent of all the pages of this extreme left press.[4] Consequently, the emphasis of the radicals on ideology was combined with a focus on events; the relationship between their ideas and the reported daily occurrences should give insight to Cordelier thinking and behavior.

When the men of the extreme left press reported events, customarily they were observing men and institutions that were contestants in the struggle for power. This statement could be made for the large majority of all the papers of the Revolution, since they too were particularly concerned with laws and demonstrations, with plots and acts of repression. This general orientation toward political "sources," however, represents a decisive break with the perspective of the Old Regime press. The journals of the eighteenth century did not report the happenings at court except in a cursory manner. While there is as yet no statistical information concerning the prerevolutionary press, a perusal of these papers reveals an obvious contrast. Rather than an emphasis on political sources, as in 1789 and after, there was a focus on graphic art, book reviews, foreign news, travel information, and the like. Although the journals published edicts and made surreptitious political allusions, they did little more, and the controversy that surrounds the right to publish political articles is part of the history of 1789.[5]

The radicals almost completely abandoned the traditional "sources" for news. Less than four percent of the articles, whose total length comprised only two percent of the press, were drawn from the activities of foreign governments. This "source" of news, important during the Old Regime, fell to a faint shadow of its former stature. But this decline does not completely reveal the total extent of the decrease, for domestic politics was the primary concern of almost three-quarters of those articles based on foreign governmental actions.[6] The radicals might report the passing of imperial troops near the French border, but the men of the left were not interested in military affairs or the strength of the Austrian government. Rather their interest was to prevent collusion between these soldiers and the French "aristocrates," who were, according to the journalists, anxious to overthrow the revolutionary government.[7] These newspapermen gave somewhat more attention to other traditional "sources" —plays, books, circulars, letters, and pamphlets—as eight percent (five percent of the total volume of the journals) of all stories reported were based on events in the written and visual world.[8] Nonetheless, over eighty percent of these articles, obstensibly devoted to the world of letters, actually dealt with French politics.[9] The plays discussed, such as André Chenier's *Charles V*, had greater political than literary interest.[10] Generally, indeed, those written works that were a "source" for the journalists were directly related to politics. Typical was Marat's review of an essay that discussed the rights of the Parisian sections and of the French citizen.[11]

Not only did the radicals, and the other revolutionary journalists as well, forsake traditional "sources," i.e., traditional newsmakers, for political ones, but they also narrowed their focus of attention to the specifically political activities of the new "sources." The impact of political institutions upon the nonpolitical world went largely unnoticed in the extreme left press. For example, the radical publicists ignored the National Assembly's regulation of rural life. Of every five Frenchmen, four were peasants, and nearly everyone owned or worked some land; yet only three articles on three separate events were devoted to the cultivator. Other gross omissions are equally easy to cite. The Revolution was born of a financial crisis and sustained by food crises, but those events, impinging both on the fiscal stability of the state and the difficulties of procuring food, received slight notice. There were seventy-seven articles (seven percent of the total number of stories and six percent of the total mass of newsprint) in these two very crucial areas. It is, I believe, fair to argue that this degree of attention, minimal though it was, was only that large because the radicals perceived a vague relationship between the fiscal and economic welfare of the nation and the continuance of the revolutionary regime. There was also very little interest in events that were related to social services. Although these newspapermen of the extreme left were close to the Parisian poor and interested in their welfare, the journalists rarely mentioned those projects and efforts designed to help the poorer citizenry. Only six articles, comprising 0.16 percent of the total newsprint, reported on this subject. Lastly, articles on ecclesiastical affairs are almost entirely absent. In all, about eighty percent of the articles and an equivalent amount of space were given to activities in the domestic political sphere, while the arts and music, economics and social welfare, foreign affairs, and farming interests were mostly overlooked.[12] All of this concentration on politics is to be expected from men whose interests were political and who lived in a city captivated and mesmerized by the political world. It may well be that this highly political emphasis was one factor that encouraged Parisians to channel their economic discontents into political demands.

Thus, the radicals shared with the majority of the revolutionary journalists an interest in politics. Nonetheless the centrist press—and this is a wide group of revolutionaries from Pierre Victor Malouet through Jacques Pierre Brissot—focused on different groups and individuals ("sources") and on different affairs ("types") than the men of the radical left. Again, neither statistical information nor any collective study of a large group of journals now exists; but a review of a number of prominent centrist newspapers reveals that most of their journalists looked to the activities of constituted bodies, with an overwhelming interest in the National Assembly. Furthermore, this press concentrated on parliamentary debate and the precise content of various legislative proposals. To be sure, they wrote of many other things; yet so many times the bulk of reporting was simply a transcription of the daily activities of the National Assembly with occasional digressions to report the debates of the Parisian Municipality. If they thought of popular involvement, it was mainly in terms of electing representatives to those legal bodies. If they reviewed new books, it was usually those written to propose various constitutional forms. The daily efforts of formal governing captivated their attention.[13]

The radical press also included many articles whose "source" was one of the constituted political bodies. Like the bulk of the Parisian newspapers, the extreme left most often drew their accounts from the debates, the decrees, and the regulations of the National Assembly. In fact, the *Révolutions de Paris*, the *Mercure National*, and the *Journal Universel* carried a regular report of the discussions of the representatives. So great was the interest of these three papers that their National Assembly reports alone often composed more than thirty percent of all their weekly news. Furthermore, around one-fifth of the articles (and approximately the same percentage of newsprint) were based on the affairs of other legally constituted bodies. Among these institutions were the Parisian and provincial national guards, departmental assemblies and directories, municipalities, and courts. Ten percent of the volume of the news had these lesser organs as their "source." An almost equivalent amount of attention was given to the actions of the king and his ministers, whose efforts during this experimental period of constitutional monarchy were likewise legal. It is interesting to note that the ministers received almost four times as much attention as the king. The revolutionaries were, indubitably, more concerned with the king's council than with Louis, because they believed that the monarch was rather passive and was manipulated by evil ministers. Thus, the radical press gave much attention, some sixty percent of their papers' total volume, to those same "sources" of news that were widely employed by almost all Parisian journalists.[14]

Although the extreme left focused on the usual "sources," they reported substantially less about the usual activities of these sources. Interest—in elections, in progress on the Constitution, in the regulation of differences between governmental bodies, and in the details of debates —was, in fact, low. Only seventeen percent of the articles and twenty-five percent of all newsprint were devoted to those activities, to those "types" of events, which focused on the establishment and regulations of government. This small percentage represents, if the current notion of the centrist press stands, a significant departure from the principal part of the Parisian press.

Since the radicals held the same overwhelming interest in politics as did most of the Parisian press and since the radicals relied heavily on the same "sources" as the Parisian centrist press, what precisely was the difference between the radical journalists and their counterparts of the center? First, the left looked to some atypical "sources" for news. In fact, thirty percent of the articles and twenty-three percent of the papers' pages were based on occurrences where informal bodies, both pro- and counter-revolutionary, were the principal actors. The radicals found space in their journals to report the maneuvers of revolutionaries who found a role outside of the constituted assemblies. We read, for example, of a district that had arrested men implicated in a conspiracy,[15] or of the Cordelier Club's efforts to plot against the state.[16] But the efforts of these organized, although informal, institutions, were only marginally reported when compared to the interest taken in spontaneous popular action. Twelve times as much paper (twelve percent to one percent) went into reporting these latter events. Fréron noted the action of the crowd at the Palais-

Royale in silencing the insults of "Riquetti-Cravatte," Mirabeau's younger brother and a virulent reactionary.[17] The *Mercure National* informed its readers of a popular festival at Nancy to celebrate the Revolution.[18] One can also learn from the Cordelier press of the cordial reception given by the Parisians to the federal troops arriving from the provinces.[19]

Not only the spontaneous actions of the radical's allies but also those of their enemies were reported. About ten percent of the total newsprint (twenty-three percent for all spontaneous activity) was devoted to chronicling the counterrevolutionaries, or, as the radicals always tagged them, the *"aristocrates."* The escape of the chevalier de Bonne-Savardin, implicated in plots against the revolutionary government, evoked wide interest from the radical press.[20] Gouvelet, an agent of Artois, was the subject of a report found in the *Orateur du Peuple*.[21] This list might be extended tediously, but the point is clear that the left press very frequently looked at "sources" other than the legally constituted bodies.

When the centrist journalists reported about the National Assembly or other constituted bodies, they generally focused on those matters relating to the construction of a new state. As noted above, the radicals viewed these affairs with less interest. What did they substitute? What "types" of activities interested them? In sum, the radicals concerned themselves with those activities impinging on or exemplifying participatory politics.

Marat, Fréron, the Roberts, and the others were, indeed, obsessed by events involving civil liberties. They felt strongly about freedom of expression, freedom for political gatherings, and access to equal justice. Tightly linked to these concerns was an interest in the nature of public force in society—the military, the courts, the national guard, and the police—as the policies of these institutions would, in the final analysis, determine the extent of civil liberties. The role of the authorities in determining political freedom was always apparent to the radicals who, both under the monarchy and under Bailly and Lafayette's regime, had to preserve their own civil liberties against repression. It is useful to imagine the leftists' daily difficulties with haughty officers and overbearing soldiers who, in a café dispute, might abuse their authority by arresting anyone who dared to disagree. The relationship, the connection, between force and freedom was, moreover, permanently reinforced by memories of Bastille Day, where liberty was won by the defection of the king's troops.[22] The radicals' ideas about public force and public freedom were discussed in more detail earlier; but suffice it to say, they were more than a little interested in these matters. One-third of the newsprint and thirty percent of the articles were concerned with such interests. For example, the most reported event during this sample period was the suppression of a mutiny at Nancy.[23] There, the rights of soldiers to resist arbitrary orders of their officers and to act for the Revolution were the center of discussion. A more symbolic issue of the same genre was the debate over whether the seal to be stamped on National Guard buttons should include the word *roi* with the consequent implication of obedience to the king.[24] Further, Audouin reported a denunciation of the National Guard's staff as guilty of falsifying orders and of limiting freedom.[25] Although the struggle to control and influence public force went on apace, the fight over civil liberties, over the freedom to act politically, was no less intense. Fréron wrote of the *Châtelet*'s efforts to reduce the freedom of the press[26] and the printers' demonstration to defend these rights.[27] The *Révolutions de Paris* examined the culpability of a bookstore owner who claimed that she was not responsible for slanderous pamphlets against the duke of Orléans that were discovered for sale in her shop.[28] From these examples, which could easily be multiplied, one can grasp the type of event that, in mid-1790, predominated in the minds of the radicals.

Events concerning civil liberties, crucial in shaping the extent of popular activity, were rivaled as an object of radical interest only by events in which spontaneous efforts themselves were described and evaluated. The interests of the revolutionaries in general, and the men of the extreme left in particular, balanced between faith in the good acts of the populace and paranoia about "ubiquitous" aristocratic plots. And in fact, both revolutionary efforts and counterrevolutionary machinations loomed very large in the radical press. One-third of the articles and thirty percent of the total volume of the papers were devoted to spontaneous action. For example, Desmoulins's *Révolutions de France et de Brabant* noted an aristocratic uprising in the East Indies,[29] while another article detailed the endeavors of the National Assembly to stop "aristocratic" scheming.[30] Fréron described a popular gathering where the names of "*aristocrates*" were burned in effigy,[31] and the *Révolutions de Paris* reported the indignation of the citizenry over the bravado of a robber and their prompt punishment of this thief.[32]

Consequently, the radicals, like other journalists, relied on political institutions and political activities for the events that were reported. Nevertheless, the politics of the radicals were not those of the centrist press. The left looked to the field of spontaneous action for their news stories; they were more concerned with those elements of the government that regulated participatory, not parliamentary, politics. They did not watch constitution making so much as they did counterrevolutionary and prorevolutionary popular action. This emphasis was quite natural because of the journalists' close relationship with the Cordeliers and their own struggle for freedom of the press. Indeed, the radical publicists were more concerned with the battle for the preservation of their political role and with schemes and legislation to control them, than with elections, general parliamentary debates, and organizational details. Their emphasis in reporting events was reinforced by their ideological commitment to popular sovereignty, a belief that drew the journalists' attention to the political participation of the average citizen. The radicals, enamored with the crowd action of July Fourteenth and captivated by belief in popular sovereignty, kept the riots of Bastille Day before their eyes and grappled with those elements that threatened and encouraged popular involvement.

Having described the general pattern of attention of the six journals under consideration, I believe that these trends are fairly indicative of the tendencies throughout the radical press. Nevertheless, the trends vary somewhat from week to week and from journal to journal, and these differences may prove to be instructive.

First, as table 1 in appendix B reveals, the pattern of attention for each of the individual papers is not uniform. One finds in this table variations between the *Orateur du Peuple* and the *Mercure National*, which stand, in most categories of interest, on opposite ends of the radical spectrum.[33] The other four journals, however, fall much closer to each other and to the mean as well. It is important, however, not to overemphasize differences between the two extremes, as figures 4.1a–c indicate.

These graphs reveal that, rather than sharp differences in coverage, there is a fairly uniform pattern in the attention of all six newspapers. To be sure, some discontinuities do exist—for example, the interest in National Assembly activities is markedly high for the *Mercure National* and strikingly low for the *Orateur du Peuple*. Furthermore, Fréron's interest in parliamentary politics is quite low, but these are the exceptions to the uniform proportions characterizing the graphs.

Nonetheless, the minor differences among journals do reveal some interesting correlations. First, those journalists who looked more to constituted bodies outside of the National Assembly and less to the National Assembly itself were also more interested in informal political groupings and in spontaneous political activity. All of this is revealed graphically in figure 4.2. (Compare bar 1 with bars 2 and 3 and then compare all three with bar 4.) Thus, there is a direct correlation between interest in the constituted bodies other than the National Assembly and concern about popular action. Why should this be the case? On one hand, the National Assembly was highly involved in regulating popular action and often debated such subjects, but, on the other hand, the National Assembly appeared to be above the daily struggle between the "*aristocrates*" and the *peuple*. Did not the National Assembly have an aura of working on something permanent, something above petty disputes of the city? And, in fact, even when the National Assembly did interfere in these

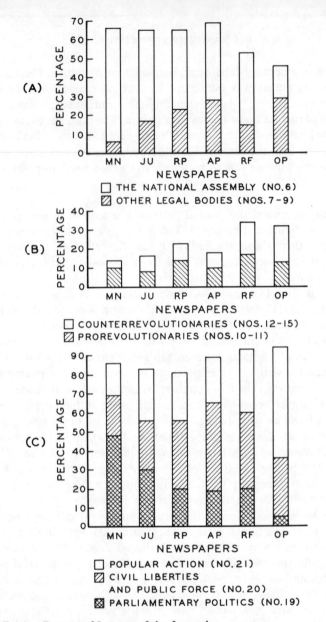

FIGURE 4.1. Pattern of Interest of the Journals

A. Percentage of Newsprint Devoted to Legally Constituted Bodies.
B. Percentage of Newsprint Devoted to Informal Political Groups.
C. Percentage of Newsprint Devoted to Selected Activities.

SOURCE: Appendix B (all figures)
NOTE: The abbreviations that follow apply to all figures.

| AP | *Ami du Peuple* | OP | *Orateur du Peuple* |
|----|-----------------|----|---------------------|
| JU | *Journal Universel* | RF | *Révolutions de France et de Brabant* |
| MN | *Mercure National* | RP | *Révolutions de Paris* |

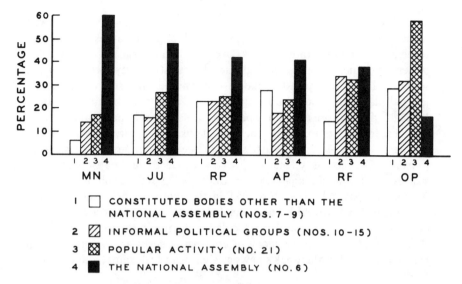

FIGURE 4.2. Attention of Journalists (Percentage of Newsprint Devoted to Selected Activities and Sources).

SOURCE: Appendix B, table 2

local matters, the municipality, or the ministers, or the *Châtelet* usually implemented the decisions. Consequently, for those who were most interested in popular action, these lesser legal bodies were often the visible agents of repression and consequently, the center of attention for the radicals.

Another interesting relationship is apparent here. While it would be well to minimize the differences among journals, it is also true that those papers whose passion for Cordelier politics was least, were most concerned with parliamentary affairs. Indeed, the *Mercure National* and the *Journal Universel* tended to focus on the National Assembly and away from other formal and informal bodies and from popular stirrings. Since they tended to be more conciliatory and less suspicious, their confidence in the Constituent Assembly was greater, and they reported more faithfully the affairs of this body. This tendency on the part of Robert and Audouin was, indeed, reflective of the direction of the centrist press, whose interests lay almost exclusively with legalism and constitutionalism.

While variations in coverage from journal to journal were, on the whole, not very significant, the deviations in the writers' interests from week to week are larger and far more important. A quick look at table 1, appendix B, reveals that the gyrations from week to week were large. To find out which weeks vary meaningfully from the average, one can chart table 1 to find those weeks where the emphasis on the major "sources" or "types" of activities is markedly different from average.[34] Specifically, I would define an atypical week as one in which major areas of coverage received fifty percent more or less coverage than their usual coverage. To understand the rationale behind the choice of ± fifty percent as the selection figure, one must visualize this number in terms of the actual journal pages. In general, no single "source" or "type" or activity would be dealt with in more than forty percent of the journals' pages and twenty-five percent was more nearly the case. Thus, the major areas of interest averaged seventy-five pages per week of the three hundred pages for all journals. Consequently, one long extra article or one half-dozen short stories concerning a single "source" or "type" of event could increase the number of pages by one-third, yet in the mind of the reader and the journalists, there would be no special emphasis in that particular area of coverage. For this reason I have decided that a minimum variation of fifty percent in at least one category of concern is necessary before one can legitimately regard the week's news as significantly deviant from the usual fare.

Using the method above, I have found the following results as shown in table 4.1. Thus, four weeks show no sharp variance from the mean, while six weeks do. To find out the causes of these distinct changes, one should, it seems to me, look most closely at those weeks (i.e., numbers one, two, and eight) where about half of the major areas of coverage showed large deviation. There were, of course, many influences on what would be reported. There surely were the whims of the writers. But the most apparent commonality among those three abnormal weeks was that all were weeks where one event, reported in at least five of the papers and occupying over one-quarter of the newsprint, dominated radical coverage. Furthermore, of the six weeks where interests deviate somewhat from the standard, four have one occurrence that is "dominant," and none of the remaining weeks have this characteristic.[35] Consequently, there can be no doubt of the high correlation between one "dominant" event monopolizing the news and an alteration of the journalists' pattern of attention. In addition, I would claim that it is the intrusion of this "dominant" event that *causes* a change in the pattern of attention, since one can easily observe that the rude change in the pattern of attention corresponds to and follows sequentially the major themes of the emerging occurrence.

To recapitulate, the average pattern of attention is not representative for all weeks. On some occasions, it is simply the case that there are wide deviations; moreover, these variations are caused by a "dominant" event that actually reoriented the pattern of attention according to its "source" and "type" of activity. How lasting is this change? Does the pattern of attention permanently alter? To answer this question requires only a glance at the preceding chart, which clearly shows a return to the norm

TABLE 4.1
Deviations in Coverage (by Week)

| Week Number* | Number of Major Sources or Types of Events Changing More than 50% |
|---|---|
| 1 | 3 |
| 2 | 3 |
| 3 | 0 |
| 4 | 2 |
| 5 | 1 |
| 6 | 2 |
| 7 | 0 |
| 8 | 4 |
| 9 | 0 |
| 10 | 0 |

*For the dates corresponding to those numbered weeks, see note to tables, appendix B.

after each significant deviance.[36] To understand why these "dominant" events do not have a more lasting effect on the writers' interests requires delving into the weekly range of events. This investigation will, in fact, show that these "dominant" events were not characteristic of the occurrences that were typically covered in the radical press. Also a closer look at those "dominant" occurrences may help us to understand more clearly the role of events in determining the newspapers' content.

To explain why "dominant" events had only a temporary impact on the pattern of attention and to shed light on the import of events to the radicals, one must initially tour the disparate occurrences of an "ordinary" week. Such a week, in which there was a wide variety of events, was August 10 to 16, 1791.[37] In this period, each of the weeklies and the daily *Journal Universel* published as usual, while the *Orateur du Peuple* and the *Ami du Peuple* each produced only six issues. The collective length of these journals was around three hundred twenty-five pages; but, subtracting for all the blank spaces and all the areas given over to the vanity of the editors, who often brandished the title of their journal more prominently than the news, there are somewhat fewer than three hundred pages of newsprint. Within these three hundred pages were ninety-four articles of varying lengths and about varying subjects. These articles were based on sixty-three different events. Fifty-eight events were each reported by a single article, while the other five events had twenty-four articles devoted to them. Twelve articles of the ninety-four were editorials. Moreover, the articles of different word lengths were somewhat unevenly distributed among the three categories. Approximately forty percent of the newsprint (twenty-four articles) was devoted to the five principle events; fifty percent to those fifty-eight events that were reported only in single articles; and ten percent (twelve articles) to editorials.[38]

Two of the five events that were more widely reported received scarcely more attention than the fifty-eight others; these two affairs, the possibility of Jacques Necker's departure and the action of the National Guard to rescue some thieves from an angry mob were reported twice each and together received only four and one-half percent of the newsprint. But a major share of attention actually went to the debates of the National Assembly, which the *Journal Universel*, the *Révolutions de Paris*, and the *Mercure National* covered as a regular feature. The most important event of this week under consideration was the *Châtelet's* efforts to bring charges against the very popular Mirabeau and Orléans for inciting the crowd in the October Days. All the papers except two, the *Mercure National* and the *Journal Universel* (always less anxious to provoke emotions), carried an article on this event, and only one of the other four, the *Révolutions de France et de Brabant*, did not place the article on its front page. The other event occasioning notable interest among the journalists (again the Roberts were not included) was a duel between the Jacobin Antoine Pierre Barnave and the royalist Jacques de Cazalès, an action seen as part of a wider attempt of the *aristocrates* to assassinate their adversaries, the "virtuous" Jacobins. Although these events appeared as giants compared to the other reported occurrences, their coverage was rather limited as well. The debates of the National Assembly received the greatest single bloc of newsprint (seventeen percent of the week's total) but found space in only three papers. Although the Barnave-Cazalès duel and the *Châtelet's* action interested more journalists, the two events received but 6.5 percent and twelve percent respectively of the total newsprint.[39]

With only this moderate concern over these five events, the journalists' interest in the week of August 10-16 was directed elsewhere. Indeed, these press radicals devoted over fifty percent of their newsprint to covering the fifty-eight events reported only once in the six journals. Although an all-inclusive list must be reserved for appendix C, an enumeration of a few representative articles is appropriate here. Included among the fifty-eight occurrences that interested only one radical newsman on a single occasion were many events from the sphere of parliamentary politics that were widely mentioned in the centrist press. The *Révolutions de Paris* devoted three pages to Armand Camus's denunciation of Necker's financial report while in a similar but unrelated story, Audouin praised the assault of Camus on the practice of granting royal pensions. Marat noted that the National Assembly had forbidden the opening of a packet of possible espionage materials. Also the radicals reported various spontaneous activities supporting the Revolution. The *Révolutions de Paris* extolled the *fête* given in memory of Benjamin Franklin by some simple *ouvriers*, and Robert printed a letter that glorified the efforts of the Englishman Dr. Price on behalf of the French Revolution. In the *Journal Universel*, Audouin noted the desire of the French artists abroad to wear the revolutionary cockade despite opposition from their conservative patrons. For those interested in foreign affairs, Audouin gave this subject some attention by reporting the truce arranged between Prussia, Hungary, and the Ottoman Empire.

But if international relations, parliamentary procedures, and popular activity favoring the Revolution interested the radicals, plots by the "*aristocrates*" were their stock-in-trade. There were *aristocrates* in Guadalupe to worry about, and there were machinations by former deputies of the second estate directed against the National Assembly and of concern to any revolutionary. Fréron warned of the plots by the cardinal of Rohan against public order in Strasbourg; and the *Mercure National* raised the possibility of foreign invasion in reporting the passage of imperial troops across France's northeastern frontier. Marat counseled that even the reliable Jacobin, Charles Malo François de Lameth, was implicated in a plot against the gains of the Revolution. In short, between August 10 and August 16, the radical newspapermen were not obsessed with any single event. They ranged widely over the field of occurrences and spoke primarily of little-known and now generally forgotten affairs.

The diversity present in the reporting in mid-August 1790, (in our one week sample) is representative of the general trend found in the six newspapers during the entire ten-week period. The coverage of individual events was for the most part brief and most often restricted to a single newspaper. The general lack of attention given to most individual events is startling. For the average week, just under one-half of the papers' newsprint would be devoted to some sixty events. Of this myriad number of events, none would receive over five percent of the news production. To understand exactly how minuscule this coverage was, one must realize that these percentages mean that each of these sixty events (ninety-five percent of the total number of events covered) received an average of two and one-half very small pages of news coverage in a week. This coverage was sometimes divided among more than one of the papers. In short, the Cordeliers spread themselves thin, and most reports were cursory. The other half of the newsprint was devoted to stories on three to four events. The breakdown may be found in table 4.2.

From the chart is is apparent that, despite the general diversity of radical reporting, there were a few events that interested the journalists sufficiently for them to make a very lengthy investigation. Occurrences that were not given more attention than ten percent of a week's production, that is, somewhat less than thirty pages, perhaps split among several

TABLE 4.2
Coverage of Events in an Average Week

| Length of Coverage (Percentage of One Week's Newsprint) | Average Number of Events Covered | Percentage of the Week's Newsprint Occupied by This Material |
|---|---|---|
| 0–5 | 59.6 | 45 |
| 5–10 | 1.4 | 10 |
| 10–20 | 1.1 | 16 |
| 20–30 | .6 | 15 |
| 30+ | .2 | 7 |
| Total | | 93%* |

*Seven percent of the average week's newsprint was allotted to editorials.

papers, did not constitute objects of great concern. On the other hand, events that absorbed or exceeded one-fifth of an entire week's projection must be considered to have been of some significance to the journalists. Each week there were generally about two of these events that received enough attention to be noticeable in the midst of so many other occurrences virtually lost in the mass of newsprint. One can, in fact, identify exactly nineteen such events in the entire ten-week period. Of these nineteen, however, only three were reported in five of the journals, and only a single event found a place in all six journals.

But even these four events, which dominated reporting at least for a week, were rapidly deserted by the journalists. As figure 4.3 indicates, the radicals were unable to sustain a common propaganda effort based on an event. Here we see that one event, the national *fête*, remained important, in fact "dominant," for two weeks. Nevertheless, all three events, after a brief period of intense interest, experienced a precipitous drop in concern and passed into oblivion in the radical mind.

By contrast, diversity in reporting was persistently sustained. In one particular week, almost sixty percent of the papers' pages was taken up by occurrences mentioned only once in one journal. In the entire ten-week period, forty-three percent of the print was devoted to events reported only in a single paper. Thirty-eight percent of the pages contained information on developments that either two, three, or four publicists found of interest. This last percentage reveals certain common concerns, but it certainly does little to remove the overall impression of a press that had very disparate interests. In sum, when over eighty percent of the newsprint (ninety-nine percent of the event-oriented articles) was devoted to events unreported in at least two journals,[40] it is impossible to

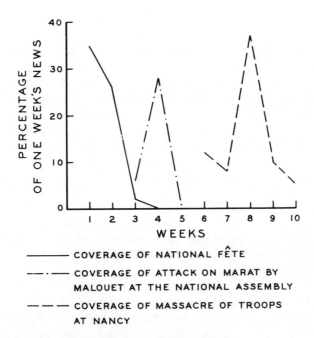

FIGURE 4.3.    Coverage of "Dominant" Events

SOURCE: Appendix B, table 5

conclude that these six papers shared common reporting even though their political positions were similar.[41]

Emerging from this description is a picture of six papers whose coverage, for the average week, was based largely on a multitude of events. Usually only one journalist was concerned with an event and then but for a few pages. Each week did have two or more events, nineteen for the entire period, that received substantially more purview than the others; but in fifteen of these cases the reporting of these events was restricted to four or fewer papers. Moreover, the other four issues, widely covered, were forgotten soon enough. They appear as anomalies. To be certain, when these four events occurred, they reduced the amount of newsprint devoted to events reported only by a single journal;[42] moreover, for three (weeks 1, 2, and 8) of these four periods, there was a major shift in the pattern of attention. The other "dominant" event, Marat's battle with the National Assembly, altered the journalists' attention, albeit with somewhat less amplitude. But because concentration on "dominant" events was not the thrust of the press, because diversity and brevity were more important than concentration of attention, the effect of these four occurrences was quite limited. The leftists evinced a certain reluctance to focus directly on single events. True, they were willing temporarily to shift their emphases, their pattern of attention, but that transitory shift was the extent of their commitment.

But why did the "dominant" events diminish so quickly as objects of radical interest and concern? Why did the journalists prefer diversity of materials and brevity of treatment to a single-minded sustained effort? Was this because there were no significant events of this period that were grist for the mill of the radical point of view? Did they abandon reporting the "dominant" activities, the big crises of the Revolution, because these were inconvenient to the political purposes of the press? A look at the well-covered occurrences, the radicals' *causes célèbres* will quickly dispel this supposition, for all the events focused on in these weeks coincided with the ideological considerations of the journalists. The articles on the national *fête* dealt principally with informal efforts to celebrate the conquering of the Bastille, while Marat's battle with the National Assembly over his incendiary pamphleteering focused interest on the regulation of the right to publish, the cornerstone of a free press. The struggle between the officers and regular troops at Nancy concentrated attention on the regulation of public force. Thus, rather than blunting the thrust of the radicals' primary point, these "dominant" events stimulated interest in those areas that related to participatory politics and that served to distinguish the radical from the centrist press. In fact, the radicals concentrated only on occurrences that fell within their political interests. There were events in this period whose importance to most Parisians should have justified extensive press coverage, but, because they lay outside the central concerns of the radicals, the Cordeliers overlooked them. There was widespread anxiety over the king's health, thought to be perilously poor at this time, and over the National Assembly debate on *assignats*; but there is little information on these matters in the radical press. Such concerns over a monarch or over fiscal affairs failed to spark these journalists' attention. But if they failed to dwell on any events in depth, it was not because events would necessarily detract from their purpose; in fact, the events that they did cover strongly supported their positions.

The journalists, however, failed to extend the coverage of the very events that might best serve their cause. They had flagrant examples of aristocratic malevolence in their hands, they had an aroused public, yet they often turned to some new issue after a short exploitation. They did not act for long in unison on any event. It seems ironic that men so interested in changing their world would fail to coordinate their actions in the press.[43] They may have acted with this apparent political naiveté because of a proprietary attitude toward their respective papers. The radicals had a myriad of interests, many of which were very personal or occasionally shared with one or two other journalists. One need only witness the amount of press coverage given by each journalist to his own tribulations and the use of the word "je" in so many instances. The radicals may be best viewed as men, possessed by certain common attitudes and emotions, who developed individual areas of new coverage based on their shared ideas. Over time they continued to specialize in certain private interests. It must not be forgotten that some events break this pattern, but, as I have argued, these are rare.

Secondly, the journalists avoided concentrating on "dominant" events because they did not wish to abdicate interest in the legitimate political sphere. They still believed, throughout this period, in the Constitution and to some extent in the officials of the present government, and they thought it necessary and proper to encourage some popular interest in these institutions. Also, they were aware that decisions made by parliamentary bodies influenced them, and they wished to exert some influence on legislation.

Finally, it appears that the rush of events was so great that the radicals were unable to focus on single occurrences or regard these occurrences as significant. The Old Regime had provided the journalists with only negligible experience in these sorts of political affairs. Their background made them uninterested in events; it had encouraged their interest in ideology. In sum, the journalists did not concentrate on "dominant" events on which men of their political movement were in accord. They did not reject common action or a common pattern of attention. They welcomed both, but each believed his diverse interests essential to the common cause.

Consequently, the journalists were concerned with a variety of individual events, but this interest was very limited. The brevity and diversity of their reporting are indicative of their typical fleeting, if passionate, approach to events. Though specific occurrences may have been of limited significance, the general characteristics of these events, discussed in the first half of this chapter, were crucial. The journalists doggedly maintained the same pattern of attention over time.[44] As was shown, this pattern of attention was common to all radical journalists and represents their mutual predisposition in favor of participatory politics and popular sovereignty. The radicals were committed to these general views; it was in this area of common perspective that the radicals came together in a common front. It was here where they acted jointly to influence opinion. Thus, it was a belief in participatory politics and in popular sovereignty, not a concern about events, which continuously energized and motivated the radicals.

# 5

# The Treatment of
# Individuals and Institutions
# in the Radical Press

E HAVE SEEN that in the radical press, events were
subordinate to ideology. While the publicists passed
hurriedly over specific occurrences and skimped in
their descriptions, they repeatedly selected events
that would validate and emphasize their concern with popular sovereignty. In a similar way, the institutions and individuals treated in the
radical press were superseded by ideology. First, only those groups with
some role in the struggle for popular sovereignty were likely to receive
much coverage. Second, the radicals found it difficult to describe or
evaluate these groups without reference to popular sovereignty.

Although the coverage of institutions and individuals was greatly
influenced by ideology, this reporting must itself be considered. The
radicals believed themselves to be judging these bodies by their actual
performance, and they were not totally inaccurate. The radical press was
especially attentive to the activities of certain institutions—particularly
the court at Versailles, the ministers, the monarchical family, the church,
the Jacobins and Cordeliers, the Paris Municipality, the National Guard,
and the National Assembly. In addition, the journalists of the six papers
singled out the preeminent members of these bodies—Necker, Jean
Sylvain Bailly, Lafayette, Louis XVI, and Marie-Antoinette—for special
treatment. Thus, to extend our answer to the question, What did the
radical press say? we must now investigate the treatment of the individuals and institutions thought to be important by the Cordeliers. This
chapter, then, begins with those men and institutions that the Cordeliers
despised (the villains), proceeds to those they idolized (the heroes), and
concludes with those first praised but ultimately condemned. The chapter

92

focuses on the quality of and the changes in the radical descriptions of these bodies and their leading members. Finally, consideration will be given to the role ideology played in the radical viewpoint.

## DURABLE VILLAINS AND DURABLE HEROES

From the onset of the Revolution in July 1789, the royal court was the object of much abuse by the radical press. The brothers and cousins of the king (Orléans usually excepted), dukes, peers, ladies-in-waiting, upper clergy, high nobles—all of court society was attacked, both individually and collectively, as the center of iniquity, as the *aristocratie* of the *aristocratie*. Fréron insisted that "it was the court which nourished the audacity of all our enemies."[1] Prudhomme condemned the court, whose example had encouraged the luxurious habits of the *aristocratie* and had caused the impoverishment of the peasants, who had to pay directly and indirectly for the aristocratic life style.[2] Moreover, in the eyes of the radicals, the mainspring of court opposition to the Revolution was the ministers. Detesting the court as the core of the *aristocratie*, the radicals thought of its power largely in terms of what the ministers were capable of doing.[3]

And, for the Cordelier journalists, the ministers were pointing toward a single goal—counterrevolution. They conspired with foreign governments; they manipulated elections; they played a nefarious role in the grain trade. Nothing—nothing that could upset the Revolution—escaped their purview. For example, Desmoulins insisted that the ministers oversupplied the army garrisons to quell just popular uprisings. Also, he listed ministerial appointments to military posts, claiming that these new officers were nothing but counterrevolutionary conspirators.[4] Audouin likewise found that the regulations in the army imposed by the ministers were all part of an effort to corrupt the military in order to effect a counterrevolution.[5] For Marat, the goal of the ministers was a war whose horrors would discourage popular support for the Revolution.[6] The list of ministerial actions, alleged by the radicals as efforts to overthrow the new regime, could be indefinitely extended, but Fréron has epitomized the radical view of ministerial intentions: "The Constitution has no more heated enemies than the ministers; they might present to the nation the cup of peace. I would break the chalice against the altar of liberty because this goblet would be full of the most fatal poison."[7]

Moreover, this hostile treatment was continued even for ministers who had the general approval of most revolutionaries. The treatment of Necker, the secretary of finance, is a case in point. Although he was admired by most revolutionaries and his removal from office precipitated street protest that led directly to the seizure of the Bastille, the radicals detested him and accused him of conspiracy. As early as September 1789, when his public credit was quite high, he was assailed by Marat for undermining the National Assembly and for working to reestablish despotism. Not much later, Marat attacked Necker as a speculator, a charge often repeated by the radical press.[8] The rest of the Cordeliers, previously neutral, followed the lead of Marat and began to defame Necker in the first few months of 1790. In April, Desmoulins termed the minister a hypocrite, and on May 2, Audouin recommended his exile.[9] Likewise, in early April, the *Révolutions de Paris*, which had briefly supported Necker, insisted that he had libeled the National Assembly.[10] Furthermore, as Necker failed to right French finances and consequently lost popularity among more moderate revolutionaries, the radicals increased their abuse. In July 1790, Marat arraigned Necker as the soul of all the plots in the country. The article went on to assert that Necker had feigned patriotism as a ploy to gain the funds necessary to corrupt the National Guard, the National Assembly, the patriotic writers, and the *Châtelet*.[11] The *Révolutions de Paris* chided itself for its earlier support of Necker and soundly condemned the minister as a liar, speculator, and a counterrevolutionary.[12]

The Cordelier journalists not only assailed Necker, they contended that all the ministers, regardless of their reputations, worked for the *aristocratie* and against the Revolution. By the time the Cordelier press had been established, those ministers irrevocably opposed to the Revolution had been replaced. By midsummer of 1789, the ministers in office, Saint Hérenn Montmorin, Saint-Priest, La Tour du Pin, Luzerne, and Champion de Cicé were willing to work with the National Assembly. But their willingness spared them nothing. The radicals asserted that these ministers were involved in the vilest plots against the Revolution. Fréron and Prudhomme implicated all of them by name in plots to overthrow the new regime.[13] Each ministerial decision provoked virulent attacks from the Cordeliers. Commenting on a ministerial investigation of a meeting in Marseilles, Desmoulins designated Saint-Priest as the leader of the ministerial efforts to destroy the new order.[14] The *Mercure National* contended that some new administrative regulations on coin and grain were ministerial efforts to monopolize these products and to overthrow the government of the *peuple*.[15] Finally, the radical press had an opportunity to join in a successful campaign to oust these ministers.

By mid-summer of 1790, many others, especially the Jacobins in the National Assembly, shared the radical antipathy for the ministers. The Revolution had run into difficulties with finances and with the church, and a scapegoat was required. This widespread anxiety coalesced around a demand for the "recall" of the ministers, who were actually removed in early November, 1790. Montmorin, the minister of war, was excepted because public opinion still considered him a friend of the Revolution.[16] Although the radicals were probably not the most influential participants in this coalition, they were the most aggressive and the most longstanding enemies of the ministry. They gave free vent to their hostilities and were pleased with the ouster of these opponents. Nonetheless, their habitual hatred of ministers precluded any favorable reception of the new appointees.

The radicals should have been completely intoxicated with this shared victory, for the new ministry favored the Cordelier positions far more than the old. Their old *bête noir*, Necker and his cabinet, had been replaced by four cronies of Lafayette, still popular in 1790, and by Adrien Duport de Tertre, a comrade of Lameth, the current darling of the radical press.[17] But the ministers, no matter what their politics, were an anathema to the Cordeliers. After a brief respite, in which the radicals promised to judge the new ministers fairly but circumspectly,[18] the journalists launched new assaults as vitriolic as the old. Drawing attention to the permission given to Austria to move troops through French territory, Marat insisted that the new ministers had arranged for a foreign attack. He predicted that these ministers would continue all the iniquitous projects of their predecessors.[19] The *Révolutions de Paris* and the *Révolutions de France et de Brabant* asserted that the ambassadors appointed by Montmorin were part of a plan to engage foreign assistance against the Revolution.[20] Fréron warned also of the counterrevolutionary dangers posed by the new ministers.[21]

Ministers, new and old, regardless of their past or current records, were constantly attacked for their political actions. Every incident, important or inconsequential, revealed to the radicals the treasonous actions of the ministers. The grounds for this hostility were complex, many based on specific grievances, and often peculiar to an individual journalist. Nonetheless, two general antagonisms do emerge. First, the radicals assumed that one could not be a minister and maintain allegiance to the *peuple*. In the *Mercure National*, François Robert voiced his doubts that ministers could be loyal. In refuting some comments of Duport de Tertre, Robert remarked that a minister could never preserve the "dignity of a man." Exposed to the court, a minister would be easily seduced and corrupted by its mores.[22] Marat likewise insisted that the court could easily manipulate and corrupt any minister in its midst, no matter how high-minded his principles were on assuming office.[23] Thus, because the court, the epitome of the *aristocratie*, was incorrigible in its hatred for the Revolution, there could be no hope for the ministers who worked in such a milieu. Ironically, the radicals also believed that it was the ministers who directed the court's machinations against the Revolution.

Second, the Cordelier writers reviled the ministers because these journalists, like other revolutionaries, required a scapegoat for the personal and policy failures of the king. For most of the period 1789 to 1791 they wanted to absolve Louis of his failure to accept the radical program, and consequently, they asserted that it was the ministers with aid from the court who were responsible for royal errors such as Louis's delay in signing the Declaration of the Rights of Man and his continued taste for a luxurious life style. Fréron insisted that all the ministers were corrupt and took advantage of the vacillating personality of the king to perpetrate their schemes.[24] Marat likewise faulted Louis's advisers for monarchical error and compassionately sympathized.

> It is not against the king that I have wished to oppose the arguments of justice and reason, but against his counsellors. . . . No one can appreciate as well as I the natural goodness of the king and the unfortunate position of this monarch, who is surrounded by knaves who abuse his confidence each day and who will end by making him lose the love and esteem of his comrades . . . the *peuple*. . . .[25]

Ministers, as described in the radical press, were durable villains, who, under the influence of the court, were completely committed to the service of the *aristocratie* and would spare no means to overturn the Revolution. Perhaps, the underlying reason for this trenchant criticism was the desire of radical publicists to excuse serious royal shortcomings.

The second of the villains was the queen, Marie-Antoinette. However, while the radical press treated her with contempt, they portrayed her in a substantially different manner than did the Paris "grub-street" writers of the 1780s. For the latter group she was extremely important, if not central, to their disillusionment with the Old Regime. She represented to the "grub-street" radicals the moral degeneracy of the court. In their essays, the queen was dangerous because of her incessant involvement in scandals where the king was humiliated and where sexual license and impulse replaced calm reflection as a basis for public appointments and decision making.[26] By contrast, the Cordeliers did not regard Marie-Antoinette as a very important opponent, and these former "grub-street" radicals did not see her in 1789 as a major threat to the morality of society.

In fact, the radical newspapermen tended to ignore Marie-Antoinette from 1789 to 1791. It would be difficult for a reader to find many references to the queen in the radical press. This was especially true from 1789 to mid-1790, and the remarks that were made were only mildly or indirectly hostile to the queen. Of the radical journalists, Camille Desmoulins was most hostile to the queen, but even his animosity was guarded. Although he believed that the principles of the Revolution required changing the status of Marie-Antoinette from queen to the wife of the king, his arguments relied on involved references to the Salic Law and to the Declaration of the Rights of Man rather than on a direct attack on the person of the queen.[27] True, such references were only a sophistic cover for Desmoulins's hostility; true, contemporaries and the queen herself were well aware of his below-the-surface anger; but, still, Desmoulins hesitated to make open charges against the queen. Moreover, other radical journalists gave more neutral treatment to the queen. Reporting the arrival of the royal family in Paris in October 1789, Prudhomme addressed himself to Marie-Antoinette. He observed that, in general, the *peuple* had been mistreated by the queens of France, but that the present queen still had an opportunity to reverse this sad history. Her arrival from Versailles had made him optimistic; now it was up to her to confirm his hopes by demonstrating her patriotism.[28] True, there was some concern that the queen might be a villain, but the tone of the article was one of hopeful confidence in her. In sum, until the middle of 1790, the radical newspapermen seldom mentioned Marie-Antoinette, and when they did they evinced only a mild animosity.

Although the radicals generally continued to ignore the queen throughout 1790 and 1791, their occasional remarks became markedly more hostile. During this period, the Cordelier publicists warned that the queen's every action was designed to foment counterrevolution. Abandoning the charge of the "grub-street" radicals that Marie-Antoinette debased public morals, the radicals attacked her for her political machinations. Marat posited that the aunts of the king should not be permitted to emigrate because of the perilous situation faced by the nation. Among such perils was the fact that the queen was "the sister of a tyrant who is armed and waiting at our frontiers, and she only breathes for the moment when she may bathe herself in the blood of the French. . . ."[29] Marat was seconded by the other radicals in his conviction that Marie-Antoinette was an avid conspirator for the counterrevolution. The Cordeliers, indeed, often insisted that the center of such plotting was a group of the queen's advisers, which they dubbed the Austrian Committee. The name given to this group indicates the radicals' obvious belief in the queen's involvement, for she was the sole Austrian that the radicals or their readers knew. And, in order that there could be no mistaking the complicity of the queen, the journalists sometimes wrote of the "comité autrichienne."[30] The use of the feminine gender of Austrian to modify the masculine noun *comité* was, of course, grammatically incorrect. Nonetheless, this usage was politically intentional, for it indicated to the naive reader and listener that the committee was inspired, not only by an Austrian but also by a female Austrian. Only the most ignorant French reader could fail to guess the identity of the chief conspirator.

In brief, although the radicals increasingly treated the queen as a villain from 1789 to 1791, she was ignored in most of their articles. It is not quite clear why Marie-Antoinette was treated so mildly in 1789 to 1791 after the blistering attacks of the 1780s, but this difference in reporting suggests that the former "grub-street" radicals redirected their attention to other villains during the first years of the Revolution.

The radicals also treated the Catholic church as a durable villain. From the very first, the newsmen identified the nonparish clergy, both monastic and regular, with the *aristocratie* and with opposition to the Revolution. The church hierarchy was guilty, so said the Cordeliers, of participating in the counterrevolution to protect their property and lascivious opulence.[31] The hostility of the radicals for the upper clergy certainly contributed to a picture of a church mired in self-indulgence, luxury, and conspiracy.

Early in the Revolution, the radicals had adopted the notion of a parish clergy united with the *peuple*.[32] This alliance saved the church from blanket condemnation for a brief period, but it was not long before these journalists began to harass the lower clergy as well. By mid-1790, the radicals were accusing the parish priests of working with the regular clergy to preserve a haughty, useless materialism and to overturn the Revolution. Prudhomme, or perhaps one of his associates, expressed his reaction to the clerical resistance to the Civil Constitution of the Clergy. He insisted that the *curés* had allied politically with the bishops simply to continue enjoying an insolent luxury.[33] Other journalists insisted that the parish priests were dedicated to maintaining luxury and halting the Revolution. Reasoning much as Prudhomme, Audouin wrote:

> Yes, the race of priests is an evil race! I except a small number of virtuous and good ministers; because certainly there are a few who are respectable and respected, who never dishonor their ministry by a shameful irreligion, by thirst for gold or blood, by a rage of passion against the decrees of a free and sovereign nation. . . .[34]

The attack, widened to include the parish priest as well as bishops or abbots, could hardly fail to tarnish further the damaged image of the church.

Finally, the picture of the church was still more clouded by radical skepticism of the validity of church doctrine. Usually, even when the radicals violently assailed the hierarchy of the church, they accepted the spiritual functions of the church as necessary and desirable.[35] Nonetheless, there were scattered attacks on Catholic teachings as well as on "clericalism." Desmoulins noted in a sarcastic passage that Paul was unintelligent and mistaken in his teachings.[36] Fréron asserted that the doctrines of Christianity were unbelievable to modern man.[37] Although such remarks were the exception in the radical press, they represented a growing attack on the church—already conceived of as an institution infected by villains who were trying to preserve "aristocratic" ostentatiousness and self-indulgence, and who were conspiring to destroy the Revolution.

Thus, in the minds of the radicals, the villainous ministry, the queen, and the entire clergy were actively plotting against the Revolution. Further, as we shall see, the National Assembly, the Parisian authorities and the king were later to join these original conspirators. Opposing these groups and institutions was a beleaguered group of steadfast men of principle, durable heroes—chiefly the Cordeliers and the Jacobins. These durable heroes, few in number, were praised from 1789 to 1791 for all their actions, whether or not these actions were central to, or even consistent with, Cordelier "philosophy." A few examples should clarify this statement.

In an article entitled "Quelques réflexions sur le club des Jacobins et sur le club 89," Robert lauded the Jacobins for their support for the issuance of the *assignats*, for the bill ascribing war-making powers to the nation, and for their decorum in the National Assembly. In the case of the *assignats*, Robert praised the Jacobins for their fiscal wisdom, not for their moral purity or commitment to popular sovereignty. He backed them specifically for their position without any extrapolation or claims that by this action the Jacobins had proved any extraordinary revolutionary ardor or had any special commitment to popular sovereignty.[38] This praise for a specific meritorious action should be contrasted with the remarks of the radicals about the villains, whose every action was interpreted not on its own characteristics but as part of a design either to ensure outrageous opulence or to facilitate the counterrevolution.

The other radical journalists praised the durable heroes in the same specific way. Fréron examined the disgruntlement of the Cordeliers with Lafayette and praised them specifically for their move to censure the general.[39] But, in addition, Fréron and his comrades often used an action of this heroic organization to illustrate a conformity with general radical principles. For example, when the Cordeliers protected Marat in one of his encounters with the Paris Municipality, Prudhomme lauded the district for its defense of the rights of the individual and waxed eloquent over the commitment of the district to the Revolution and to popular sovereignty.[40]

Finally, whether the radical journalists restricted their praise to the specific action or expanded their praise to include ideology, they were unrestrained in their enthusiasm for the Jacobins and the Cordeliers. Audouin reported Cordelier resistance to a municipal decision that would forbid the posting of criticism of the political authorities. He praised their position, associated himself with the Cordelier cause, and then concluded.

> Our blood [the Cordeliers'] will be the fecund germ of a new generation of patriots. The municipality wishes to prevent us from revealing the plots of the enemies of the Revolution and the vices of the administrative bodies . . . but despite our enemies, these so-called friends of the law, public understanding will make irresistible progress each day, the love of liberty will triumph over all obstacles and will assure the happiness of future generations. Indeed our patriotism, our virtue, our persecution, perhaps even our blood will have cemented this happiness.[41]

Audouin may have limited his praise to the Cordeliers' posters and to their defiant desire to keep them in circulation, but he obviously did so in the most extravagant fashion. The Jacobins were treated to similar, though not quite so hyperbolic, plaudits by the radical newspapers. Their policy of exclusive membership and their frequent capitulation to the National Assembly cost them a measure of adulation, but they were still widely applauded.[42] Audouin asserted that the Jacobins were the highest moral force in the Revolution.[43] Likewise Desmoulins affirmed that the Jacobin Club, for its efforts on the *Journée des Poignards,* was the "most wonderful institution that has ever existed."[44] Thus, the Jacobins like the Cordeliers were abundantly praised from 1789 to 1791 for diverse activities and in a diverse pattern that included both specific remarks and general ideological approval.

## FROM HEROES TO VILLAINS:
## THE PARIS MUNICIPALITY, BAILLY,
## LAFAYETTE, THE NATIONAL GUARD

Following the opening of the Estates-General, the police and executive bodies that had administered Paris either atrophied or were purposely dismantled. This decay continued at an accelerated rate after the seizure of the Bastille. All that remained to fill the local power vacuum were the electoral districts of the capital, which, their original function having been completed, had become almost dormant by July 1789. However, in July when the arrival of royal troops threatened the Revolution, the district councils revitalized and assumed local leadership. Under their aegis, the National Guard was formed and the Revolution secured. But coordination among the districts was needed and to this end a central body, the municipality, was formed. In addition, a mayor, Bailly, and a commander for the National Guard, Lafayette, were elected. In July 1789, Bailly,

Lafayette, the municipality, and the National Guard, so recently created by the districts, shared the support, indeed, the acclaim, of all those who approved the direct action taken by the district leadership. The radical press joined in unbridled and unreflective praise for these new institutions and their leaders. Bailly, Lafayette, and the municipality, the creation of the districts, and the institutional embodiment of popular sovereignty, enjoyed an imposing mandate that precluded criticism. But this acclaim did not long endure. By 1791 the radical journals would insist that each had abandoned the principles of popular sovereignty and had committed other transgressions that justified acid attacks in all six papers.[45]

First to come under criticism was the municipality. The Cordeliers granted some grudging admissions of respect,[46] but very soon after the events of July, the municipality found itself indicted by the extreme-left press. The initial radical complaints centered on two charges—one, that the municipality was trying to usurp the powers of the districts, and two, that the municipality was composed of "corrupt" men. On September 25, 1789, the *Révolutions de Paris*, after reporting some recent decisions of the ministers, demanded that the municipal authorities give up efforts to usurp the legislative powers of the sixty districts. This journal returned to its defense of district sovereignty in October. Its editors claimed that the municipality was attempting to deny the citizenry the right to remonstrate.[47] Not much later, Marat agreed with the *Révolutions de Paris* that the districts were being denied their right to deliberation; however, Marat directed his charge more at immorality within the municipality. Reviewing the actions of the municipality, he asserted that their meeting place, the *Hôtel de Ville*, was filled with the *aristocratie*, disreputable characters, hoarders of coin and grain, and agents of the ministers.[48]

These lines of attack were repeated by both journals and later were echoed by the entire radical press. In October 1790, Desmoulins noted the closing of the *Parlement* by the municipality and launched a diatribe against the pomp displayed by the Paris officials on this occasion. He assailed their ostentatious attire and their inflated honor guards.[49] Elsewhere, complaints about the usurpation of powers by the municipality persisted. Audouin noted in early 1791: "Why is the Municipality of Paris already incorrigible? Why does it play with despotism? Why does it frequently arrogate to itself an unconstitutional authority?"[50] Thus, dating from September 1789, and persisting through 1791, there were attacks on the municipality for its efforts to ape the ostentatiousness and manners of the *aristocratie* and for its "unconstitutional" assault on popular sovereignty.

But this loss of faith led to a more serious charge against the municipality. No longer were its members simply *debauchés* or even dangerous usurpers of power; they were active counterrevolutionary plotters. In September 1790, Marat claimed that the municipal officials had formed *compagnies de famine,* whose ultimate purpose was to weaken the resistance of the *peuple* to the armed counterrevolution.[51] This same charge was sounded by Fréron a few months later.[52] Relating another theory of conspiracy, Audouin insisted that it was through misappropriation of funds that the city officials favored the "aristocratic" plot.[53] In brief, the municipality enjoyed only a short-lived popularity in the radical press, and it soon joined the durable villains as a participant in the effort to overthrow the Revolution.

The head of the municipality, Bailly, enjoyed only a slightly longer period of grace. In late 1789 when Marat launched his attack on the municipality, he remained relatively silent about Bailly's complicity in its actions. The mayor, the executor of municipal decisions, seemed immune to Marat's scathing pen. Possibly, the mayor's charisma, shown by his courage at the *Jeu de Paume,* restrained Marat. However, in December 1790, Bailly drastically reduced the number of hawkers permitted to peddle journals in the street. Marat immediately accused him, not of obstruction of political rights, but of threatening the financial support of the journals. Marat exploded:

> . . . you have become insensitive the moment you were presented some honors. Success then hardens the heart of a *philosophe* as much as a common man. . . . Drawn in a shiny carriage, you cover us with mud in the streets, you drink our blood in cups of gold.[54]

Although Bailly would later be accused of many crimes by the radical press, this caricature of an intellectual, addicted to pomp and luxury, would often return to haunt him.

In fact, only a week after Marat's accusation, Desmoulins attacked an agent of the *Hôtel de Ville,* Boucher d'Argis, for his overbearing pride and then blamed the example of Bailly for the vanity of his subordinate. According to the journalist, the ostentatiousness of the mayor had infected local government and caused a certain *"petitesse."*[55] Despite the attacks of Desmoulins and Marat early in 1790, the other journalists remained silent or defended the character of Bailly for a few more months. For example the *Révolutions de Paris* lauded the mayor specifically for his assiduous scavenging of grain for Paris and, elsewhere, praised him generally for his support of popular sovereignty.[56] But Bailly was seldom mentioned or only neutrally discussed by the other journalists, though he received criticism from Marat and Desmoulins for his superfluous display.

By the second half of 1790, this relative respite from criticism had ended. First, Desmoulins and Marat broadened their charges against Bailly. In May 1790, Marat blamed Bailly for the proposal to destroy the districts and asserted that the mayor wished to obstruct popular sovereignty.[57] Two months later Desmoulins reached the same conclusion. Noting the boundaries and the hurried organization of the newly formed sections, Desmoulins asserted that the mayor intended to destroy the right of the *peuple* to self-government.[58]

The other publicists, perhaps swayed by Bailly's role in the suppression of the districts, joined in the assault. In September, Fréron called Bailly a pompous, inconsequential man.[59] The editors of the *Mercure National* joined in discrediting Bailly with the serious charge that he, with Lafayette, had designed a plan to corrupt the National Guard.[60] In October, Audouin questioned Bailly's support for certain decrees proposed by the ministers, and by November he had concluded that Bailly was in league with these "villains."[61]

In fact, by the end of 1790, all the radical journalists were charging Bailly with complicity in counterrevolutionary plots. Earlier the defender of Bailly, the *Révolutions de Paris* now noted that the mayor had refused to present the demands of the sections to the National Assembly and concluded that he had joined with the ministers in suppressing such complaints.[62] Fréron also asserted that Bailly was an active conspirator who had personally designed a "project" to induce a civil war.[63] Charges of counterrevolutionary plotting continued unabated from the end of 1790, and continued into 1791; predictably Bailly's earliest opponents, Marat and Desmoulins, joined in this campaign. In April, Marat informed his readers that the mayor was a member of a coalition whose goal was to make Alsace the first theater of civil war.[64] Desmoulins reinforced Bailly's image as a conspirator by charging that he had aided the flight of Louis XVI to Varennes in June 1791.[65]

Thus, in a relatively short period from 1789 to 1791, Bailly had passed from fame to infamy. All the stages of this transformation would be impossible to trace, but the radicals first pointed to his opposition to district sovereignty and his ostentatiousness. Once Bailly was distrusted for his pomp and his local political policies, the radicals began to regard his actions as conspiratorial. Bailly's reputation declined more slowly than that of the municipality; nonetheless, by 1791 he was associated with the durable villains and by 1793 he would face the guillotine.

Although historians have found it difficult to differentiate between the policies of Bailly and those of Lafayette, the radicals apparently believed them to be quite distinct. At a time when the radical editors were either opposed or indifferent to Bailly, they were effusive in their praise for his counterpart, the general and commander of the National Guard. Indeed, during all of 1789 and the first five months of 1790, nothing but praise for Lafayette appeared in all six journals.

Lafayette must have felt encouraged about his political security by the complimentary remarks of the radical press. Marat found him to be a man suited for freedom[66] and Desmoulins could write unashamedly about a painting of Lafayette: "Then let me prostrate myself before this image. . . . I love to contemplate it, not as an ideal, but as the object of our dearest hopes." While there was some hint here that Desmoulins did not want such adulation to go too far, his affection was open and obvious.[67] Indeed, despite his commitment to weak government, he praised Lafayette for the able use of spies to stifle "conspiracies" in Paris.[68] This dithyrambic praise was especially persistent in the *Journal Universal,* where Audouin as late as mid-May 1790, lauded the general for his role in the National Assembly.[69] The hyperbolic remarks of an anonymous poem were not uncommon fare for the readers of this paper. One author wrote in January of 1790:

Ah! que plutôt sous le glaive assassin,
Puisse tomber ma tête, ou s'ouvrir *tout* mon sein,
Avant que La Fayette ait, d'un trait homicide,
Reçu le coup fatal, dont menace un perfide—!
Dieu juste, Etre éternel, prononce, et j'obéis
Ouvre-moi le tombeau; j'y défends à ce prix
Sans effroi, sans regret, je donnerai ma vie
Pour sauver le Héros qui sauve ma Patrie.

Par Madame de M——[70]

There was no single style for their praise. These plaudits might be limited to a single action, or they might praise Lafayette for contributions to freedom and popular sovereignty in general. But their passion and enthusiasm for the "Hero of Two Revolutions" was uniform.

Yet, the affection of the radicals was soon to wane. By spring of 1790, some faint rumblings could be heard against Lafayette. The editors of the *Révolutions de Paris* and the *Révolutions de France et de Brabant* criticized Lafayette's vanity,[71] and Marat impugned his organization of the National Guard.[72] Although these criticisms were meant only to correct and not to vilify the general, they tarnished his image as a hero and warned of future disintegration of his popularity among the radicals.

In June 1790, Marat turned sharply against Lafayette and expanded his earlier criticism about the structure of the National Guard. He insisted that the National Guard had obstructed the sovereignty of the *peuple.*[73] Marat's charges increased in intensity, climaxing with the following indictment on June 28, 1790:

I will not paint here the picture of your [Lafayette's] old demerits; I will not cry again how your conduct is contrary to the principles that you claim; I will not oppose here your devotion to the court, whose interests you feign to neglect, to your disloyalty for the *peuple* whose cause you feign to serve; I will not speak here of your connivance with the ministers. . . . I will speak to you of the composition of your general staff . . . the action of your paid troops . . . and the spirit of the National Guard.

Marat went on to claim that the general staff, the paid troops, and the haughtiness of Lafayette's soldiers jeopardized the ability of the *peuple* to govern themselves.[74] The status of this hero was, thus, seriously endangered. While hesitating to charge Lafayette openly as a conspirator, Marat depicted him as a threat to popular sovereignty.

In mid-July, Desmoulins's *Révolutions de France et de Brabant* launched the second assault against Lafayette. Desmoulins complained of the idolization of Lafayette, which had attained dazzling heights at the first anniversary celebration of the fall of the Bastille. At this festival, Desmoulins observed the growth of a development he greatly feared. In the hero worship for Lafayette, Desmoulins saw the emergence of a vanity, a pride, commonly associated with the *aristocratie*. He hoped that the general would renounce these attentions, but, in fact, Lafayette had cultivated them. Desmoulins, with his confidence in his hero broken, concluded by echoing the charges of Marat:

> Thus, after the destruction of arbitrary *ordres,* M. Motier [Lafayette] has raised a new order, the most formidable of all, the order of citizens armed with rifles and sabers. . . . M. Motier, in place of royal censors, has substituted 30,000 municipal censors armed with bayonets, of whom a great number cannot or do not wish to read.[75]

For Desmoulins as well, Lafayette had created a National Guard willing to stifle the political expression of the *peuple.*

In the first week of August, Prudhomme and his chief journalist, Loustallot, joined the ranks against Lafayette and blasted him with attacks that paralleled those of Marat and Desmoulins. Precipitating this new hostility was a decision by the general to expand further the responsibilities of the National Guard in order to guarantee law and order. To Prudhomme, this decision was no less than a declaration of war on the sovereignty of the *peuple* in particular and on the Revolution in general. It was also convincing proof that the praise tendered Lafayette had corrupted him. He had become an egotist, seeking to aggrandize his position at the expense of the *peuple.*[76]

But the three other radical journals restrained themselves. No longer did they shower Lafayette with extravagant praise, but they did avoid attacking him. However, in the wake of the massacre at Nancy in mid-August, Fréron and the Roberts joined in the assault on Lafayette. François Bouillé, a known royalist, had led an attack on some mutinous army regiments and had left 3,000 soldiers dead. Lafayette was implicated in this disaster because he had supported the repression of these mutineers, because he was the brother-in-law of Bouillé, and because he was active in trying to make this slaughter more palatable to Parisian opinion. The radicals, by principle and political association, shared the viewpoint of the rebellious troops at Nancy, whose complaints had centered upon the right of the common soldier to review and appeal orders and decisions made by the officer corps. Consequently, the radicals, as a group, were outraged by the killing of so many who stood for a good cause. They anathematized those who supported either the sending of troops or the "cover-up" that followed. The participation of Lafayette in this incident cost him almost all his remaining support in the radical camp.[77]

Fréron found Lafayette's role in suppressing the complaints of the Nancy garrison sufficient reason to end his silence and to attack the general openly. He charged Lafayette with abetting the *aristocratie* by defying the right of the troops to regulate their affairs.[78] The subsequent concealment of the incident at Nancy outraged the Roberts. They asserted that it was the vanity of Lafayette, his need for recognition, that had encouraged him to try to justify this massacre. Hoping for the luxuries and the prestige that the court could provide, Lafayette had done what he could to aid their cause.[79]

Only Audouin hesitated to attack the general, but he was soon to fall into step. In late October, Audouin appealed to Lafayette to prove that he was not controlled by the ministers.[80] In the following month, Audouin's suspicion deepened that his former hero was a conspirator. However, it was not until February 1791, that he finally concluded that Lafayette had deceived the public and was working for the counterrevolution.[81]

While Audouin was growing distrustful, the other radical newspapers were stiffening their charges. At first they had claimed that Lafayette was either an egotist needing adulation or an opponent of popular sovereignty; in late 1790 and early 1791, they came to consider him a zealous conspirator in the service of the counterrevolution. Robert, in the *Mercure National,* labeled Lafayette a traitor and claimed that he desired to massacre half of the Paris population in order to overturn the Revolution.[82] The editors of the *Orateur du Peuple* and the *Révolutions de France et de Brabant,* alarmed by the machinations of the general, called for his death.[83] And in the *Ami du Peuple,* Marat wrote:

> It is with this plan of organization [described in detail in a passage omitted here] that the counterrevolutionnary Moitié has succeeded in forming, in all the realm, an innumerable army of satellites. He flatters himself that with these men he will be able to overturn the altar of liberty. His first try was at Nancy. But since this horrible massacre, how many other attempts has he made to cause a civil war! In these attempts, when they have failed, he never misses a chance for a "cover-up" or a deception. Such were the massacres at Rapée and at La Chapelle.[84]

Thus, while Lafayette had escaped the radical attack longer than Bailly or the municipality, he finished in the same way. Lauded in 1789 and in early 1790, he was brutally condemned in late 1790 and 1791.

Last of the Parisian governmental institutions to come under radical attack was the National Guard. Although it is difficult to distinguish the activities of this body of citizen-soldiers from the other authorities of the city, it received no criticism for a long period. When Cordelier opinion did change, there were only infrequent and unsystematic allegations. Possibly, the radicals spared the National Guard because they believed it to be composed largely of the "beloved" *peuple*.

While the radicals usually left the National Guard unmentioned and unassailed, they accused the general staff, Lafayette's hand-picked subordinates, with the same vigor and at about the same period as they criticized the general himself. For example, throughout July 1790, the *Révolutions de Paris* insisted that the general staff was trying to "establish servitude" for the *peuple*.[85] Further, the *Orateur du Peuple* attacked the general staff along with Lafayette for collusion with the ministers.[86] Likewise, when the *Mercure National* called Lafayette a conspirator against the Revolution, it named the general staff as accomplices.[87] This distrust for all these leaders must reveal a certain distrust for the National Guard itself.

Nonetheless, only infrequently was the guard as a whole maligned and denigrated. In April 1790, there was a growing concern about the National Guard. By the middle of 1790 all the journalists had stopped praising the guard and had become either neutral or noncommittal in the treatment of this body; occasionally a publicist would launch a limited attack. These charges recommended that the guard correct certain abuses, but these complaints did not impugn its general character.[88] A good example of radical anxieties was the challenge of Audouin that the National Guard patrols were too numerous. He did not find conspiracy or an attack on popular sovereignty in this hyperactivity; rather he chose to refer to the problem as a "misunderstanding" and proposed the very practical solution of publicizing the schedule of patrols in order to reduce possible confrontations between the citizenry and the soldiers.[89]

For most of the journalists such mild rebukes were the extent of their disillusionment with the guard, but in August 1790, Marat changed course. He stated that there must be an insurrection of the *peuple* to secure their needs, since there could be no reliance on the National Guard in the struggle for the popular cause. Claiming that these soldiers were haughty and blinded by their leaders, Marat found them an obstruction to, not an instrument of, popular sovereignty.[90] Marat continued his attacks throughout 1790 and 1791 and finally gained an ally in April 1791.

TABLE 5.1
"Key" Events of the
Paris Revolution, 1789–91

| | |
|---|---|
| *1789* | |
| August 4 | Abolition of "feudalism" |
| October 5–6 | October Days |
| November 2 | Nationalization of church lands |
| | |
| *1790* | |
| February 5 | King speaks to Assembly |
| May 22 | Decree on right of declaring war |
| June 19 | Nobility abolished |
| July 12 | Civil Constitution of the Clergy |
| July 14 | Fête of Federation |
| August 15 | Nancy mutiny and suppression |
| | |
| *1791* | |
| February 20 | Departure of king's aunts |
| February 28 | *Journée des Poignards* |
| April 18 | King's effort to journey to Saint-Cloud |
| June 21–3 | Flight to Varennes |
| July 17 | Champ de Mars massacre |

Like Marat, Audouin assailed the National Guard for suppressing the political activity of the "passive citizens."[91] But only these two were willing to assault the guard directly. The others might attack the leadership and implicitly attack those who obeyed such leaders, but generally the publicists refused to do more than question specific practices of the citizen army.[92]

Therefore, in widely varying degree, all major components of the revolutionary government of Paris were discredited. First to be attacked was the municipality, then Bailly and Lafayette, and finally the leaders of the National Guard. Was there a connection between the changes in editorial opinion and the events of the Revolution? Did radical views shift following "key" events, such as the October Days or the flight of the king—events that historians have commonly felt explained major shifts in public opinion? Consider first figures 5.1, 5.2, 5.3, and table 5.1.[93]

A careful survey of these tables indicates that, from Bastille Day, there was no single month and no single event that coincided with a uniform shift in radical opinion of either the municipality, or Bailly, or Lafayette. Further, only one journalist, Fréron, altered his opinions of all three authorities at the same time or following a single event. Consequently, in these cases, the impact of single (even the so-called key) events on

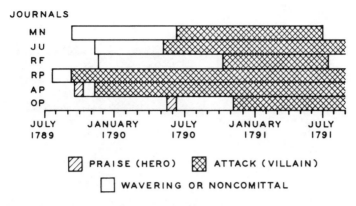

FIGURE 5.1. The Paris Municipality in the Radical Press

SOURCE: Appendix D

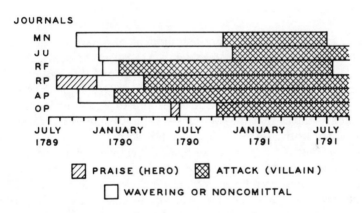

FIGURE 5.2.   Mayor S. Bailly in the Radical Press

SOURCE: Appendix D

editorial opinion was limited, and one must look elsewhere for the influences that changed the editorial views of the radical press. This negative conclusion may seem obvious enough here, but one should recall the persistent efforts of historians to explain the "course of the Revolution" in terms of these "key" events, such as the massacre at Champ de Mars, as the prime movers of public opinion.

On the other hand, there does emerge some commonality in the qualitative treatment of these institutions and individuals. At first all were

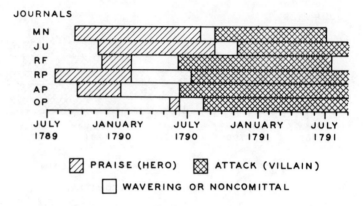

FIGURE 5.3.  Lafayette in the Radical Press

SOURCE: Appendix D

heroes, and they were often praised, in ideological terms as defenders of the *peuple* and of popular sovereignty. On other occasions, the praise was specifically related to the action performed, and the substance of this praise had little to do with radical ideology. Recall, for example, the support given to Lafayette for his spies and to Bailly for his help with provisions—topics that the journalists did not relate to Cordelier ideology. Subsequently, these groups and their leaders moved into a period where the journalists gave them neutral treatment, but where specific actions were subject to criticism. At this stage praise and criticism were usually unaccompanied by any political overtones or ideological elaboration. For example, Marat's first objections to Lafayette were constructive ones, designed to assist in a practical reorganization of the National Guard. Finally, as trust evaporated, as former heroes appeared to be villains, the journalists turned to a stylized treatment. Villains acted, not from sheer stupidity, or from any misguided practical considerations, but because they were haughty and egotistical, or because they were opposed to popular sovereignty, or because they conspired against the Revolution. While heroes and "semi-heroes" could be judged with no particular pattern in mind, villains were attacked in a systematic fashion that was dictated by the ideology of popular sovereignty. One should have no difficulty in recognizing the similarity between the conspiratorial, haughty, and antipopular villain, and the *aristocrate*. This villain of the radical press was hated for the very same crimes as the *aristocrate*. The treatment given by the radicals to the National Assembly and the monarch will substantiate and give depth to this pattern.

## FROM HEROES TO VILLAINS:
## THE MONARCH AND THE NATIONAL ASSEMBLY

Like the Parisian revolutionary government, the king, Louis XVI, passed from hero to villain in the radical press. Despite a general hatred of monarchies and suspicions about the Bourbon monarchy, the radicals initially applauded Louis XVI. In fact, most revolutionaries praised Louis throughout 1789. They approved of his reliance on Necker, then thought to be a champion of liberal reforms, and they credited the king for the doubling of the representation of the third estate. Overlooking Louis's shortcomings, the revolutionaries blamed mistakes on his advisors and eagerly pointed to those royal actions that could be interpreted as signs of the king's advocacy of the revolutionary cause.[94] Apparently, radical writers were in agreement with the general revolutionary sentiment, since 1789 found the press replete with the praises of Louis XVI.

It was February 1790, before any significant rumblings of discontent appeared in the radical newspapers, and some Cordelier journalists persisted in praising the king long after that date. Figure 5.4 should make this clear.

Several conclusions can be drawn from the following diagram. The radicals' initial disenchantment with Louis closely paralleled in time their discontent with Lafayette. However, soon after they had begun to lose faith in the general, they attacked him sharply as a pompous *aristocrate,* an opponent of popular sovereignty, and a conspirator for the counterrevolution. On the other hand, the radical journalists were loathe to discredit Louis in any irretrievable or definitive way. They all wavered for at least seven months after July 1789, some for over a year, about whether they should attack the monarch. Just as they could not decide whether or not France should depose its monarchy, they were undecided as to whether or not France should depose its monarch. But while the publicists failed in 1791 to advocate a republic explicitly, they eventually agreed, by June 1791, that though the monarchy might remain, Louis must go.

Further, when the radical journalists did change their opinion of Louis XVI, they acted at about the same time. True, they did not shift in unison following a single event; each journalist changed his mind at a different time after a different event. Nonetheless, these changes did occur within a limited time. All began to waver in early 1790; four newspapers changed between May and July. All began to distrust the king completely the following year; four journalists adopted a hostile stance from April to June, 1791.[95] In sum, for the king as well as for the Parisian authorities, no single event swayed opinion. On the other hand, the shifts in the treatment of the king did occur in a relatively brief period of time. A search for the causes of their shift is beyond the scope of this book, but

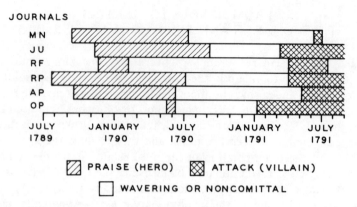

JOURNALS

FIGURE 5.4.   The Monarch in the Radical Press

SOURCE: Appendix D

the cultural milieu of the radical editors seems a more promising area of research than a detailed chronology of political events. In short, this study suggests the need for a social history of ideas in the Revolution itself with emphasis on the ideological formation of the would-be opinion makers of the decade.

The qualitative substance of radical writing about Louis closely paralleled the treatment of other "fallen" heroes of the Revolution. The king was praised by the radical press throughout 1789 and into the first few months of 1790. The Cordelier journalists lauded Louis in a variety of ways. They sometimes praised him for his specific policies; on other occasions they used his actions to describe him as defender of the Revolution and of popular sovereignty. The editor of the *Révolutions de Paris* acclaimed the king for a series of activities—among them an effort to procure grain for the capital in October 1789, and a conciliatory speech on February 4, 1790. In the first case, the journalist applauded the king as an honest supplier of grains; while in the second instance, he claimed that Louis was an advocate both of the Revolution and of popular sovereignty.[96] Audouin likewise approved Louis's speech of February 4 as evidence of the king's revolutionary ardor. Desmoulins praised the king as a man who generously donated supplies for the Parisian winter.[97]

But the praise of these journalists usually centered on the good intentions of the king, not on his actions, which they believed were effectively thwarted by the court, the ministers, and even the National Assembly. The publicists credited him with a variety of worthwhile desires, even if he was unable to enact them. Marat insisted that the king himself had no wish to make the French citizenry "his personal chattel," as the ministerial language often implied. Rather, Louis sincerely believed that he was dependent on the nation and was a true advocate of popular sovereignty.[98] Robert, speculating about the intentions of the monarch, characterized him as an honest man who was unfortunately surrounded by courtiers and by a tradition that encouraged corruption.[99] Prudhomme likewise attributed to the king the desire to prevent efforts of the National Assembly to restrict the suffrage and limit popular sovereignty.[100]

Trusting the actions or at least the good intentions of Louis, the radical journalists indulged in some extravagant praise for the king. Not only did they mimic other revolutionaries in acclaiming Louis the "Restorer of Liberty," but they even surpassed the adulation of many of the supporters of a constitutional monarchy as shown in the following exclamation of Audouin after the speech of February 4, 1790: "Louis XVI, whom one may justly call the father of his *peuple,* has given yesterday yet another dazzling proof of his love for his subjects and of his desire to see them finally finish the great work of the Constitution."[101] Fréron lauded Louis as the "Citizen-King," and Prudhomme exhorted his readers to yearn for freedom in order to be worthy of having Louis for king.[102]

Nonetheless, this surfeit of praise diminished in the latter half of 1790 as the radicals began to mix their approval with gentle criticism. At first they had believed that the king, besieged by courtiers and ministers and unable to execute his good actions, would still maintain a favorable disposition toward the Revolution. Now they began to worry. Their confident assurances of the loyalty of the king alternated with troubled questions about Louis's judgment. There was much criticism of the royal request concerning the king's domain. The radicals were shocked at the size of the request, but they ended by suggesting a reduction in the amount of the petition, no more. They did not charge that the king was a haughty egotist or a conspirator, only that he was too demanding.[103] Similarly, the radicals suggested that Louis cease hunting, his favorite pastime. The radicals questioned whether this was a proper use of his time or a dignified pursuit for a monarch.[104] For the most part, at this stage the radicals kept their criticism within bounds of monarchical loyalty and civic propriety.

But if they usually avoided emotional and ideological charges, the publicists issued some strident reprimands to the monarch where they attacked him in the most vitriolic manner. In these assaults the publicists never called Louis a pompous *aristocrate.* No—much worse, he was pictured as a conspirator for the counterrevolution. Indeed, for several months in the second half of 1790 the radicals interspersed praise, mild criticism, and defamation of the king in their press. Witness some of these extreme blasts against Louis occurring within a period when the norm was a favorable or only mildly critical portrait of the king. Marat was the first to write of the monarch's collusion in the "aristocratic conspiracy," and in a later report he concluded that the king actually was its leader.[105] Fréron complained that Louis had not promulgated the Constitution of the Clergy and asserted: "Finally Louis XVI has torn up the Declaration of Rights, which is the main foundation of the sovereignty of the *peuple,* and now he openly declares war on the Constitution, and he rebels against the laws of his country."[106] In sum, praise, moderate criticism, and occasional acid attacks all coexisted from about July 1790 to early 1791 in each of the radical papers.

By mid-1791, the radicals had ended entirely their laudatory remarks, ignored their former limits on criticism, and multiplied their assertions that Louis XVI was a willing partner, if not the leader, in the plots to overthrow the Revolution. In April 1791, when Louis proposed to journey to Saint-Cloud for Easter as he had done the year before, Fréron exploded:

> But your decision is taken, you are starred for despotism. Ah, well, if you leave, we shall no longer see in you but Tarquin chased from Rome. We shall seize your chateaus . . . your palaces, your civil list; we shall proscribe your head.[107]

For Robert, the flight to Varennes was sufficient proof that Louis was involved in the counterrevolution.[108]

Other journalists concurred at about the same time. While Marat had long insisted that Louis was deeply implicated in conspiracy, the "Friend of the People" wavered in his treatment of the king until April 1791. Subsequently, whatever the monarch's action, Marat was able to link it to Louis's role as leader of the counterrevolution. When it was rumored that Lebègue Duportail, then minister of war, would retire, Marat saw in this resignation an effort by the king to lull the *peuple* into false security and to foment counterrevolution.[109] Later, when the king fled to Varennes, convincing most people of his antirevolutionary sentiments, Marat stiffened his attack: "The thirst for absolute power which devours his soul will soon render him a ferocious assassin; soon he will swim in the blood of his citizens who have refused to submit to tyranny."[110] By June, all the journalists ceased wavering, stopped speaking of the good intentions of the king, and treated him as counterrevolutionary. Their hatred led them to advocate his removal from the throne, his imprisonment, and even his death.[111]

To recapitulate, the monarch followed the fate of the revolutionary authorities of Paris. Widely praised at first for all his actions, the king saw his popularity decline among the radicals during the second half of 1790. For most of the next nine months, he was still applauded or criticized only in a limited way, although signs of his future harsh treatment began to appear. But by March 1791, there was consensus among the radicals that the king was not to be trusted—that he was actively undermining the Revolution.

The National Assembly followed much the same pattern as the Parisian authorities and the monarch in the radical press. Throughout 1789, the radicals glowingly praised the National Assembly. They applauded first and foremost the adoption of the Declaration of the Rights of Man. Had the National Assembly done nothing but formulate this document, the Cordeliers would have still regarded this body as the fount of revolutionary heroism. In this Declaration of the Rights of Man, the radicals could find support for their ideology of popular sovereignty. In their own minds, the declaration substantiated their political, economic, and social assumptions. Furthermore, the Assembly's resistance to the first two orders in May, June, and July 1789, and the policies adopted on August 4 won this body acclaim from revolutionaries in general and the radicals in particular.[112] In sum, it is no surprise to find these six journals praising the National Assembly with unremitting enthusiasm and without qualification.

But this period of praise was brief as figure 5.5 reveals. With the exception of the *Mercure National,* the radical press by early 1790 had turned from praising the National Assembly to treating it either with some reservations or with unmitigated disdain. At one extreme was Marat, the editor of the *Ami du Peuple,* who after losing his passion for the National Assembly, quickly slipped into censuring all its actions. At the other pole, the editors of the *Journal Universel* and the *Mercure National* hesitated to make villains out of the representatives, and it is apparent from the chart that from 1789 to 1791 they never totally condemned the National Assembly. True, in mid-1791 they assailed the National Assembly as counterrevolutionary. Nonetheless they did not consistently maintain this view, as they interspersed their virulent attacks against the National Assembly with recommendations that the public support the delegates on this or that point.[113]

Such wavering on the National Assembly was characteristic of the radical press. In addition to the mixed portrait drawn by the *Mercure National* and the *Journal Universel,* Fréron vacillated for six months and Prudhomme for almost a year. Desmoulins wavered for six weeks, then attacked for four months, and then hesitated again for another six months.[114] Why was there a strong tendency toward wavering by men whose habit elsewhere was to regard men and institutions as either heroes or villains? One possible explanation is that the court, the ministers, the church, the staff of the National Guard, and the Parisian Municipality, all acting behind closed doors, could be more readily seen as monolithic, composed of individuals who were unanimous or at least uniformly duped in their dedication to counterrevolution. But in the case of the

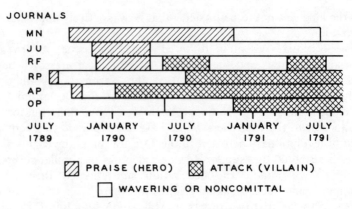

FIGURE 5.5.    The National Assembly in the Radical Press

SOURCE: Appendix D

National Assembly, with its open meetings, public debates, clearly identifiable factions, and published records, the radical publicists had to accept the existence of an opposition, of a division of view, and it proved more difficult to apply to this institution the stereotyped label of hero or villain. The radicals were surely loathe to condemn the Jacobins, one of the major groups within the National Assembly. Thus, aware of competing factions among the delegates, the radicals might label the National Assembly the bastion of counterrevolution on one day and on another the rallying point of the Revolution. Only when the radical journalists could believe that the Jacobin deputies were turncoats to the Jacobin Club, or completely uninfluential delegates, might they systematically assail the National Assembly.[115]

In short, only after mid-1790 did even half of the newsmen attack the National Assembly. They all began their attacks at different times and as a result of different events. These times were so infrequently spaced that there must have been no coordination in the timing of these shifts. Nonetheless, although this change took place according to the pace of each individual journalist, there was a commonality in the tone of radical reporting. When the radicals did praise the National Assembly, these plaudits all sounded somewhat the same from paper to paper. This same commonality existed as well when the radicals attacked or wavered on the National Assembly.

The radicals usually limited their praise of the National Assembly to applauding specific achievements. Sample the treatment given by Audouin to the National Assembly. After reading the record of the pensions administered by Necker prior to 1789, the journalist lauded the

National Assembly for its decision to relieve Necker of his post.[116] Likewise, the writer flattered the delegates for their efforts to prepare the Constitution. He stated in March 1790:

> The accomplishments of the National Assembly, their efforts on the Constitution, increasingly admired and cherished, will silence all by their quality, by their beautiful simplicity, by their useful grandeur. They will inevitably form the code of human reason and the code for all the French.[117]

This unqualified flattery was matched by other journals. Applauding the efforts of the representatives to assure grain and to complete the Declaration of the Rights of Man, Prudhomme wrote:

> The representatives of the nation continue their work with an unparalleled zeal. They hold two sessions daily. . . . Such a visible ardor when linked to brilliant insights that one sees sparkle each day in this august Assembly, can only produce excellent results.[118]

Such examples should make clear the character of the plaudits for the National Assembly. The praise for the representatives conformed to no general political principles; it was limited to the specific action they performed. When they were lauded for finding grain, they were trumpeted as heroes because of their diligence and judgment, not because of any ideological contribution to the Revolution.

But the glorification of the delegates in the radical press was not to last long. At first, while continuing to praise the National Assembly, the publicists criticized them in a manner designed to correct but not to oust their representatives. Their criticisms usually focused on a single issue with a suggestion of how to resolve the problem. However, over several months the tenor of these criticisms changed. The National Assembly was vigorously attacked, not only in a limited way but also as the center for "aristocratic" conniving. These vicious assaults alternated with praise for, or at least acceptance of, the National Assembly.[119] Finally by 1791, four of the journalists lost all faith in the representatives and considered them full partners in the counterrevolution.

Thoroughly distrustful of the National Assembly, these four editors attacked them in much the same manner as they had attacked the Parisian authorities. No matter what the activity, the radical journalists saw the representatives acting for personal wealth and self-indulgence, against popular sovereignty, or for the counterrevolution. The treatment given to the National Assembly by Marat should serve as an adequate example. Once he had decided, in the last days of December 1789, that the delegates were unworthy of any praise, he initiated a campaign to prove that they wished to block popular sovereignty. Pointing to the desire of the National Assembly to establish a new municipal structure, Marat observed that their real goal was to deprive the citizens of the right to govern themselves. Not much more than a week later, he described the National Assembly's handling of an accused counterrevolutionary. Here again Marat saw in the action of the representatives an effort to usurp the rightful powers of the *peuple*. [120] Marat continued to condemn each move of the National Assembly as an assault on popular sovereignty until mid-September 1790, when he also began to include counterrevolutionary plotting and a wish to share in "aristocratic" luxuries as motives for the misdeeds of the nation's delegates.

Now the various activities of the National Assembly were part of a conspiracy to overturn the Revolution. Marat informed his readers that the deliberations and decisions of the National Assembly on the massacre at Nancy were governed by the delegates' desire to curb the Revolution. Indeed, Marat repeatedly found the National Assembly members acting as counterrevolutionaries. For example, after describing in detail a new measure calling for increased appropriations, Marat speculated about the underlying motives for this bill. He finally concluded with the assertion that this expenditure was passed simply to finance counterrevolution. [121]

In late 1790, Marat also began to attribute the positions of the National Assembly to a third factor—the desire of the delegates to imitate the ostentatious life of the *aristocratie*. Increasingly Marat attributed the uncivic actions of the representatives to their high living, to their need for silver to underwrite superfluous spending. In despair over the delegates' lenient treatment of the king after the flight to Varennes, Marat listed the crimes of the National Assembly, concluding that: "It [the National Assembly] has perfidiously betrayed the nation, selling itself to the prince for a part of the gold that it had extracted for him from the rights and interests of the *peuple*." [122] In sum, Marat, once he was distrustful, often saw the legislative bills, directives, and the decisions of the National Assembly as instruments against the sovereignty of the *peuple* and against the Revolution. Somehow, the rest of the Assembly's actions were aimed at obtaining the luxuries necessary for those delegates who aped the *aristocratie*. The treatment of the National Assembly in the *Ami du Peuple* was echoed in much of the radical press. Three other Cordelier journalists, at first dazzled by the National Assembly, came to regard the delegates as villains, whose vices were the same as those of the antipopular, antirevolutionary, and luxury-loving *aristocrate*. Audouin and the Roberts resisted this extreme, but their treatment of the National Assembly, save for an occasional laudatory remark, was scarcely less hostile than that of their comrades.

We return to our starting point: What did the radical press say about the individuals and institutions that concerned them? What were the characteristics of their qualitative treatment? The Cordelier journalists depicted men and institutions as either heroes or villains or as a mixture of the two. They lauded their heroes in the most extravagant manner. But, though the praise was undeniably characterized by the incessant use of superlatives, it was most often limited to approval for a specific act. If an institution had successfully acquired a quantity of grain or had worked to increase suffrage, the radicals tended to praise it only for such actions. Sometimes the radicals used such efforts as an occasion to recite an ideological apotheosis, attributing to the hero special commitments to morality, to the Revolution, and to popular sovereignty. But generally they praised the specific action of the hero and left ideology for other situations.

As these newspapermen became partially disillusioned, they would alter their treatment of these individuals and institutions. They might continue the same praise, but they also initiated some restrained criticism. In these times, the journalists attacked the actions of the former heroes, but they did so in a fashion designed to correct, not condemn, their subjects. This mild treatment revealed some disagreement without a fundamental loss of faith in the institution under consideration. The journalists also might take a more neutral and noncommittal stance in their reporting during these periods of partial disillusionment. Finally, on rare occasions, even while their overall treatment remained favorable or at least noncommittal, the publicists would publish biting articles condemning these "semi-heroes" as counterrevolutionaries.

Finally, when these heroes had become villains in the opinion of the radicals, or when durable villains were under consideration, the newspapermen ignored their former flexible and diverse lines of attack. With heroes and semi-heroes, the publicists usually varied their remarks according to the issues; with villains, the publicists employed a very repetitive treatment. No matter what the action taken by a villain, the radicals reported it as part of a larger effort to ensure a wealthy lifestyle, or to obstruct popular sovereignty, or to defeat the Revolution through conspiracy. They repeatedly described the villains at least one of these three ways, though the political crimes of the villains received greater emphasis than their propensity for a life of luxury. Not only was the treatment of villains stereotyped, but it was also ideologically determined, for the misdeeds of the villains were exactly those of the *aristocrates*. Apparently, after the level of distrust was so great as to preclude an impartial evaluation, the journalists relied on their ideology for a response and accused existing institutions of the crimes they imagined their enemies would commit.

Therefore, as the number of heroes decreased and the number of villains rose, the coverage of the radical press grew proportionately more ideological. Indeed, by the opening of the Legislative Assembly, the only significant institutions not considered as villains were the Jacobins, Cordeliers, and usually the National Guard. All the rest were heartily assailed; consequently the newspapermen were relying increasingly on ideology to interpret the actions of those men they reported.

It would be an important addition to the current understanding of the Revolution if one could ascertain the cause of the radical disaffection with the major institutions and individuals of revolutionary France. A complete answer would be beyond the scope of the study, but we can tentatively state that no single event was responsible for significant alterations in radical opinion. Chapter four has already demonstrated the relative unimportance of events, and figures 5.1 through 5.5 confirm this. These diagrams clearly reveal that the journalists never collectively shifted their opinions on any one subject at the same time and, therefore, as a direct result of any particular event.

It should also be noted that each journalist usually changed his opinions about these men and institutions one at a time. But even in the two cases where a journalist recast several of his opinions in only a month, a single event did not precipitate this shift. In June of 1790, Fréron stopped praising and began to waver on the merits of the municipality, Bailly, and Lafayette. However, this change was only vaguely related to the occurrence of a particular event; rather it resulted from Fréron's peculiar situation. He had only begun publishing his paper on May 22, 1790, and had probably treated the Parisian authorities mildly to avoid undue attention. After all, he had signed a contract agreeing not to publish a competing newspaper. Thus, one month later when he revealed his first doubts about Bailly, Lafayette, and the municipality over one of their united efforts, he was probably not showing a change of opinion. Rather he was then daring to show his true opinions, which dated from before the establishment of his newspaper. Similarly, in July 1790, Prudhomme stopped treating the king as a hero and began virulently attacking Lafayette and the National Assembly. However, a closer look at this newspaper reveals that these shifts of opinion came after a series of different, if closely spaced, events. In short, such exceptions do little to weaken the assertion that the journalists did not change a group of their opinions because of a particular event. Consequently, in searching for some general causes for these shifts of opinion, one might well discount cataclysmic events as an answer.

If the causes of these changes of radical opinion must remain obscure, one can at least attempt to determine when they took place. The timing of the changes may even help to explain why they occurred. This information is available to us in figures 5.1 through 5.5.[123] To ascertain the shifts in radical opinion, one must analyze the tenor of the press for each month. For example, in July 1791, two journalists wavered about the National Assembly, while the other four attacked it. Thus, two-thirds (sixty-seven percent) of the newspapers were hostile to the National Assembly, while one-third (thirty-three percent) were undecided. One may repeat this process for radical opinion in July in regard to Bailly, Lafayette, the municipality, and the king. Indeed, all six journals were attacking all these bodies and consequently were completely unfavorable (one hundred percent). A compilation of the attitudes for July 1791 of these six newspapers for the five institutions, is shown in table 5.2. Thus, an average of each column of percentages shows that the approach of the radical press to these individuals and institutions was six percent undecided or wavering and ninety-four percent hostile. There was no evidence at all (zero percent) of unqualified praise. Admittedly, these numbers by themselves would be a crude way of characterizing the treatment given these institutions in the radical press; but here they should serve, not to replace, but only to summarize earlier qualitative description. With that qualification, one may forge ahead to calculate the tenor of the treatment for each month. The result is shown in figure 5.6.

The smooth curves of this graph reconfirm the assertion that there were no precipitous changes of opinion in any short period, that is, in relation to any single event. The curves do, however, indicate certain broad time spans that witnessed significant changes. Through January 1790, the general opinion given of the king, Lafayette, Bailly, the National Assembly, and the municipality by the radical press was favorable. In this period, one could most often expect to find these institutions being treated as heroes. However, the praise diminished so that in March 1790, wavering on these institutions had become the predominant approach of the radical press. This condition lasted only a few months, for by October 1790, the Cordelier publicists were primarily referring to the Parisian authorities as villains. Increasingly, the radical journals abandoned any wavering, and by May 1791, there was little indecision, only extreme distrust, of all these institutions.

The significance of the timing should not be overlooked. Long before the flight to Varennes or the massacre at the Champ de Mars, the radicals were very hostile to their institutions and their leaders. It was in the first half of 1790 that they wavered over their opinions of their governing bodies. It was in the last half of 1790 and early 1791 when they made up their minds. Too much has been made of the emigration of the king's aunts (January 1791), the *Journée des Poignards* (February 1791), the king's abortive departure to Saint-Cloud (April 1791), and the king's flight to Varennes (July 1791), as the collective cause for the efforts of the Cordeliers at the Champ de Mars.[124] Apparently, the developments in 1790 warrant more attention than they have received.

TABLE 5.2

Percentage of Newspapers Praising, Wavering,
or Attacking Various Institutions in July 1791

| Institutions | Percentage of Newspapers | | |
| --- | --- | --- | --- |
| | Praise | Wavering | Attack |
| King | 0 | 0 | 100 |
| National Assembly | 0 | 33 | 67 |
| Municipality | 0 | 0 | 100 |
| Lafayette | 0 | 0 | 100 |
| Bailly | 0 | 0 | 100 |
| (Average) | 0 | 6 | 94 |

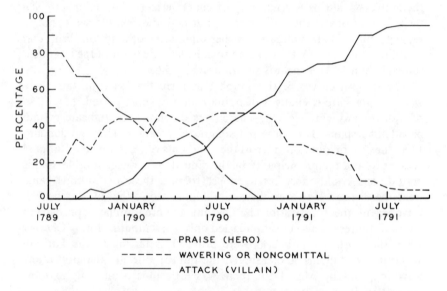

FIGURE 5.6.   Percentage of Radical Newspapers Praising, Wavering, or Attacking Selected Institutions and Individuals, 1789–91

SOURCE: Appendix D
NOTE: See text and note 123 for selection

The radicals, then, did not shift their opinions of men and institutions
because of a sequence of the "key" events of 1791. Rather, their changes
coincided more with a series of relatively obscure occurrences in 1790. We
may rightly question whether these isolated and mostly forgotten incidents of 1790 were the main cause of the radical disillusionment. Is it not
rather to the ideological predelictions and cultural milieu of the editors

that we must look? The personal frustrations of the radical publicists before 1789 and their participation in the underground "grub-street" society made them likely to distrust any constituted body and to see haughtiness and "aristocratic" conniving in any effort to govern. The efforts of Bastille Day, the passage of the Declaration of the Rights of Man, and the decrees of August 4, assuaged this fundamental distrust, but the respite was only temporary. Without repeated covenants of cooperation between the *peuple* and the government, the tendency of the radicals was to focus again on their old antagonist—constituted authority. Inevitably, they mounted the battlements once again, ready to train their weapons upon these villains, the enemies of the *peuple*.

# 6

# Conclusion

INALLY, armed with a list of responses, we can return to the question, What did the radical press say? Or alternately stated, we can now answer the questions, (1) What were the Parisian radicals thinking from 1789 to 1791? and (2) What was the content of this major source of information for the Parisian public? Indeed, this press is a crucial source for an understanding of the radicals, for the Cordeliers, like most Frenchmen of the time, resisted formal party organization. Their meetings were spontaneous and ill-organized, and the journalists with a continuous forum for their opinions exercised a predominant influence on radical thought.[1] Furthermore, many Parisians were regular followers of the popular political press, and we can state with some confidence that its impact was widespread. Thus, the following summary of reporting in the radical press provides not only an insight into the radicals' thinking but also an account of one segment of opinion that shaped the views of the public.

The message found in the radical press focused primarily on the propagation of a political ideology, however rudimentary and unsophisticated. Although almost all the articles were written as a response to some particular event, there was no great concern with the events themselves. Events were reported briefly. Even those occurrences that precipitated shifts in radical opinion were isolated and relatively unimportant in themselves, and they certainly are not the "key" events regarded by most historians as determining the course of the Revolution. Indeed, the events reported by radicals were ignored by most of the Parisian press; the radical newspapermen concentrated instead on events relating to the success or failure of popular sovereignty. Consequently, events, insofar as they had import, were significant largely as symbols of the radical commitment to the ideology of popular sovereignty.

Nonetheless, the radical newspapermen were involved in reporting and evaluating the activities of the powerful individuals and institutions of the capital. In fact, for the heroes and "semi-heroes," the reporting in the radical press was largely based on their actual activities. However, villains were castigated not for what they did, but as haughty, antipopular, conspiratorial *aristocrates*. Because the radicals interpreted, according to their own ideology, the actions of those they distrusted, these attacks were a confirmation of the ideology of popular sovereignty as much as they were a castigation of a certain group or individual. With almost all groups being treated as villains by 1791, the message of the papers was in fact increasingly stereotypical and ideological.

What, then, was the ideological position of the radical press? In brief, the radicals believed that, by an accident of history, a moral, egalitarian *peuple* had developed. This *peuple* embraced brotherhood and desired no more wealth, or power, or prestige, than their comrades. Confronting the *peuple,* however, was an *aristocratie* who wished both to preserve their old power and luxuries and to monopolize any new positions created by the Revolution. While the *peuple* disdained wealth, the *aristocrates* coveted it in order to provide themselves with luxuries and with offices. Moreover, if money or influence in high places would not arrest the progress of the *peuple,* the *aristocrates* were capable of resorting to any tactics—even the most violent—to achieve their ends.

To counter the "aristocratic" menace to the social ideal of the *peuple,* the radicals proposed a literal adherence to popular sovereignty. Already imbued with a morality of concern for their fellows, the *peuple* would make certain that government could do nothing contrary to their wish. Government would be left weak with vigorous action reserved to the *peuple* themselves, who could be trusted never to abuse their power. Also, cultural life would be organized so that the *peuple* could express their opinions freely and so that the influence of the *aristocratie* would be severely restricted. In the realm of economics, the radicals were more reticent in redefining conditions. Here they did not advocate destruction of the accumulated wealth of the *aristocratie*. Although they believed only a member of the *aristocratie* would want more than did his neighbors, they did not sanction equal fortunes. Generally, they avoided proposing any specific means—such as a limit to free trade or a progressive income tax—that might reduce or redistribute the wealth of the *aristocratie*. Also, while they advocated a guaranteed minimum subsistence, they were very vague about how it would be provided. They relied on moral suasion to convince the wealthy to pay high wages and to spend more money in order to stimulate the economy.

Thus, from 1789 to 1791, the Parisian radicals were obsessed with this ideology of popular sovereignty. Their treatment of events, individuals, and institutions only served to highlight radical ideology. In emphasizing ideology, they were not very different from the "grub-street" radicals, similarly unconcerned with mundane activity. They were also similar in their indifference to, and in their hostility for, constituted authority. The professional and social rejection in the 1780s had made them resentful of the "establishment," and this bitterness influenced their revolutionary activities. But the radicals did not continue their prerevolutionary behavior without modification, for after 1789 they spoke prudishly, not pornographically. They constantly warned of the sharp and dangerous horns of the *aristocratie,* rather than the foolish and witless horns of the cuckold. Before the Revolution, the radicals had envisioned a moral *peuple,* who were opposed to a degenerate, debauched *aristocratie.* After 1789, they continued to believe in this same moral *peuple,* but this time their opponents, if they still lusted after wealth and indulgence, including the sins of the flesh, were now aggressive and active—and capable of effective political machinations. The Cordelier lack of interest in Marie-Antoinette clearly reveals that their chief target was no longer private morality, for the queen certainly would have been more frequently mentioned if sexual indiscretions had been a principal point of the radical focus. In the Revolution, radical attacks on licentiousness changed to attacks on political persuasions.[2]

On the other hand, there was little substantive difference between the ideology of the Cordelier radicals of 1789–91 and the Jacobin radicals of 1793–94. Although it is difficult to define precisely the radicals and radicalism of the later period, one can compare the earlier militants both with the "most advanced" Jacobins of 1793–94 and with the *sans-culottes* of the Year II as described by Albert Soboul. The similarity between the "most advanced" Jacobins, Robespierre and his followers, and the Cordeliers of 1789–91 is striking. Of course, Robespierre and his associates were concerned with planning and manipulating daily politics, but their social, political, and economic ideals are impossible to differentiate from those of the early radicals. Both groups favored social equality, popular sovereignty, and a minimum subsistence for all. Both favored free trade and opposed the indiscriminate sequester of the fortunes of the wealthy *qua* wealthy. This similarity is confirmed by the fact that the Cordeliers supported Robespierre wholeheartedly from 1789 to 1793. For example, of the newspapermen who were regular contributors to the radical press, fourteen of the seventeen were political allies of Robespierre in the Year II.[3]

Furthermore, the early Cordeliers differed from the *sans-culottes* in the same way as the "most advanced" Jacobins. The *sans-culottes* agreed with the Jacobins and the Cordeliers in their politics and social ideology, but they wished to limit free trade to guarantee themselves adequate supplies. This difference on economic policy and principle was partially responsible for dissolving the coalition between the *sans-culottes* and the Jacobins. Nonetheless, the similarities in ideology between these two groups were considerable, and as Soboul points out, it was not exclusively the dispute over economic issues that split the *sans-culottes* from the Jacobins. It would seem rather that their problems were exacerbated much more by the fact that the Jacobins occupied the central government and the *sans-culottes* the local centers of authority. The dissolution of their coalition was caused, not so much by fundamental ideological disagreement, but by a struggle for power.[4]

On an ideological level at least, the *sans-culottes* may be considered the heirs of the Cordeliers. The "most advanced" Jacobins, moreover, inherited both ideology and personnel from these Cordeliers. It is significant that there is this coherence between the militants of 1789–91 and those of 1793–94. It is now apparent that the positions taken by the *sans-culottes* and Robespierre and his followers were not, for the most part, new positions, born of political exigencies of the moment. Their principles were most certainly articulated in the radical press beginning in 1789. As we shall see, the longevity and stability of these opinions cast some doubt on the findings of M. J. Sydenham and Richard Cobb.

Michael J. Sydenham has insisted that there were no serious ideological differences between the Jacobins and the Girondins. Although he notes that one issue, the Girondist hostility to Paris, divided these two groups, he considers that this single issue was relatively minor compared to the many points of political agreement. He emphasizes that a "Girondist" was really only a political opponent of Robespierre without any ideological distinctions between "Girondist" and Jacobin.[5] My study, however, indicates that the dissension between Robespierre and his opposition was far more than simply political. Indeed, the one ideological difference that Sydenham does cite—the Gironde's animosity to Paris—is not a small exception. Rather, it was crucial because hostility to Paris meant hostility to the long term ideology of the Jacobins described in this book. Since 1789 many of the Jacobins had advocated an ideology that called for social equality and popular sovereignty. Because Paris was the workshop of these ideals, the Girondist opposition to Paris could not be taken lightly by the "most advanced" Jacobins. Their belief in Cordelier ideology and in Paris was no creation of the political strife of 1792–93: it was their longstanding guideline; it dictated that those who distrusted Paris must be eliminated. Thus, the division over Paris was not a simple, possibly reconcilable, difference, for the Jacobin position was founded upon a four-year commitment to an ideology that had been nurtured and guided by the capital.

Similarly, the persistence of this Cordelier ideology from 1789 to 1793 testifies against Richard Cobb's assertion that sans-culottism was a fleeting, unsubstantial movement. He has argued that the political power of the *sans-culottes* was based on an unusual confluence of certain conditions and that their destruction requires no explanation—especially not that of Albert Soboul.[6] To some extent, Cobb is correct. Nonetheless, the existence and incessant propagation of Cordelier ideology by the journals cannot be dismissed as insignificant. Since the efforts of these newspapers were supplemented by the efforts of a host of clubs, there was a solid experience of four years underlying *sans-culotte* agitation. Their existence and prosperity should be no surprise, and Soboul's explanation of their demise is certainly warranted.

Just as these six newspapers are a source for radical thought from 1789 to 1791, they are also a source for the thought of some segments of the Parisian population at large. Few outside the Cordeliers thought precisely the same way as these newspapermen, but many were strongly influenced by them. Thus, since the radicals were fiercely ideological, since they supported social equality and popular sovereignty, and since they were moderate and restrained in their economic goals, we might expect those under their influence to think somewhat along those lines. While it is impossible to discover who subscribed to radical views, one might logically assume that the members of George Rudé's crowd were among the most likely believers in the radical cause. The assumption that the crowd shared Cordelier ideology makes its activities easier to explain. The political awareness of the crowd, its idealism, its choice of political goals over economic ones all make sense if one accepts the notion that they were greatly influenced and patterned by the radicals' idealism and political views.[7] This is not to say that the crowd was created or totally shaped by the radical press. Rather, it is simply to suggest that at least in part the behavior of the crowd was determined by the news reports they read or heard—not exclusively by material conditions of life.

The stress of the radical press on ideology, their persistent advocacy of direct popular sovereignty and of vigilance against the *"aristocrates,"* raises again the role of ideas on the course of the French Revolution. Since the demise of H. Taine's "conspiracy of ideologues," French revolutionary historiography has leaned heavily on nonideological explanations of revolutionary actions. These have ranged from the "theory of circumstances" of Aulard and the "premature class struggle" of Mathiez to the "power struggle" of Sydenham and the "release of capitalist enterprise" of Soboul. To explain the Terror, the role of the *sans-culottes*, and the grand *journées* of Paris, historians have offered corollary and supplemental hypotheses including crowd action, political organization, secular religion, and personal rivalries—indeed, almost every explanation except political ideology.[8] This book does not intend to resurrect Taine's assertions; but it does raise doubts for his opponents. The Cordeliers, at least, acted and argued primarily from their ideology. This ideology was not a sophisticated political theory, but its tenets were completely understood and accepted by the radical journalists. The ideas probably originated in the past poverty and career frustrations of the Cordelier journalists, but by 1789 they existed independently of their origins.[9] Further, these ideas were repeatedly trumpeted in the radical press—they echoed throughout Paris—and with the rise of the radicals to power, were greatly influential in determining the course of the Revolution. Furthermore, these concepts were so powerful that even the Thermidoreans, the Directory, and Napoleon could not suppress them, and they persist to the present day.[10] The radical journalists, who brought these ideas into focus and then popularized them, were thus responsible for many of the developments of 1789, 1790, 1791, and beyond.

# Appendixes

# APPENDIX A
# METHODOLOGY:
# AN EXAMINATION OF EVENTS
# IN THE RADICAL PRESS

To ascertain the radicals' treatment of events, I found inadequate a traditional qualitative assessment of the events included in the radical journals. I had some general impressions from my research about what types of events were reported, but these impressions were too uncertain to go untested. The sheer mass of newsprint and the multitude of reported events required some standard evaluation process; quantification could provide a more exact assessment of the value of my notions about reported events.[1] Thus, after weighing my expectations carefully, I formalized them into a set of hypotheses, which, generally, state that the men of the radical press watched those occurrences that were related primarily to the politics of popular sovereignty and not to parliamentary procedure. Specifically then, they were concerned with those institutions and activities that infringed directly on popular sovereignty. Second, despite the journalists' enormous interest in events, their attention span was short, and while they might concentrate much writing on a particular event for a short period of time, this event was often soon forgotten.[2] To test these notions and others, I devised a "score sheet" to be used to analyze the event (if there was one) that was the source of each article. This score sheet follows:

## Score Sheet

I. General information
   1. Journal name, volume, issue, page
   2. Date
   3. Event discussed (code number assigned)
   4. Non-event discussed
   5. Length of article
II. Source, that is, the group, individual, or institution that initiates the event
   6. The National Assembly ⎫
   7. Miscellaneous legal bodies: departments, municipalities, courts, National Guard general staffs ⎬ Formal governmental activity
   8. Ministers and their subordinates
   9. Monarch ⎭

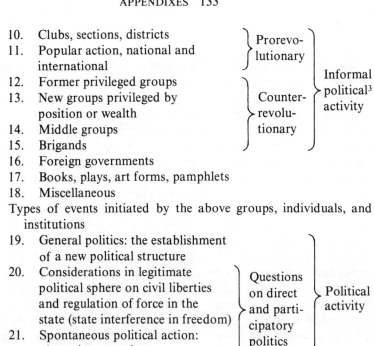

10. Clubs, sections, districts
11. Popular action, national and international
12. Former privileged groups
13. New groups privileged by position or wealth
14. Middle groups
15. Brigands
16. Foreign governments
17. Books, plays, art forms, pamphlets
18. Miscellaneous

III. Types of events initiated by the above groups, individuals, and institutions
19. General politics: the establishment of a new political structure
20. Considerations in legitimate political sphere on civil liberties and regulation of force in the state (state interference in freedom)
21. Spontaneous political action: plots, riots, meetings
22. Fiscal affairs
23. Economics of dearth
24. Arts
25. Social services
26. Foreign affairs
27. Ecclesiastical affairs
28. Affairs of the cultivators
29. Miscellaneous

As is apparent, slots 1, 2, and 5 were used merely to identify the location and length of a particular article. To ascertain the length of any article, I counted the number of pages in each account.[4] For a worded description of the event involved, I employed line 3; or, if the article were in fact purely editorial and not based on any identifiable occurrence, I used line 4 to identify the subject of the article. Based on the event described in line 3, I then assigned the article a code number that was the same for all articles written about a similar event. Then I used slots 6 through 18 to identify the institutions, individuals, or groups that the journalists were considering when they wrote about an event. On line 19 through 26, I recorded the "type" of action taken by the various institutions, groups, or individuals that had attracted the journalist's eye in the first place.

In summary, in order to understand the journals' patterns and spans of attention in their treatment of events, I took each article and ascertained the event that occasioned the article, if, indeed, an occurrence was responsible. Then I linked together all the articles based on the same happening, assigned a common code number, and finally registered the "source" and "type" of each event. I have endeavored to be aware of the possible pitfalls involved in categorizing and in quantifying qualitative data and have been tortured often by the difficulty of placing information of this type, unique by its very nature, into numbered categories. To compensate for the ever-present ambiguities and nuances, flexibility was built into the scoring procedure. When there was uncertainty about which group, constituted body, or individual was responsible for an event or about the "type" of this event, I assigned credit to all claimants according to the amount of coverage, that is, the number of pages devoted to them. This division of responsibility often involved a subjective judgment on my part; but making this decision seemed more accurate than giving equal credit when such was obviously undeserved. Also, the categories were designed to avoid any foreseeable overlap, and miscellaneous areas were assigned to remove the necessity for forcing material into inappropriate categories. Perhaps a few examples will clarify my procedure.

In Fréron's *Orateur du Peuple*, there is a half-page article on the National Assembly's efforts to crush Marat.[5] After recording the information on the length and location of this article, I determined that the National Assembly's legislation against Marat was an "event" and the basis for this article. Thus, the "source" of the event was checked as the National Assembly, while the "type" of this activity involved was listed under the category, "the considerations in the legitimate political sphere on civil liberties." Having read Fréron's account, that the action taken by the Assembly against the journalist was to control his alleged libels, I reasoned that these activities were designed to regulate the exercise of civil liberties and could rightfully be placed in category 20. Finally, since other journals reported this same event, I was careful to assign a code number that was the same for all articles based on this event.

Another item illustrative of this scoring technique is a long article in the *Révolutions de Paris* on the actions of the National Assembly, ministers, and the Parisians concerning a military mutiny at Nancy.[6] Because of the various actors in this article, I divided the responsibility for the "source" of the event among the three categories above according to their relative number of pages in the writings of the journalists. Consequently, I assigned forty percent of the pages to both the National Assembly and the ministers and half that to the popular action of the

Parisians. Since all of these groups focused their attention on the army officers' control of public political participation, I again assigned category 20 as the "type" of activity involved.

These examples could be multiplied indefinitely but perhaps one more will be satisfactory. In July 1790, the *Mercure National* carried a story that compared the French and English revolutions.[7] As this article seemed to me to be purely editorial, I recorded that the item was not founded on any event and consequently there was no particular "source" that the writer was watching. Nevertheless, since the journalist expressed a definite interest in the reorganization of the French state, I recorded that he was interested in a certain "type" of event, that of category 19, namely, those concerning the reconstruction of the political order.

Hopefully, these examples make the scoring method clear and reveal the difficulties and ambiguities inherent in such work. No one can deny that making objective judgments about such data is fraught with dangers; no one should claim that the statistical results are as reliable as those available in the physical sciences; nonetheless, I would assert that this quantification is absolutely necessary to arrive at any results of substantial validity. Reliance on impressions and the use of selected examples to support a particular hypothesis are, it seems to me, much less reliable (given the overwhelming amount of data) than a systematic, though not completely objective, method of analysis. And the reader should be reminded that this methodology is designed ultimately to illuminate, as accurately as possible, what interest the radicals had in events through the "types" and "sources" of reported activities and through the time and space devoted to particular occurrences.

As the volume of newsprint made a quantitative analysis useful and necessary, so this very same volume requires that this assessment of events be restricted to a limited time period. As the average week of newsprint includes more than one hundred articles, an assessment of twenty-eight months of six papers was not feasible. I have employed instead a ten-week period, July 13 to September 20, 1790, a time when all six papers were operative, and selected from the middle point of those years, 1789 to 1791, which are under examination here. To validate the results obtained from this period, I picked, at random, from a period as far removed as possible from mid-1790, another small span for one newspaper, the *Journal Universel*, for ten weeks, February 1 to April 11, 1791. If the events of this latter study conform to the same generalizations as the events of the larger sample, then it is fairly safe to assume that the results from 1790 are valid for the entire period under consideration.[8]

# APPENDIX B
# EVENTS IN THE RADICAL PRESS

TABLE 1

Percentage of Newsprint
Devoted to Various Sources
and Types of Activities (By Week)

| Sources | Weeks[a] | | | | | | | | | | Average |
|---|---|---|---|---|---|---|---|---|---|---|---|
| | 1 | 2 | 3 | 4 | 5 | 6 | 7 | 8 | 9 | 10 | |
| (4)[b] | 6 | 10 | 11 | 4 | 9 | 4 | 5 | 7 | 4 | 10 | 7 |
| (6) | 30 | 26 | 29 | 57 | 43 | 46 | 44 | 44 | 51 | 37 | 41 |
| (7) | 13 | 7 | 5 | 15 | 17 | 2 | 5 | 7 | 12 | 18 | 10 |
| (8) | 3 | 2 | 21 | 2 | 6 | 7 | 2 | 27 | 5 | 4 | 8 |
| (9) | 0 | 1 | 2 | 1 | 0 | 2 | 7 | 0 | 1 | 1 | 2 |
| (10) | 2 | 1 | 5 | 2 | 1 | 0 | 1 | 1 | 0 | 1 | 1 |
| (11) | 26 | 30 | 5 | 4 | 6 | 15 | 7 | 5 | 5 | 11 | 12 |
| (12) | 9 | 7 | 7 | 7 | 7 | 15 | 8 | 3 | 7 | 7 | 8 |
| (13) | 2 | 0 | 1 | 1 | 0 | 5 | 2 | 0 | 3 | 0 | 1 |
| (14) | 0 | 3 | 0 | 0 | 0 | 0 | 1 | 0 | 0 | 0 | 0+ |
| (15) | 1 | 1 | 1 | 0 | 0 | 0 | 4 | 0 | 0 | 2 | 1 |
| (16) | 1 | 5 | 0 | 2 | 3 | 0 | 3 | 2 | 1 | 2 | 2 |
| (17) | 4 | 6 | 10 | 2 | 5 | 4 | 9 | 3 | 7 | 4 | 5 |
| (18) | 3 | 1 | 3 | 3 | 3 | 1 | 2 | 1 | 4 | 3 | 2 |
| *Activities* | | | | | | | | | | | |
| (19) | 25 | 30 | 20 | 20 | 16 | 41 | 35 | 17 | 27 | 20 | 25 |
| (20) | 16 | 14 | 25 | 50 | 37 | 36 | 27 | 59 | 23 | 43 | 33 |
| (21) | 53 | 49 | 37 | 23 | 37 | 15 | 25 | 15 | 32 | 15 | 30 |
| (22) | 1 | 1 | 7 | 2 | 4 | 2 | 6 | 2 | 11 | 10 | 5 |
| (23) | 1 | 0 | 2 | 0 | 0 | 3 | 1 | 1 | 0 | 3 | 1 |
| (24) | 0 | 0 | 1 | 1 | 0 | 0 | 0 | 0 | 0 | 0 | 0+ |
| (25) | 0 | 0 | 0 | 0 | 0 | 0 | 0 | 0 | 1 | 1 | 0+ |
| (26) | 0 | 1 | 2 | 1 | 1 | 1 | 4 | 1 | 1 | 1 | 1 |
| (27) | 1 | 1 | 1 | 0 | 2 | 1 | 1 | 1 | 0 | 1 | 1 |
| (28) | 0 | 0 | 0 | 1 | 0 | 0 | 0 | 0 | 2 | 0 | 0+ |
| (29) | 3 | 4 | 5 | 2 | 3 | 1 | 1 | 4 | 3 | 6 | 3 |

NOTE: (These notes apply to tables 1–7. Rounding numbers has caused some of the rows to add up to slightly more or less than 100 percent. Also some averages have been rectified to compensate for rounding.)

[a]The numbered weeks correspond to the following dates:

| | | | |
|---|---|---|---|
| 1 | July 13–19, 1790 | 6 | August 17–23, 1790 |
| 2 | July 20–26, 1790 | 7 | August 24–30, 1790 |
| 3 | July 27–August 2, 1790 | 8 | August 31–September 6, 1790 |
| 4 | August 3–9, 1790 | 9 | September 7–13, 1790 |
| 5 | August 10–16, 1790 | 10 | September 14–20, 1790 |

[b]The numbers in parentheses, which stand for various sources and types of activities, correspond to those numbers on the score sheet (appendix A) where the various categories of sources and actions are described.

[c]AP  *Ami du Peuple*            OP  *Orateur du Peuple*
JU  *Journal Universel*       RF  *Révolutions de France et de Brabant*
MN  *Mercure National*        RP  *Révolutions de Paris*

TABLE 2

Percentage of Newsprint
Devoted to Various Sources
and Types of Activities (By Newspaper)

| Sources | Newspapers[c] | | | | | | Average |
|---|---|---|---|---|---|---|---|
| | MN | JU | OP | AP | RF | RP | |
| (4)[b] | 7 | 9 | 14 | 5 | 3 | 4 | 7 |
| (6) | 60 | 48 | 17 | 41 | 38 | 42 | 41 |
| (7) | 5 | 10 | 19 | 14 | 4 | 12 | 10 |
| (8) | 1 | 3 | 10 | 13 | 9 | 10 | 8 |
| (9) | 0 | 4 | 0 | 1 | 2 | 1 | 2 |
| (10) | 1 | 2 | 1 | 2 | 0 | 1 | 1 |
| (11) | 9 | 6 | 12 | 8 | 17 | 13 | 12 |
| (12) | 1 | 6 | 14 | 6 | 12 | 8 | 8 |
| (13) | 3 | 0 | 1 | 1 | 3 | 1 | 1 |
| (14) | 0 | 1 | 2 | 0 | 0 | 0 | 0+ |
| (15) | 0 | 1 | 2 | 1 | 2 | 0 | 1 |
| (16) | 3 | 1 | 4 | 1 | 1 | 0 | 2 |
| (17) | 8 | 5 | 1 | 5 | 6 | 7 | 5 |
| (18) | 2 | 4 | 3 | 2 | 3 | 1 | 2 |
| Activities | | | | | | | |
| (19) | 48 | 30 | 5 | 19 | 20 | 20 | 25 |
| (20) | 21 | 26 | 31 | 46 | 40 | 36 | 33 |
| (21) | 17 | 27 | 58 | 24 | 33 | 25 | 30 |
| (22) | 5 | 8 | 2 | 3 | 3 | 6 | 5 |
| (23) | 1 | 1 | 0 | 2 | 1 | 0 | 1 |
| (24) | 1 | 0 | 0 | 0 | 0 | 0 | 0+ |
| (25) | 0 | 0 | 0 | 0 | 0 | 2 | 0+ |
| (26) | 1 | 2 | 1 | 1 | 1 | 4 | 1 |
| (27) | 2 | 1 | 0 | 0 | 1 | 3 | 1 |
| (28) | 0 | 0 | 0 | 0 | 1 | 1 | 0+ |
| (29) | 4 | 5 | 3 | 5 | 1 | 3 | 3 |

TABLE 3

Percentage of Event-Oriented Articles
Devoted to Various Sources and Types of Activities

| Source | Number of Articles | Percentage |
|---|---|---|
| (6)[b] | 310 | 31 |
| (7) | 145 | 15 |
| (8) | 62 | 6 |
| (9) | 21 | 2 |
| (10) | 27 | 2 |
| (11) | 129 | 13 |
| (12) | 118 | 12 |
| (13) | 8 | 1 |
| (14) | 6 | 1 |
| (15) | 12 | 1 |
| (16) | 37 | 4 |
| (17) | 79 | 8 |
| (18) | 46 | 5 |
| *Activities* | | |
| (19) | 188 | 17 |
| (20) | 324 | 30 |
| (21) | 371 | 34 |
| (22) | 64 | 6 |
| (23) | 13 | 1 |
| (24) | 2 | 0+ |
| (25) | 6 | 1 |
| (26) | 24 | 2 |
| (27) | 19 | 1 |
| (28) | 3 | 0+ |
| (29) | 83 | 8 |

TABLE 4

Percentage of Event-Oriented Articles
of Each Source Devoted to Each Different Type of Activity

| Sources | Activities | | | | | | | | | | |
|---|---|---|---|---|---|---|---|---|---|---|---|
| | (19)[b] | (20) | (21) | (22) | (23) | (24) | (25) | (26) | (27) | (28) | (29) |
| (6)[b] | 23 | 31 | 20 | 12 | 2 | 0+ | 1 | 3 | 3 | 0+ | 4 |
| (7) | 13 | 53 | 26 | 0 | 1 | 0 | 0 | 0 | 0 | 0 | 7 |
| (8) | 5 | 50 | 26 | 11 | 2 | 0 | 0 | 0 | 0 | 0 | 6 |
| (9) | 48 | 14 | 14 | 5 | 0 | 5 | 0 | 0 | 5 | 0 | 10 |
| (10) | 15 | 37 | 33 | 4 | 0 | 0 | 0 | 0 | 4 | 0 | 7 |
| (11) | 12 | 32 | 46 | 0 | 2 | 0 | 0 | 0 | 1 | 0 | 5 |
| (12) | 10 | 16 | 62 | 1 | 0 | 0 | 0 | 0 | 2 | 0 | 10 |
| (13) | 7 | 21 | 43 | 14 | 0 | 0 | 0 | 0 | 0 | 0 | 14 |
| (14) | 5 | 19 | 40 | 16 | 0 | 0 | 0 | 0 | 2 | 0 | 18 |
| (15) | 17 | 17 | 67 | 0 | 0 | 0 | 0 | 0 | 0 | 0 | 0 |
| (16) | 3 | 3 | 68 | 0 | 0 | 0 | 0 | 19 | 3 | 0 | 5 |
| (17) | 30 | 23 | 26 | 9 | 0 | 0 | 0 | 5 | 0 | 1 | 5 |
| (18) | 20 | 11 | 30 | 2 | 0 | 0 | 2 | 2 | 2 | 0 | 30 |

TABLE 5

Coverage of Events by Number of Papers
Covering that Event (Percentage of Newsprint)

| Weeks[a] | Number of Journals in Which Event Is Reported | | | | | | Editorials* |
|---|---|---|---|---|---|---|---|
| | 1 | 2 | 3 | 4 | 5 | 6 | |
| 1 | 35 | 8 | 4 | 16 | 0 | 35 | 3 |
| 2 | 40 | 4 | 22 | 0 | 26 | 0 | 7 |
| 3 | 51 | 2 | 6 | 33 | 0 | 0 | 8 |
| 4 | 30 | 11 | 23 | 4 | 28 | 0 | 2 |
| 5 | 49 | 0 | 20 | 13 | 7 | 0 | 11 |
| 6 | 59 | 3 | 0 | 36 | 0 | 0 | 6 |
| 7 | 51 | 8 | 23 | 14 | 0 | 0 | 5 |
| 8 | 30 | 1 | 0 | 28 | 37 | 0 | 4 |
| 9 | 30 | 5 | 0 | 52 | 10 | 0 | 3 |
| 10 | 53 | 18 | 25 | 0 | 0 | 0 | 4 |
| Average | 43 | 6 | 12 | 20 | 11 | 4 | 5 |

*The percentage of Editorials is lower here than in tables 1 and 2 because, when the same editorials appeared in more than one paper, I assumed common interest among journalists, and I treated the editorial subject as an event, not as an editorial.

TABLE 6

Coverage of Events by Length of Coverage

| Length of Coverage (Percentage of One Week's Output) | Average Number of Events Covered at That Length | Percentage of the Ten Weeks' Newsprint Occupied by This Material |
|---|---|---|
| 0–2 | 54.4 | 31 |
| 2–5 | 5.2 | 14 |
| 5–10 | 1.4 | 10 |
| 10–20 | 1.1 | 16 |
| 20–30 | .6 | 15 |
| 30+ | .2 | 7 |

TABLE 7
Corroborative Study—Pattern of Interest
of the *Journal Universel*,
February 1 to April 11, 1791
(Percentage of Newsprint)

| Sources | JU$^c$ 1790 | JU$^c$ 1791 |
|---|---|---|
| (4)[b] | 9 | 4 |
| (6) | 48 | 45 |
| (7) | 10 | 12 |
| (8) | 3 | 3 |
| (9) | 4 | 1 |
| (10) | 2 | 3 |
| (11) | 6 | 9 |
| (12) | 6 | 13 |
| (13) | 0 | 0 |
| (14) | 1 | 1 |
| (15) | 1 | 0 |
| (16) | 1 | 2 |
| (17) | 5 | 6 |
| (18) | 4 | 1 |
| *Activities* | | |
| (19) | 30 | 37 |
| (20) | 26 | 22 |
| (21) | 27 | 26 |
| (22) | 8 | 4 |
| (23) | 1 | 2 |
| (24) | 0 | 0 |
| (25) | 0 | 0 |
| (26) | 2 | 0 |
| (27) | 1 | 5 |
| (28) | 0 | 0 |
| (29) | 5 | 4 |

# APPENDIX C
## SUBJECTS OF ARTICLES FOR
## WEEK OF AUGUST 10–16, 1790

*Journal Universel*

National Assembly reports
Abbé Gouttes did check cheating
The provinces mobilize against the Austrians
Foreign courts have gathered gold
*Aristocrates* try to have National Guards back their projects
Boucher has spoken at the National Assembly
The people from Lorraine are helping the Brabançons

Barnave beats Cazalès in duel
Riquetti-Cravatte has disappeared
I have battled with some National Assembly *aristocrates* over October
   Days and the *Châtelet*
Praise to patriots
The National Assembly forbids dueling
French artists abroad wish to retain the cockade
The *Châtelet* is trying to condemn the Revolution
A resident of the *Châtelet* speaks
What of Necker's accounts?
*Aristocrates* attack in Guadaloupe
Truce is arranged between Prussia, Hungary, and the Turks
Affairs at Liège
National Guards save five from the gallows
Two municipalities unite
Regent, in 1718, was ready to reduce the clergy in status
Gouvelet has been released
De Riolles retained
Praise on a work by Cloots
Dueling is terrible
Letter accuses *Journal Universel* of error in case of soldier
The National Assembly has passed a law limiting plays
Camus attacks pensions
Legal cases disposed of
Robbers protest their innocence
Necker gives his accounts

*Révolutions de Paris*

The *Châtelet* has revived the October Days trial
The electoral system is bad
Barnave and Cazalès duel
Camus denounces Necker
Jacobins of Lorraine call for arms
Franklin is praised by simple workers in a *fête*
French army is in insurrection after thefts by its officers
Colonel Guerchy is a friend of the Constitution
The owner of the *cirque* of the Palais-Royal is not guilty of despotism
The municipality of La Rochelle denies having obstructed the *fête*
The municipality of Clermont-Ferrand defends legitimacy of their elec-
   tion
The Jacobin Clubs are everywhere
The Revolution must be made in spirit

*Gardes des Corps* are aristocratic
National Assembly reports
List of subscribers to statue for J.-J. Rousseau

## *Ami du Peuple*

The *Châtelet* tries to convict on October Days
The National Assembly deals with finances
Various plots
Necker's plan for the *don patriotique*
The National Assembly rejects the *Châtelet*
The National Assembly decrees against the opening of *pacquet* by municipality, St.-Aubin
*Ami du Peuple*, you are effective—elections have changed
The municipal officers will try to retain their positions
Barnave and Cazalès duel
Lameth implicated in a plot
*Noirs* ought to be wiped out
Lafayette is negligent in recent duel
Attack on ministers for role in army affairs
National Assembly passes decree on regulation of play
National Assembly acts on a conspiracy of Toulouse-Lautreck
Municipality of Balan makes an arrest
The municipal committee attacks *Châtelet* over October Days
Marat defends against Desmoulins

## *Mercure National*

Which country will follow France's lead?
The municipality reports on the Bonne-Savardin affair
Foreign troops pass near us (at Nancy)
Letter from Quimper Jacobins to Dr. Price
National Assembly reports
There are guns at Cherville
Leopold and Prussia sign a peace agreement

## *Révolutions de France et de Brabant*

Bailly is reelected mayor
Malouet attacks Marat and me
The National Assembly opposes the decree of the *Châtelet* on October Days
Cazalès and Barnave duel
Necker is not guilty of monopolizing grain
The former noble deputies have protested against the National Assembly

*Orateur du Peuple*

The *Châtelet* has acted against Mirabeau and Orléans
The ministers plot against us
Pitt has been replaced
Rohan responsible for disturbances in Strasbourg
Soldiers of Regiment of Flanders defend themselves
The ministers conspire against us
Duel between Cazalès and Barnave
Ministers arrested as they begin to flee
All the foreign countries are beset with internal disintegration
The National Guards of Stenay disperse plot
The National Assembly has seized an illicit parcel
The *Châtelet* charges Mirabeau, Orléans, and the patriotic writers
Court acts to reconstitute the king's bodyguard
An old man has been oppressed by a minister
The National Guard is attacked by the crowd

## APPENDIX D
## THE PARIS MUNICIPALITY, BAILLY, LAFAYETTE,
## THE KING, AND THE NATIONAL ASSEMBLY
## IN THE RADICAL PRESS

### Mercure National

| Institution | Praise | Wavering | Attack |
|---|---|---|---|
| Municipality | None | Sept., 1789–June, 1790 | June, 1790–July, 1791 |
| Bailly | None | Sept., 1789–Sept., 1790 | Sept., 1790–July 1791 |
| Lafayette | Sept., 1789–Aug., 1790 | Aug., 1790–Sept., 1790 | Sept., 1790–July, 1791 |
| King | Sept., 1789–July, 1790 | July, 1790–June, 1791 | June, 1791–July, 1791 |
| National Assembly | Sept., 1789–Nov., 1790 | Nov., 1790–July, 1791 | None |

### Journal Universel

| Institution | Praise | Wavering | Attack |
|---|---|---|---|
| Municipality | None | Nov., 1789–April, 1790 | April, 1790–Oct., 1791 |
| Bailly | None | Nov., 1789–Nov., 1790 | Nov., 1790–Oct., 1791 |
| Lafayette | Nov., 1789–Sept., 1790 | Sept., 1790–Nov., 1790 | Nov., 1790–Oct., 1791 |
| King | Nov., 1789–Sept., 1790 | Sept., 1790–March, 1791 | March, 1791–Oct., 1791 |
| National Assembly | Nov., 1789–May, 1790 | May, 1790–Oct., 1791 | None |

### Révolutions de France et de Brabant

| Institution | Praise | Wavering | Attack |
|---|---|---|---|
| Municipality | None | Nov., 1789–Oct., 1790 | Oct., 1790–July, 1791 |
| Bailly | None | Nov., 1789–Jan., 1790 | Jan., 1790–July, 1791 |
| Lafayette | Nov., 1789–Feb., 1790 | Feb., 1790–June, 1790 | June, 1790–July, 1791 |
| King | Nov., 1789–Feb., 1790 | Feb., 1790–April, 1791 | April, 1791–July, 1791 |
| National Assembly | Nov., 1789–April, 1790 | April, 1790–May, 1790 and Sept., 1790–April, 1791 | May, 1790–Sept., 1790 and April, 1791–July, 1791 |

### Révolutions de Paris

| Institution | Praise | Wavering | Attack |
|---|---|---|---|
| Municipality | None | July, 1789–Sept., 1789 | Sept., 1789–Oct., 1791 |
| Bailly | July, 1789–Nov., 1789 | Nov., 1789–March, 1790 | March, 1790–Oct., 1791 |
| Lafayette | July, 1789–Feb., 1790 | Feb., 1790–July, 1790 | July, 1790–Oct., 1791 |
| King | July, 1789–July, 1790 | July, 1790–April, 1791 | April, 1791–Oct., 1791 |
| National Assembly | July, 1789–Aug., 1789 | Aug., 1789–July, 1790 | July, 1790–Oct., 1791 |

### Ami du Peuple

| Institution | Praise | Wavering | Attack |
|---|---|---|---|
| Municipality | Sept., 1789–Oct., 1789 | Oct., 1789–Nov., 1789 | Nov., 1789–Oct., 1791 |
| Bailly | None | Sept., 1789–Dec., 1789 | Dec., 1789–Oct., 1791 |
| Lafayette | Sept., 1789–Jan., 1790 | Jan., 1790–June, 1790 | June, 1790–Oct., 1791 |
| King | Sept., 1789–June, 1790 | June, 1790–April, 1791 | April, 1791–Oct., 1791 |
| National Assembly | Sept., 1789–Oct., 1789 | Oct., 1789–Jan., 1790 | Jan., 1790–Oct., 1791 |

### Orateur du Peuple

| Institution | Praise | Wavering | Attack |
|---|---|---|---|
| Municipality | May, 1790–June, 1790 | June, 1790–Nov., 1790 | Nov., 1790–Oct., 1791 |
| Bailly | May, 1790–June, 1790 | June, 1790–Sept., 1790 | Sept., 1790–Oct., 1791 |
| Lafayette | May, 1790–June, 1790 | June, 1790–Aug., 1790 | Aug., 1790–Oct., 1791 |
| King | May, 1790 only | May, 1790–Jan., 1791 | Jan., 1791–Oct., 1791 |
| National Assembly | None | May, 1790–Nov., 1790 | Nov., 1790–Oct., 1791 |

NOTE: These months should be read as approximate measures, because usually the editors' attitudes changed gradually, taking some weeks to settle.

## APPENDIX E
### TITLES AND DATES
### OF APPEARANCE OF THE DIFFERENT VERSIONS
### OF THE *MERCURE NATIONAL*

| | |
|---|---|
| *Journal d'Etat et du Citoyen* | August 13, 1789– December 27, 1789 |
| *Mercure National ou Journal d'Etat et du Citoyen* | December 31, 1789– August 30, 1790 |
| *Révolutions de l'Europe et Mercure National Réunis* | September 11, 1790– September 14, 1790 |
| *Mercure National et Révolutions de l'Europe* | September 14, 1790– March 29, 1791 |
| *Mercure National et Etranger, ou Journal Politique de l'Europe* | April 16, 1791– July 5, 1791 |

# Notes

## CHAPTER 1

1. *Feuille du Jour,* vol. 10, December 10, 1790, p. 75. For more information on the turmoil in Paris and throughout France, see Samuel F. Scott, "Problems of Law and Order during 1790, the Peaceful Year," *American Historical Review* 80 (1975): 859–88.
2. In July 1790, the sixty districts that had been organized for the elections to the Estates-General were disbanded; and forty-eight sections, drawn with entirely new boundaries, replaced them.
3. A clear picture of the deluge of papers will be given in the second half of this chapter.
4. Here I mean to strip from the words *radical* and *extreme left* all their modern connotations and use them only to identify the group at the most revolutionary end of the political spectrum in 1789.
5. Claude Bellanger et al., *L'Histoire générale de la presse française* (Paris: Presses Universitaires de France, 1969), pp. 451–62.
6. Alphonse Aulard, *The French Revolution: A Political History,* trans. Bernard Miall, 4 vols. (New York: Scribner's and Brothers, 1910), passim.
7. Eric Thompson, *Popular Sovereignty and the French Constituent Assembly, 1789–91* (Manchester: Manchester University Press, 1952), pp. 18–20.
8. Both Michael J. Sydenham, in *The French Revolution* (New York: Capricorn Books, 1966), p. 65, and Norman Hampson, in *A Social History of the French Revolution* (London: Routledge and Kegan Paul, 1953, and Toronto: University of Toronto Press, 1963), p. 100, describe the growth of the radical movement and its leadership by the Cordeliers. This leftist agitation in Paris and the Cordeliers' primary role has been well documented in monographs by Georges Garrigues, *Les Districts parisiens pendant la Révolution française* (Paris: Editions Spès, n.d.), passim, and Isabelle Bourdin, *Les Sociétés populaires à Paris pendant la Révolution* (Paris: Recueil Sirey, 1937), passim. Another historian who points to the leadership of the Cordeliers is Albert Mathiez in *Le Club des Cordeliers pendant la crise de Varennes et le massacre du Champ de Mars* (Paris: Librairie Ancienne H. Champion, 1910), pp. 3–41. Contemporary politicians also believed that the radical movement was led by the Cordeliers. The repeated attacks of the central authorities on the Cordeliers' effort to maintain a power base have not been chronicled systematically, but such assaults have been individually treated (e.g., Louis Madelin, *Danton,* trans. Mary Loyd (London: William Heinemann, 1921), pp.

147

39–44). These sustained efforts are a strong indication that the Cordeliers were envisioned by the Paris government as too extreme to be tolerated and as a center of radicalism.

9. Sigismond Lacroix, *Actes de la Commune de Paris pendant la Révolution* (Paris: Société Française d'Editions d'Art, 1895–1909) 2: 471. For a full account of the Cordeliers' reverence for the principles of popular sovereignty, see Garrigues, *Les Districts parisiens*, passim, and Bourdin, *Les Sociétés populaires*, passim.

10. Emmanuel Joseph Sieyès, *What Is the Third Estate?*, trans. M. Blondel and S. E. Finer (London: Pall Mall Press, 1963), p. 10.

11. Georges Lefebvre, *The Coming of the French Revolution*, trans. Robert R. Palmer (New York: Vintage Books, 1947), p. 189.

12. Garrigues, *Les Districts parisiens*, pp. 155–60.

13. Louis R. Gottschalk and Margaret Maddox, in *Lafayette in the French Revolution through the October Days* (Chicago: University of Chicago Press, 1969), passim, describe in excellent detail the chaotic situation that determined the "law-and-order" position taken by the National Assembly, the municipality, and Lafayette himself.

14. J. M. Thompson, *The French Revolution* (London: Hazell, Watson, and Viney, Ltd., 1943), p. 124.

15. Bellanger et al., *L'Histoire de la presse*, pp. 423–33. In this book, Jacques Godechot explains the conditions which created the freedom of the press. For more detail on the ability of the left—in the Assembly, the districts, and the streets—to restrict prosecution, see Eugène Hatin, *Histoire politique et littéraire de la presse en France*, 8 vols. (Paris: Poulet-Malassis et de Broise, 1859–61) 6:7–200.

16. Lefebvre, *The Coming of the French Revolution*, pp. 133–56.

17. For more detail on press technology, see Bellanger et al., pp. 3–23 and Gérard Martin, *L'Imprimerie* (Paris: Presses Universitaires de France, 1963).

18. Hatin, *Histoire de la presse* 4:13–17.

19. Bourdin's *Les Sociétés populaires* and Garrigues's *Les Districts parisiens* are obvious exceptions to this rule. They both employ fairly modern techniques although both books are old. Bourdin's effort dates from 1936, and although Garrigues's book is not dated, the most recent work that he cites was written in 1924. Nonetheless, these books are quite solid and cover important ground. However, the overwhelming majority of the latest research on the political history of the period was done at the turn of the century by Aulard and his students. These works are often marred by political bias and outmoded technique, although they do treat their chosen topic with great sensitivity.

20. Alfred Bougeart, *Les Cordeliers, documents pour servir à l'histoire de la Révolution française* (Caen: Henri Delesques, 1891), and Mathiez, *Le Club des Cordeliers*, cited above.

21. George Rudé, *The Crowd in the French Revolution* (Oxford: Clarendon Press, 1959), passim.

22. Albert Soboul, *The Parisian Sans-Culottes and the French Revolution*, trans. Gwynne Lewis (London: Oxford University Press, 1964), pp. 249–61.

23. Richard Cobb, *The Police and the People* (Oxford: Clarendon Press, 1970), pp. 185–90.

24. Robert Darnton, "The High Enlightenment and the Low-Life of Literature in Pre-Revolutionary France," *Past and Present*, no. 51 (1971), pp. 81–115.

25. Michael J. Sydenham, *The Girondins* (New York: Athlone Press, 1960), passim.

26. Madeleine Varin d'Ainville, *La Presse en France, genèse et évolution de ses fonctions psychosociales* (Paris: Presses Universitaires de France, 1965), pp. 149–167. This book has an interesting theoretical framework, but it lacks hard data to back many precarious assertions.

27. William J. Murray, "The Right-Wing Press in the French Revolution, 1789–1792" (dissertation, Australian National University, 1971).

28. For example, one can select the most recent theses on the Parisian press of the Revolution. See P. Laborie, "Le Patriote Francais" (dissertation, Université de Toulouse, 1961); J. Benétruy, "L'Atelier de Mirabeau" (dissertation, Université de Paris, 1962); A. Laurens, "Les Actes des Apôtres, journal contre-révolutionnaire" (dissertation, Université de Toulouse, 1963); François Sabatier, "Etude de la 'Feuille Villageoise'" (dissertation, Université de Montpellier, 1963); Melvin A. Edelstein, " 'La Feuille Villageoise,' Communication and Rural Modernization in the French Revolu-

tion" (dissertation, Princeton University, 1965); and Max Fajn, "Le Journal des Hommes Libres" (dissertation, University of Chicago, 1971). There are some older studies where the press has been collectively analyzed, but the periods of concentration have been too brief to afford many definite general statements. The best of these, in my estimation, is G. Michon's *Le Rôle de la presse en 1791–1792, la Déclaration de Pillnitz et la guerre* (Paris: TEPA, 1941). Despite this lacuna for the Parisian press, there have been several collective studies of the provincial press, the most recent being Georges Clouse, "La Presse de la Marne pendant la Révolution" (dissertation, Université de Paris, 1971).

29. Bellanger, et al., pp. 405–548. The writers of texts on the press have had, from the first, to limit themselves to a sequence of descriptions of various journals. See Léonard Gallois, *Histoire des journaux et des journalistes de la Révolution française, 1789–1796,* 2 vols. (Paris: Au Bureau de la Société de l'industrie fraternelle, 1845–46).

30. To count or select or arrange newspapers also requires a definition of a newspaper. A common-sense definition related to the realities of periodical production in 1789 is best here. To conform to this standard, I have defined a newspaper (or a journal, periodical, or paper) as a printed work that is published as a part of a series, where current developments are considered in each issue.

31. These statistics on the number of journals produced between 1789 and 1791 are at best just a minor foray into a vast uncharted territory. My only goal is to indicate the size of the press and to justify the selection of a sample. There are obviously many other valid questions to be asked of this material. For example, one might query whether daily periodicals were more or less popular at different times in the Revolution or whether weekly papers survived longer than dailies. These questions and others deserve study. The primary source for the data provided here is André Martin and Gérard Walter, *Catalogue de l'histoire de la Révolution française,* vol. 5 (Paris: Editions des Bibliothèques Nationales, 1940). I have taken the advice of Jacques Godechot (Bellanger, et al., *L'Histoire de la presse,* p. 588) and of A. Terroine (in her "L'Oeuvre bibliographique de M. G. Walter," *Annales historiques de la Révolution française* 20 (1948):1–26) that this catalogue does have errors and gaps; and I have made some efforts to supplement Walter's list of the newspapers with those reported in the *Catalogue collectif des périodiques conservés dans les bibliothèques de Paris et les bibliothèques universitaires,* 43 vols. (Paris: Bibliothèque Nationale, 1940–62).

32. These figures are somewhat misleading as some journals lasted longer than these statistics reveal. Some newspapers that endured only a month or two from 1789 to October 1791, are actually more substantial since they persisted into 1792, beyond our range of consideration. Obviously, the inclusion of the continued life of these journals would diminish the number of those periodicals whose existence appears so fragile. Such an inclusion would not, however, alter the general picture very much because few of the short-lived journals were among those that survived into late 1791 and 1792.

33. Arthur Aspinall, *Politics and the Press, c. 1780–1850* (London: Home & Van Thal, Ltd., 1949), p. 6.

34. Professor William J. Murray has suggested that to deal with a group of papers, one should vary one's attention according to the relative impact of each journal. I quite agree; nonetheless, because I have no accurate measure of the value of the different journals—no reliable circulation figures exist—I plan to treat them as equals and give approximately equivalent attention to each.

35. For examples, see *Ami du Peuple,* no. 447, May 13, 1791, pp. 4–8, and *Révolutions de France et de Brabant,* no. 31, June 28, 1790, p. 309.

36. *Ami du Peuple,* no. 339, January 13, 1791, pp. 4–5.

## CHAPTER 2

1. Alphonse Aulard, *Histoire politique de la Révolution française* (Paris: Librairie Armand Colin, 1901), pp. 86–87. In order to avoid confusion, I shall generally refer to this journal, despite its varied names, solely as the *Mercure National.* Only in those

cases where the accurate title is revealing will the reader be troubled by the long and difficult names employed by the editors of this journal. However, the reader who wishes to know the exact name at any particular time may consult appendix E.

2. *Mercure National*, no. 8, October 1, 1789, p. 1.
3. Ibid., Prospectus, no. 2, n.d., p. 2.
4. Eugène Hatin, *Bibliographie historique et critique de la presse périodique française* (Paris: Librairie de Firmin Didot Frères, Fils et Cie., 1866), pp. 127–28.
5. For further detail see L. Antheunis, *Le Conventionnel Belge François Robert (1763–1826) et sa femme Louise de Kéralio (1758–1822)* (Belgium: Editions Bracke Wetteren, 1955), pp. 11–13, and "Kéralio, dame Robert," *Biographie universelle, ancienne et moderne* 21:535–36.
6. M. Weiss, "Louis-Felix-Guinement de Kéralio," *Biographie universelle, ancienne et moderne* 21:535.
7. According to Hatin, *Bibliographie historique*, p. 128, one Masclet also participated in the publication of this journal, but I can find no evidence of his assistance or any biographical information about this individual.
8. For more information, see Antheunis, *François Robert*, passim, and P. Gaffarel, *François Robert, ses travaux scientifique, son rôle politique, son rôle artistique* (Dijon: Darantière, 1889), passim.
9. For a more complete account, see B. D. Prevost, "Carra (Jean-Louis)," *Dictionnaire de biographie française*, fascicule 41 (1955), p. 1218. A more recent, and more satisfactory, summary of Carra's early life may be found in Michael Kennedy, "The Development of a Political Radical, Jean-Louis Carra, 1742–1787," in *Proceedings: Western Society for French History*, ed. Brison Gooch (Dallas: WSFH, forthcoming).
10. A. Beuchot and M. Durozier, "Bassville (Nicolas Jean Hugou de)," *Biographie universelle, ancienne et moderne* 3:241–42.
11. Hatin, *Bibliographie historique*, p. 128.
12. Ogier, Mittié fils, A.-N. Courtois, and Le Brun all contributed articles after the merger with Tournon, but internal evidence indicates that none were regular collaborators.
13. "Tournon, Alexandre," *Biographie universelle, ancienne et moderne* 42:57.
14. By early 1791, all the writing was being done by Robert and his wife, as they were signing all the articles.
15. There were two other contributors, Lanthenas and Lequino, but they wrote only two articles between them.
16. Antheunis, *François Robert*, p. 16.
17. M. Michaud, Jr., "Tondu, dit 'Lebrun' (Pierre Henri-Marie)," *Biographie universelle, ancienne et moderne* 41:659.
18. André Martin and Gérard Walter, *Catalogue de l'histoire de la Révolution française*, vol. 5 (Paris: Editions des Bibliothèques Nationales, 1943), p. 355.
19. Léonard Gallois, *Histoire des journaux et des journalistes de la Révolution française, 1789–1796* (Paris: Au Bureau de la Société de l'industrie fraternelle, 1845–46) 2:491.
20. *Journal Universel*, no. 160, May 1, 1790, pp. 1278–79.
21. Robert Darnton, "The High Enlightenment and the Low-Life of Literature in Pre-Revolutionary France," *Past and Present*, no. 51 (1971), p. 103.
22. Sigismond Lacroix, *Actes de la Commune de Paris pendant la Révolution* (Paris: Société Française d'Editions d'Art, 1899) 7:461.
23. For the details of Audouin's life, I have relied on E. Franceschini, "Audouin (Pierre-Jean)," *Dictionnaire de biographie française*, fascicule 20 (1947), pp. 433–35. The interpretation of his actions is my own and is based on his journal and his speeches recorded in various volumes of the *Archives Parlementaires*, ed. M. J. Mavidal and M. E. Laurent, vols. 1–31 (Paris: Librairie Administrative de Paul Dupont, 1879–1888).
24. Jules Claretie, *Camille Desmoulins, Lucile Desmoulins, étude sur les Dantonistes d'après des documents nouveau et inédits* (Paris: Plon, 1875), pp. 78–79.
25. Claude Bellanger et al., *Histoire générale de la presse française* (Paris: Presses Universitaires de France, 1969), p. 453–54. It should be additionally noted that this newspaper was not dated, but the regularity of production and references within the newspaper itself make such dating very simple and reliable.

26. Gallois, *Histoire des journaux* 2:19-20.
27. Bellanger, et al., *L'Histoire de la presse,* p. 454; and chap. 5.
28. In mid-August, J.-F.-N. Dusaulchoy began to publish a journal, *Révolutions de France et de Brabant,* which he wished to be regarded as the successor to that of Desmoulins. But the tone and the substance of the second newspaper were clearly different, and I have chosen to regard Desaulchoy's periodical as a new journal, not to be considered here.
29. Many studies have been written about Desmoulins, although none are of great value. Among the best of this undistinguished group are Claretie, *Camille Desmoulins;* A. Chuquet, "La Jeunesse de Camille Desmoulins," *Annales Révolutionnaires* 1(1908): 1-26; Edouard Fleury, *Etudes révolutionnaires; Camille Desmoulins et Roch Marcandier. La Presse révolutionnaire,* 2 vols. (Paris: Didier, 1851); Pierre Labracherie, *Camille Desmoulins, grandeur et misère d'une âme ardente* (Paris: Librairie Hachette, 1948); Jean Matrat, *Camille Desmoulins* (Paris: Editions J. A. R., 1956); and J. B. Morton, *Camille Desmoulins and Other Studies of the French Revolution* (London: Weiner Laurie, 1950).
30. Bellanger, et al., pp. 451-52.
31. For more detail see Eugène Hatin, *Histoire politique et littéraire de la presse en France,* 8 vols. (Paris: Poulet-Malassis et de Broise, 1859-61), 6:318-20; Francisque Greppo, "Un Lyonnais, imprimeur et journaliste. Le Journal: *Les Révolutions de Paris,*" *Revue Lyonnais,* fifth series, 29 (1900):42-55; and Gallois, *Histoire des journaux* 2:230-32. I emphasize Prudhomme's role more than most historians have in the past.
32. In 1791, Prudhomme expanded his journal to fifty-six pages per issue.
33. Gallois, *Histoire des journaux* 2:202-23.
34. Because of the anonymity of the journalists, there are surely many contributors who are as yet unknown. Also there are two others, P. J. F. Robut and Sonthonax, who are so obscure that there is insufficient information for a biographical sketch. On Robut, there is nothing; for Sonthonax documents indicate that he played an active role in the Jacobins, and there exists an article on his activities by M. Sciout, "La Révolution à Saint-Dominigue. Les Commissaires Sonthonax et Polveral," *Revue des questions historiques* 64 (1898):399-470.
35. Bellanger, et al., p. 453.
36. Ibid., pp. 451-52. For more data on Loustallot, see Denys d'Aussy, "Elisée Loustallot," *Revue de la Révolution* 11 (1888):113-42; Marcellin Pellet, *Elisée Loustallot et les "Révolutions de Paris"* (Paris: Armand Le Chevalier, 1872), pp. 5-13; and Georges Villacèque, "Les Révolutions de Paris" (dissertation, Université de Toulouse, 1961), passim.
37. For more inclusive information, see C. A. Fusil, *Sylvain Maréchal ou l'homme sans Dieu* (Paris: Plon, 1936), passim, but especially pp. 108-13, and Maurice Dommanget, *Sylvain Maréchal, l'égaletaire, "l'homme sans Dieu," 1750-1803. Vie et oeuvre de l'auteur du "Manifeste des Egaux"* (Paris: R. Lefeuvre, 1950), passim.
38. There has been much written about Chaumette's activities under the Terror, but only two articles were particularly useful here. See Frédéric Braesch, "Chaumette et les *Révolutions de Paris,*" *Révolution Francaise* 76 (1923):157-59 and A. Chuquet, "La Jeunesse de Chaumette," *Revue critique d'histoire et de littérature,* (1909), pp. 1-26. For a summary of Chaumette's life, one should turn to A. Martin, "Chaumette (Pierre-Gaspard, dit Anaxagoras)," *Dictionnaire de biographie française,* fascicule 46 (1958), pp. 858-59.
39. For more details, see Alphonse Aulard, "Figures oubliées de la Révolution. Fabre d'Eglantine," *Nouvelle Revue* 35 (1885):59-86; Jules Claretie, "Fabre d'Eglantine à la Comédie Française," *Révolution Française* 33 (1897):385-404; Victor Fournel, "Fabre d'Eglantine, le comedien, l'auteur dramatique et le révolutionnaire," *Revue des questions historiques* 54 (1893):145-215; Louis Jacob, *Fabre d'Eglantine, chef des fripons* (Paris: Librairie Hachette, 1946), passim; and Marcel Rufas, "Les Origines sociales de Fabre d'Eglantine," *Annales historique de la Révolution française* 32, no. 161 (1960):294-300.
40. Martin and Walter, *Catalogue de l'histoire,* p. 65.

41. The municipality in 1791 raided a Marat printshop located on the Ile-de-la-Cité and owned by a Mme. Colombe.
42. Gérard Walter, *Marat* (Paris: Editions Albin Michel, 1933), p. 100.
43. Louis R. Gottschalk, *Jean-Paul Marat: A Study in Radicalism* (New York: Greenberg, 1929, and Chicago: University of Chicago Press, 1967), pp. 20–22. Walter (*Marat*, pp. 25–28) disagrees with Gottschalk and states that at this time Marat had already accepted revolutionary principles. Both rely on the same tract—Jean-Paul Marat, *The Chains of Slavery* (London: 1774)—to prove opposite points. I believe a careful reading of the tract shows Gottschalk's interpretation to be the correct one.
44. To a degree, Marat's judgment about the *Académie* was correct. Its members were not malicious schemers, but they were an encrusted group of old men who were quite capable of rejecting, without test, theories that challenged their own. But his intense frustration stemmed only partially from an accurate perception of injustice and primarily from his paranoia.
45. Marat's paranoia is well-documented by Gottschalk, *Jean-Paul Marat*, p. 25. Gottschalk, however, labels Marat's personality disorder as a case of *manie persecutrice*. Even if my use of paranoia is not medically precise, it is more accurate than Gottschalk's *manie persecutrice*, which, I believe, is clumsy and induces an image of a suffering poet instead of an aggressive politician. For more details on Marat's confrontation with the *Académie*, see Robert Darnton, *Mesmerism and the End of the Enlightenment in France* (Cambridge: Harvard University Press, 1968), passim.
46. Of the men examined here, Marat has been the most frequent subject of historical interest. Some of the most important books and articles follow in chronological order: Charles Brunet, *Marat, dit l'ami du peuple. Notice sur la vie et ses ouvrages* (Paris: Librairie Poulet-Malassis, 1862); Alfred Bougeart, *Marat, l'ami du peuple*, 2 vols. (Paris: A. Lacroix, Verbaeckhoven, 1865); François Chevremont, *Jean-Paul Marat, orné de son portrait*, 2 vols. (Paris: Chez l'Auteur, 1880); Louis Héritier, "Jean-Paul Marat avant 1789," *Revue Socialiste* 22 (1895):436–50; Ernest Belfort Bax, *Jean-Paul Marat, the People's Friend* (London: Grant Richards, 1900); Albert Mathiez, "Marat, père des sociétés fraternelles," *Annales revolutionnaires* 1 (1908):661–64; Ralph Catteral, "The Credibility of Marat," *American Historical Review* 16, no. 1 (1910):24–35; Louis R. Gottschalk, "Marat dans la journée du 14 juillet 1789," *Révolution Francaise* 76(1923): 13–18; René Farge, "Le Local du Club des Cordeliers et la coeur de Marat," *Annales historiques de la Révolution française* 4 (1927):320–47; Gottschalk, *Jean-Paul Marat* (1927); Walter, *Marat* (1933); Gaston Martin, *J.-P. Marat, l'oeil et l'ami du peuple* (Paris: Rieder, 1938); Jacques-Thomas de Castelnau, *Marat, "l'ami du peuple," 1744-1793* (Paris: Hachette, 1939); V. M. Daline, "Babeuf et Marat en 1789-1790," *Annales historiques de la Révolution française* 30, no. 150 (1958):16–17; Jean Massin, "Marat, un intellectuel de gauche du XVIIIe siècle," *Nouvelle Critique*, n.s., 1, no. 182 (1967):13–16; Stéphane Cordier, *Jean-Paul Marat* (Brussels: A. de Roche, 1967). While some of the works in this list were written purely to satisfy historical curiosity, many are the result of a polemical interest in Marat's ideological position, parts of which forecast Marxian thought. For example, he believed that law was only a function of the dominant group in society. Other books are written about Marat because of his identification with the introduction of "legal violence." The thinking runs that if Marat was justified, so was the Terror; if he was not, then the Terror was not. Consequently, Marat has become a *cause célèbre* for elements of the Left and a *bête noire* for much of the Right. An interesting bibliographical essay remains to be written.
47. Gallois, *Histoire des journaux* 2:233–37. The format of the *Orateur du Peuple* prevents the dating of individual issues of this paper in either the text or the footnotes. However, in chapters 4 and 5, some dating is required, and a close scrutiny of the contents of a journal usually provided sufficient detail to place a particular issue within a one-week time period. Admittedly, however, this method does not result in complete accuracy.
48. Fréron's brother-in-law, La Poype, occupied important positions in the revolutionary government from 1789, and one wonders why he did not immediately use his influence.
49. The name of the printer usually appeared within the pages of each journal.
50. Claretie, *Camille Desmoulins*, pp. 78–79.

51. For further details, see Raoul Arnaud, *Journaliste, sans-culotte, et thermidorien, le fils de Fréron, 1754–1802* (Paris: Librairie Academique Perrin et Cie., 1909), and J. Trévedy, *Fréron et sa famille* (Saint-Brieuc: 1889).

# CHAPTER 3

1. Noam Chomsky, *Language and Mind* (New York: Harcourt, Brace & World, 1968), passim, and Marshall McLuhan and Quentin Fiore, *The Medium Is the Massage* (New York: Bantam Books, 1967), passim.
2. A separate study of these rhetorical devices should focus on the physical layout of the newspapers, the use of prints, and the language and argumentative practices employed by the radicals. Perhaps the techniques of quantification could be used in such a study.
3. *Révolutions de Paris*, no. 28, January 23, 1790, p. 5.
4. *Révolutions de Paris*, no. 26, March 20, 1790, p. 16.
5. *Mercure National*, no. 8, February 14, 1790, p. 480.
6. *Ami du Peuple*, no. 451, May 7, 1791, p. 8. This is a very early use of the term *prolétaire*, later to be widely employed as a Marxist category.
7. *Dictionnaire de l'Académie française* 1 (Paris: Chez J. J. Smits et Cie., 1798): 162–63.
8. Ibid., p. 357.
9. Pierre Goubert, "The French Peasantry of the Seventeenth Century: A Regional Example," in *Crisis in Europe 1500–1660*, ed. Trevor Aston (New York: Basic Books, 1965), pp. 144–54.
10. For example, see *Ami du Peuple*, no. 179, August 1, 1790, p. 7.
11. *Révolutions de Paris*, no. 82, February 5, 1791, p. 171.
12. Ibid., no. 87, March 12, 1791, p. 456.
13. See Albert Soboul, *The Parisian Sans-Culottes and the French Revolution*, trans. Gwynne Lewis (London: Oxford University Press, 1964), passim, for the tensions that developed between these two groups.
14. *Révolutions de France et de Brabant*, no. 30, June 21, 1790, p. 304.
15. *Journal Universel*, no. 586, July 1, 1791, p. 10084.
16. *Révolutions de Paris*, no. 82, February 5, 1791, p. 174.
17. *Ami du Peuple*, no. 306, December 10, 1790, p. 7.
18. For example, see *Mercure National*, no. 41, May 27, 1791, pp. 646–50.
19. *Révolutions de France et de Brabant*, no. 34, July 19, 1790, p. 467.
20. Ibid., no. 8, January 16, 1790, pp. 337–78 and *Révolutions de Paris*, no. 6, August 22, 1789, pp. 12–22.
21. *Mercure National*, no. 25, September 29, 1790, p. 849.
22. *Révolutions de France et de Brabant*, no. 15, March 8, 1790, pp. 87–88.
23. *Mercure National*, no. 1, April 18, 1790, pp. 32–33.
24. *Révolutions de Paris*, no. 64, October 2, 1790, p. 593.
25. *Ami du Peuple*, no. 261, October 25, 1790, p. 6.
26. *Révolutions de France et de Brabant*, no. 15, March 8, 1790, pp. 87–88.
27. *Révolutions de Paris*, no. 72, November 27, 1790, pp. 361–70.
28. *Mercure National*, no. 25, May 11, 1791, pp. 396–97.
29. Ibid., no. 5, January 24, 1790, p. 225.
30. *Révolutions de France et de Brabant*, no. 30, June 21, 1790, p. 304.
31. For example, see *Journal Universel*, no. 551, May 27, 1791, pp. 8004–5.
32. Ibid., no. 358, November 14, 1790, pp. 2857–64 and *Mercure National*, no. 39, November 16, 1790, p. 1529.
33. *Ami du Peuple*, no. 193, August 16, 1790, p. 632.
34. *Révolutions de France et de Brabant*, no. 63, September 25, 1790, pp. 517–18.
35. *Ami du Peuple*, no. 362, February 5, 1791, p. 7.
36. *Journal Universel*, no. 455, February 20, 1791, pp. 3637–38.
37. *Révolutions de France et de Brabant*, no. 83, February 12, 1791, p. 211.

38. *Mercure National*, no. 12, February 15, 1791, p. 5.
39. For an extremely interesting and expansive moralization of the rectitude of home and family, see *Révolutions de Paris*, no. 83, February 12, 1791, pp. 226-35.
40. *Mercure National*, no. 14, February 22, 1791, pp. 94-105.
41. *Journal Universel*, no. 117, March 19, 1790, pp. 955-56; *Révolutions de Paris*, no. 83, February 12, 1791, pp. 226-35; and *Journal Universel*, no. 72, February 2, 1790, pp. 593-94. In this last citation, Audouin revealed not only his political prejudice against women but also a contempt for them in general. Such virulent antifeminism was rare.
42. *Révolutions de Paris*, no. 83, February 12, 1791, pp. 226-35.
43. *Mercure National*, no. 14, February 22, 1791, pp. 94-105.
44. *Journal Universel*, no. 551, May 27, 1791, pp. 8004-5.
45. *Révolutions de Paris*, no. 67, October 23, 1790, p. 78.
46. *Mercure National*, no. 24, March 19, 1791, p. 81.
47. *Ami du Peuple*, no. 271, November 4, 1790, pp. 4-5.
48. *Révolutions de Paris*, no. 1, July 17, 1789, p. 5.
49. *Journal Universel*, no. 434, January 30, 1791, p. 3470.
50. *Orateur du Peuple*, no. 38, vol. 1, n.d., p. 301.
51. *Révolutions de Paris*, no. 100, June 11, 1791, pp. 430-32.
52. *Révolutions de France et de Brabant*, no. 9, June 23, 1790, pp. 397-98.
53. Ibid., no. 1, November 28, 1789, p. 40.
54. *Révolutions de Paris*, no. 68, October 23, 1790, p. 116.
55. *Mercure National*, no. 8, April 23, 1791, pp. 113-117.
56. *Ami du Peuple*, no. 132, June 13, 1791, p. 8.
57. *Révolutions de Paris*, no. 100, June 11, 1791, pp. 430-32.
58. *Journal Universel*, no. 551, May 27, 1791, p. 8007.
59. *Révolutions de Paris*, no. 34, March 6, 1790, p. 11.
60. *Mercure National*, no. 23, May 9, 1791, pp. 353-57.
61. Regrettably for the historian, the radical journalists did not describe more expansively what nature dictated to the *peuple*, but what they have written leads to the conclusion that they were not utilitarians. The instinct of the *peuple*, so greatly valued by the radicals, did not tell the *peuple* what the greatest good was for the greatest number; rather they might learn what was natural, what nature dictated—natural law. Indeed, and this rest is speculative to be sure, the radicals were not particularly interested in satisfying the needs of the *peuple*, if such were to be placed before constructing that freedom required by natural law. Of course, the *peuple* were, in practice, the arbiters of natural law, but the journalists believed the *peuple* were merely interpreters of what nature had previously determined. Consequently, if the radicals were, indeed, advocates of natural law, then there is another kernel to add to the persistence of such theories late into the eighteenth century.
62. *Mercure National*, no. 31, October 9, 1790, p. 1097.
63. *Ami du Peuple*, no. 296, November 30, 1790, pp. 6-7. See Jacques Godechot, *The Counter-Revolution: Doctrine and Action, 1789-1804*, trans. Salvator Attanasio (New York: Howard Fertis, 1971), pp. 141-201, for the substance of these counterrevolutionary attempts.
64. *Orateur du Peuple*, vol. 3, no. 13, n.d., pp. 97-104.
65. Ibid., vol. 1, no. 3, n.d., pp. 21-23.
66. *Mercure National*, no. 42, November 26, 1790, pp. 1630-33 and *Ami du Peuple*, no. 117, May 19, 1790, pp. 5-6.
67. There were exceptions to this statement as the writers did occasionally claim that the lower clergy were conscious participants in the Revolution. For an example, see *Orateur du Peuple*, vol. 1, no. 28, n.d., pp. 209-11.
68. *Révolutions de France et de Brabant*, no. 3, December 12, 1789, p. 109.
69. *Journal Universel*, no. 16, December 8, 1789, pp. 23-24.
70. On rare occasions (see page 39) the radicals attacked the financiers for their activities in the Old Regime as *fermiers-généraux*. Generally, the journalists were silent on this issue. It would seem that the dismantling of the old financial structure had satisfied the newspapermen and the public.

71. Jean Maury was a noted royalist assemblyman.
72. *Révolutions de Paris*, no. 40, April 17, 1790, p. 118.
73. *Ami du Peuple*, no. 6, September 16, 1789, pp. 59–60.
74. *Mercure National*, no. 25, May 11, 1791, pp. 396–97.
75. See page 39.
76. *Ami du Peuple*, no. 273, November 7, 1790, pp. 1–2.
77. *Révolutions de France et de Brabant*, no. 18, March 29, 1790, pp. 135–36.
78. *Révolutions de Paris*, no. 10, September 18, 1789, pp. 20–24.
79. *Ami du Peuple*, no. 184, August 7, 1790, pp. 4–5.
80. *Orateur du Peuple*, vol. 1, no. 34, n.d., pp. 265–70.
81. While Alfred Cobban has stated (*The Social Interpretation of the French Revolution* (Cambridge: Cambridge University Press, 1965), chap. 6) that the lawyers favored the Revolution, a new study challenges this work. Lenard Berlanstein, in *The Barristers of Toulouse in the Eighteenth Century (1740–1793)* (Baltimore: Johns Hopkins University Press, 1975), chapter 6, suggests that the provincial lawyers as a group opposed the Revolution. If Berlanstein is right, then the existence of a few prorevolutionary *avocats* in the National Assembly would not have dissipated the animosity of the journalists for lawyers as a whole.
82. For an example of the rare mention of the *brigands*, see *Ami du Peuple*, no. 426, April 11, 1791, pp. 1–2. In his book *La Grande Peur de 1789* (Paris: Librairie Armand Colin, 1932), passim, Georges Lefebvre discusses the intense rural reaction to the threat of *brigands*.
83. *Mercure National*, no. 2, January 7, 1791, pp. 54–55 and *Révolutions de France et de Brabant*, no. 38, August 16, 1790, pp. 675–76.
84. *Révolutions de Paris*, no. 19, November 21, 1789, pp. 2–3. For more detail on the financiers, see John Bosher, *French Finances, 1770–1795: From Business to Bureaucracy* (Cambridge: Cambridge University Press, 1970), passim.
85. *Ami du Peuple*, no. 549, September 8, 1791, pp. 4–5.
86. *Révolutions de France et de Brabant*, no. 59, January 10, 1791, pp. 317–18 and *Révolutions de Paris*, no. 9, September 11, 1789, pp. 16–22.
87. *Mercure National*, no. 21, March 18, 1791, pp. 384–85.
88. *Journal Universel*, no. 169, May 10, 1790, p. 1350.
89. *Mercure National*, no. 11, February 11, 1791, p. 425.
90. See note 67.
91. *Révolutions de Paris*, no. 73, December 4, 1790, p. 390. See also *Journal Universel*, no. 180, May 21, 1790, p. 1440.
92. *Orateur du Peuple*, vol. 1, no. 7, n.d., p. 482. These different "orders" were based on the various tax restrictions imposed by the National Assembly on voting and office-holding.
93. *Journal Universel*, no. 443, February 8, 1791, p. 3543.
94. Robert Darnton, "The High Enlightenment and the Low-Life of Literature in Pre-Revolutionary France," *Past and Present*, no. 51 (1971), pp. 81–115.
95. Albert Soboul has already commented on this fact that the average citizen saw France in 1789 as basically divided between two groups, the rich and the poor. See Albert Soboul, "Problems of Work in the Year II," in *New Perspectives on the French Revolution*, ed. Jeffry Kaplow (New York: John Wiley and Sons, 1965), pp. 211–25.
96. See page 51.
97. Perhaps this contradiction was implicit in and inherited from the Enlightenment as Ernst Cassirer described this problem in his classic book, *The Philosophy of the Enlightenment*, trans. Fritz Koelln and James P. Pettegrove (Princeton: Princeton University Press, 1951). Also see Lionel Gossman, *French Society and Culture: Background for 18th Century Literature* (Englewood Cliffs: Prentice Hall, 1972), passim, for the role of Jansenism in this divided view of nature.
98. *Ami du Peuple*, no. 539, August 27, 1791, pp. 1–2.
99. Ibid., no. 16, September 26, 1789, p. 139.
100. *Révolutions de Paris*, no. 3, August 1, 1789, p. 10.
101. Ibid., no. 28, January 23, 1790, pp. 2–3 and ibid., no. 83, February 12, 1791, p. 211.

102. *Mercure National*, no. 37, November 9, 1790, p. 1438, and *Journal Universel*, no. 492, March 29, 1791, p. 3931.
103. *Journal Universel*, no. 226, July 6, 1790, p. 1803 and ibid., no. 492, March 29, 1791, p. 3931.
104. *Révolutions de France et de Brabant*, no. 83, July 9, 1791, p. 203.
105. *Orateur du Peuple*, vol. 2, no. 42, n.d., pp. 329-33.
106. *Révolutions de France et de Brabant*, no. 23, May 3, 1790, p. 438.
107. *Révolutions de Paris*, no. 8, September 4, 1789, pp. 2-7 and *Ami du Peuple*, no. 243, September 9, 1790, pp. 2-3.
108. *Journal Universel*, no. 537, May 13, 1791, p. 6096.
109. *Orateur du Peuple*, vol. 3, no. 58, n.d., pp. 463-66.
110. *Journal Universel*, no. 100, March 2, 1790, pp. 815-16.
111. *Orateur du Peuple*, vol. 1, no. 26, n.d., pp. 205-7.
112. *Ami du Peuple*, no. 223, September 17, 1790, p. 6.
113. *Révolutions de Paris*, no. 22, December 12, 1789, pp. 6-8.
114. Ibid., no. 63, September 25, 1790, pp. 533-38.
115. Raymond Antoine Sartine, Paul François La Vauguyon, Louis Charles Breteuil, and Charles Alexandre Calonne were all former ministers who emigrated prior to, or just after, the seizure of the Bastille and who did, in fact, work for counterrevolution. Marshall Victor François de Broglie, who followed the ministers into exile, was the commander of the troops around Paris that tried to quash this same municipal revolt of July 1789.
116. *Orateur du Peuple*, vol. 1, no. 6, n.d., pp. 44-45. For other plots, see *Mercure National*, no. 7, January 28, 1791, pp. 241-42 and *Ami du Peuple*, no. 525, August 7, 1791, pp. 3-8.
117. *Ami du Peuple*, no. 380, February 23, 1791, p. 2.
118. *Mercure National*, no. 52, December 31, 1790, pp. 2018-19.
119. *Orateur du Peuple*, vol. 5, no. 27, n.d., pp. 232-33.
120. *Journal Universel*, no. 178, May 19, 1790, p. 1420.
121. *Révolutions de Paris*, no. 8, September 4, 1790, pp. 1-7.
122. *Ami du Peuple*, no. 422, April 7, 1791, pp. 5-7.
123. For an example see *Journal Universel*, no. 64, January 25, 1790, pp. 510-11.
124. Toward the end of this period, 1789 to 1791, the radicals lost faith in the king. This lack of confidence will be discussed fully in chapter five, but for now it is only necessary to note that as the credibility of the king diminished, the radicals began to worry more about willful flight rather than abduction. Nonetheless, for most of this period, the radicals, in their concern, fretted over a forced departure by the king. The continued fear of abduction (*enlèvement*), not an escape, by even the extreme left explains how Bailly could maintain credibility with his contemporaries when he asserted that the flight of the king to Varennes (June 21-22, 1790) was an abduction.
125. *Orateur du Peuple*, vol. 2, no. 48, n.d., pp. 369-70.
126. *Révolutions de France et de Brabant*, no. 62, January 31, 1791, pp. 454-55.
127. *Ami du Peuple*, no. 106, May 18, 1790, p. 5.
128. See as well *Orateur du Peuple*, vol. 2, no. 13, n.d., pp. 97-102.
129. *Mercure National*, no. 31, May 17, 1791, pp. 481-84.
130. *Révolutions de France et de Brabant*, no. 63, February 7, 1791, pp. 544-45.
131. *Ami du Peuple*, no. 124, January 5, 1791, p. 12.
132. By this juncture in the *Ami du Peuple*, the king was under severe attack and included among the *aristocratie*.
133. Ibid., no. 350, January 24, 1791, p. 7.
134. *Mercure National*, no. 50, December 24, 1790, p. 1938.
135. *Révolutions de Paris*, no. 10, September 18, 1789, p. 10.
136. There are multitudes of examples of this wavering. On occasion the radicals expressed absolute confidence in the success of the *peuple*, while at other times they shook with disappointment. A good example of this contrast was provided by the *Mercure National*. In November 1790 (no. 41, November 23, 1790, p. 1576) this journal promised the triumphant culmination of the Revolution; but by March 1791, this

certainty had faded to the supposition that the destruction of the new regime was probable, (ibid., no. 19, March 11, 1791, pp. 297–301).

137. An initial study of this problem has already been undertaken by Eric Thompson, *Popular Sovereignty and the French Constituent Assembly, 1789–91* (Manchester: Manchester University Press, 1952), passim.

138. See the "Declaration of the Rights of Man" and the "Constitution of 1791" in John Hall Stewart, *A Documentary Survey of the French Revolution* (New York: MacMillan Co., 1951), pp. 113–15 and pp. 230–62.

139. *Mercure National*, no. 7, January 28, 1791, p. 243.

140. *Journal Universel*, no. 373, November 30, 1790, p. 2980.

141. *Révolutions de France et de Brabant*, no. 51, November 15, 1790, p. 535.

142. *Ami du Peuple*, no. 207, August 31, 1790, pp. 4–5. Although this statement by Marat surely would justify federalism, such was not his intention. He was thinking only of underlining his belief in popular sovereignty and was not considering any plan for the division of France.

143. The journalists usually estimated that from five sixths to nineteen twentieths of the populace were being eliminated from the vote, but the actual figure was much smaller—the radicals exaggerated and the officials failed to enforce this stringent regulation. In general, apathy excluded more voters than restrictions. See Leo Gershoy, *The French Revolution and Napoleon* (New York: Appleton, Century, Crofts, 1964), pp. 146–47, for details of regulation for voters, electors, and office holders.

144. For an example, see *Mercure National*, no. 48, June 3, 1791, pp. 760–61.

145. *Révolutions de France et de Brabant*, no. 60, January 17, 1790, p. 349.

146. *Ami du Peuple*, no. 110, July 1, 1790, p. 4 and *Révolutions de Paris*, no. 18, November 7, 1789, p. 19.

147. For examples of the use of the term *salut du peuple*, see *Orateur du Peuple*, vol. 2, no. 5, n.d., pp. 33–38 and *Révolutions de Paris*, no. 59, August 28, 1790, pp. 329–33.

148. *Ami du Peuple*, no. 171, July 21, 1790, pp. 6–7.

149. *Révolutions de Paris*, no. 7, August 28, 1789, pp. 6–12.

150. *Mercure National*, no. 8, June 6, 1790, p. 528, and ibid., no. 39, November 16, 1790, pp. 1494–1500.

151. Ibid., no. 16, April 12, 1790, p. 1079.

152. Ibid., no. 31, October 19, 1790, p. 1118.

153. Ibid., no. 39, November 16, 1790, p. 1529.

154. Ibid., no. 21, March 18, 1791, pp. 378–81.

155. Ibid., no. 39, November 16, 1790, pp. 1493–94.

156. Ibid., no. 23, March 24, 1791, p. 48.

157. *Journal Universel*, no. 54, January 15, 1790, p. 430.

158. Ibid., no. 358, November 14, 1790, p. 2456.

159. Ibid., no. 120, March 23, 1790, p. 980.

160. Ibid., no. 159, April 30, 1790, p. 1271.

161. Ibid., no. 61, January 22, 1790, pp. 482–87.

162. Ibid., no. 391, December 18, 1790, pp. 3124–25.

163. *Révolutions de France et de Brabant*, no. 21, April 19, 1790, p. 349.

164. Ibid., no. 5, December 26, 1789, p. 22.

165. Ibid., no. 16, March 15, 1790, pp. 97–98 and 103–6.

166. Ibid., no. 41, September 6, 1790, p. 60–61, and ibid., no. 45, October 4, 1790, p. 278.

167. Ibid., no. 3, December 12, 1789, pp. 109–11. For Desmoulins's relationship with the *lanterne*, see Pierre Labracherie, *Camille Desmoulins, grandeur et misère d'une âme ardente* (Paris: Librairie Hachette, 1948), pp. 57–66.

168. *Révolutions de Paris*, no. 74, December 11, 1790, p. 460.

169. Ibid., no. 68, October 30, 1790, pp. 113–120.

170. Ibid., no. 9, September 11, 1789, pp. 10–16 and ibid., no. 21, December 5, 1789, p. 19.

171. Ibid., no. 77, January 1, 1791, pp. 642–43.

172. Ibid., no. 67, October 23, 1790, pp. 114–15.

173. Ibid., no. 75, December 18, 1790, p. 573.

174. *Ami du Peuple*, no. 361, February 4, 1791, pp. 1–6.
175. Indeed, as early as January 1790, Marat appealed to the *peuple* to form clubs for themselves. See ibid., no. 92, January 9, 1790, pp. 4–6. One historian of Paris popular societies has asserted that Marat, because of his appeals, fathered these clubs. See Isabelle Bourdin, *Les Sociétés populaires à Paris pendant la Révolution* (Paris: Receuil Sirey, 1937), pp. 53–55.
176. There are numerous accounts of the impact of this pamphlet by Marat. An adequate summary may be found in Louis R. Gottschalk, *Jean-Paul Marat: A Study in Radicalism* (New York: Greenberg, 1927 and Chicago: University of Chicago Press, 1967), pp. 68–69. For Marat's appeals to violence see *Ami du Peuple*, no. 156, July 7, 1790, p. 8; ibid., no. 223, September 17, 1790, pp. 7–8; and ibid., no. 314, December 18, 1790, pp. 7–8.
177. *Orateur du Peuple*, vol. 2, no. 64, n.d., p. 508.
178. Ibid., vol. 5, nos. 3–6, n.d., passim.
179. Ibid., vol. 5, no. 47, n.d., pp. 395–96.
180. Ibid., vol. 5, no. 19, n.d., pp. 105–10.
181. Ibid., vol. 3, no. 6, n.d., pp. 41–43.
182. For an example, see *Révolutions de Paris*, no. 27, January 16, 1790, pp. 23–28.
183. See *Ami du Peuple*, "Third Prospectus," n.d., pp. 1–2 and *Révolutions de France et de Brabant*, no. 26, May 24, 1790, pp. 569–77.
184. In the following section, I shall discuss how the various segments of the government were limited in scope. Although I have chosen to investigate the legislature, the executive, the judiciary, and the army, the radicals themselves did not always make such distinctions. Marat occasionally questioned the need for either an executive or a judicial branch and wished to subsume both under the legislature. Generally, however, the radicals did accept the divisions of authority that I shall presently discuss.
185. *Révolutions de Paris*, no. 8, September 4, 1789, pp. 23–25 and *Ami du Peuple*, no. 53, November 21, 1789, pp. 201–2.
186. *Révolutions de Paris*, no. 9, September 11, 1789, pp. 16–22.
187. *Mercure National*, no. 18, n.d., pp. 572–75.
188. *Ami du Peuple*, no. 35, January 25, 1791, p. 4.
189. *Révolutions de Paris*, no. 56, November 6, 1790, pp. 161–70 and *Ami du Peuple*, no. 326, December 31, 1790, pp. 6–8.
190. *Révolutions de Paris*, no. 68, October 30, 1790, pp. 122–32.
191. *Journal Universel*, no. 138, April 9, 1790, pp. 1097–1104 and *Révolutions de France et de Brabant*, no. 24, May 10, 1790, pp. 479–80.
192. *Orateur du Peuple*, vol. 4, no. 21, n.d., p. 168.
193. *Révolutions de Paris*, no. 37, March 30, 1790, p. 45.
194. All except Audouin fought giving the state power of capital punishment. For examples of both attitudes, see *Journal Universel*, no. 557, June 3, 1791, p. 8050; *Révolutions de Paris*, no. 98, May 28, 1791, pp. 321–27; *Ami du Peuple*, no. 164, July 17, 1790, p. 45 and *Orateur du Peuple*, vol. 3, no. 8, n.d., p. 60.
195. For example, see *Mercure National*, no. 35, November 2, 1790, p. 1281, and *Journal Universel*, no. 11, December 4, 1789, p. 85.
196. *Révolutions de France et de Brabant*, no. 83, July 8, 1791, p. 216.
197. Ibid., no. 13, March 21, 1790, pp. 803–13 and ibid., no. 1, November 28, 1789, pp. 36–39.
198. The radicals wavered throughout 1789, 1790, and 1791 in their opinion of the monarchy. But throughout, they did profess hope that the monarchy could be saved. See, for example, *Mercure National*, no. 50, December 24, 1790, pp. 1938–39; *Révolutions de France et de Brabant*, no. 26, May 24, 1790, p. 575; and *Journal Universel*, no. 508, April 14, 1791, pp. 4063–64.
199. *Révolutions de France et de Brabant*, no. 11, September 25, 1789, passim.
200. For example, see *Ami du Peuple*, no. 501, June 25, 1791, pp. 6–8.
201. *Journal Universel*, no. 506, April 12, 1791, pp. 4043–48, and *Révolutions de France et de Brabant*, no. 7, January 9, 1790, pp. 292–95.
202. *Révolutions de Paris*, no. 37, March 30, 1790, pp. 6–7, and *Ami du Peuple*, no. 131, June 12, 1790, pp. 292–95.

203. *Ami du Peuple*, no. 278, November 12, 1790, p. 6.
204. For examples, see *Révolutions de Paris*, no. 103, July 2, 1791, pp. 604–6, or *Journal Universel*, no. 287, September 5, 1790, pp. 2285–86. Richard Cobb, *Les Armées révolutionnaires: Instrument de la Terreur dans les Départements*, 2 vols. (Paris: Mouton, 1961–63), passim, depicts a later image of the army, which was far more favorable to the radicals.
205. *Révolutions de Paris*, no. 72, November 27, 1790, pp. 336–43.
206. For examples, see ibid., no. 62, September 18, 1790, pp. 461–78, and *Journal Universel*, no. 287, September 5, 1790, pp. 2285–86.
207. The evidence for this paragraph is so overwhelming that the author must be satisfied with referring the reader to a few samples. See *Ami du Peuple*, no. 427, April 12, 1791, pp. 1–6; *Mercure National*, no. 9, February 21, 1790, pp. 568–76; and *Révolutions de Paris*, no. 12, October 2, 1789, pp. 24–26. Louis R. Gottschalk and Margaret Maddox, *Lafayette in the French Revolution through the October Days* (Chicago: The University of Chicago Press, 1969), pp. 284–307, have described in detail the National Guard of Lafayette.
208. It would be especially interesting to investigate, as well, the projected powers of the foreign affairs ministry and its ambassadors, as the radicals expected to exercise a similar veto power here as well as in other governmental affairs.
209. *Journal Universel*, no. 380, December 7, 1790, pp. 3036–37, and *Révolutions de Paris*, no. 90, April 2, 1791, pp. 581–88.
210. *Ami du Peuple*, no. 189, August 12, 1790, pp. 4–5. See Robert Forster, *The House of Saulx-Tavanes* (Baltimore: Johns Hopkins, 1971), pp. 55–108, for the pressures such a tax would have placed on a well-to-do noble.
211. *Révolutions de Paris*, no. 68, October 30, 1790, pp. 132–36.
212. For example, see *Ami du Peuple*, no. 468, May 24, 1791, pp. 6–7.
213. *Mercure National*, no. 23, May 9, 1791, pp. 353–57.
214. For example, see *Mercure National*, no. 52, December 31, 1790, pp. 2011–26.
215. For a greater discussion of the *loi agraire*, see Alphonse Aulard, *The French Revolution*, trans. Bernard Miall, vol. 1 (New York: Scribner's and Brothers, 1910), passim.
216. For an example, see *Ami du Peuple*, no. 149, June 30, 1790, pp. 1–8.
217. *Révolutions de Paris*, no. 11, September 25, 1789, p. 20.
218. Ibid., no. 69, October 2, 1790, pp. 577.
219. Grace M. Jaffé (*Le Mouvement ouvrier à Paris pendant la Révolution française, 1789–91* [Paris: Librairie Felix Alcan, n.d.,], passim.) best described the radical hostility to organizing the labor force.
220. See note 29.
221. Indeed, the radicals often openly stated their preference for the success of their political goals over their hopes for changes in the economic structure. See *Orateur du Peuple*, vol. 2, no. 44, n.d., p. 505; *Révolutions de Paris*, no. 4, August 8, 1789, p. 8; and *Journal Universel*, no. 390, December 17, 1790, pp. 3115–20.
222. See *Ami du Peuple*, no. 181, August 4, 1790, pp. 7–8. In all fairness to the radicals, it should be recalled that the unity of the *peuple* automatically defined those who would disagree as members of the *aristocratie*. Thus, the radicals would not feel compelled, in any system, to encourage diversity of opinion, although doubtless it was their extreme fear of the *aristocratie* that was responsible for all the restrictions the radicals contemplated.
223. *Révolutions de Paris*, no. 57, October 23, 1790, pp. 67–68.
224. Ibid., no. 54, July 24, 1790, pp. 73–89. For further information on revolutionary propaganda, see James A. Leith, *Media and Revolution: Moulding a New Citizenry in France during the Terror* (Toronto: Canadian Broadcasting Corporation, 1968), passim, and Cornwell B. Rogers, *The Spirit of Revolution in 1789: A Study of Public Opinion as Revealed in Political Songs and Other Popular Literature at the Beginning of the French Revolution* (Princeton: Princeton University Press, 1949), passim.
225. *Mercure National*, no. 47, December 14, 1790, p. 1814.
226. *Révolutions de France et de Brabant*, no. 61, January 24, 1791, pp. 435–36.
227. *Ami du Peuple*, no. 182, August 5, 1790, p. 6.

228. *Journal Universel*, no. 488, March 25, 1791, p. 3904.
229. *Ami du Peuple*, no. 54, July 24, 1790, pp. 73–89.
230. *Révolutions de France et de Brabant*, no. 18, March 29, 1790, p. 112.

# CHAPTER 4

1. I have defined an event for the purposes of this study to be an occurrence localized in a single place and lasting one week or less.
2. For the exact percentage of articles based on events, see tables 1, 2, and 3 of appendix B.
3. For a complete explanation of the methodology employed to select a sample and to codify and quantify the radicals' reporting, see appendix A.
4. See tables 1, 2, and 3 in appendix B. It seems necessary here to explain the range of data afforded me by the computer for this section of the study. First, I know how many articles and how many events correspond to each category of the score sheet in appendix A, and consequently I can ascertain the percentage both of articles and of reported events devoted to a certain area of interest. However, because articles and events are featured in varying length, it proved necessary to calculate the amount of newsprint given to each category. It is this last statistic that I believe to be the most significant; for the other two types of data are severely compromised by the lack of uniformity in coverage for certain articles and events. Several good examples are available. While thirty-one percent of all articles are drawn from National Assembly activity, these articles actually compose forty-one percent of the total news production. Secondly more articles are written about popular action (thirty-four percent of the total) than about civil liberties (thirty percent); but this last category received more newsprint (thirty-three percent) than the former (thirty percent). I would argue that the most significant statistic is the one that tells us the percentage of paper devoted to any category. Indeed, this account of volume gives a more accurate notion of the press's composition than merely the number of articles or events, some of which may be only short notes, practically overlooked by the writer, usually overlooked by the reader. I shall, however, be using all three sets of statistics. In appendix B, there is a selective record of the most important data. In the text, I shall be using the type of statistic that I believe to be the most accurate indicator.
5. This transformation from a nonpolitical to a political press is widely documented elsewhere. An excellent general account of this change is given in Claude Bellanger et al., *L'Histoire générale de la presse française* (Paris: Presses Universitaires de France, 1969), pp. 405–29. There is also a wealth of literature that deals specifically with this topic. Among the best books on the subject are Raymond Manevy, *La Révolution et la liberté de la presse* (Paris: Edition Estienne, 1964), and A. Söderhjelm, *Le régime de la presse pendant la Révolution française*, 2 vols. (Helsingfors and Paris: Hufvudstadsbladet, 1900–1901).
6. See table 4 of appendix B.
7. *Mercure National*, no. 6, August 15, 1791, pp. 377–80.
8. See tables 2 and 3 of appendix B.
9. See table 4, appendix B.
10. *Ami du Peuple*, no. 224, September 18, 1790, pp. 6–8.
11. *Ami du Peuple*, no. 175, August 8, 1790, pp. 1–8.
12. See tables 2 and 3, appendix B.
13. The notion of a centrist press is defined by combining Jacques Godechot's press of the moderate left and the moderate right, as he has explained it in Bellanger et al., *L'Histoire de la press française*, pp. 443–51 and 463–71. I have accepted Godechot's nominations to membership in this group, which occupied the middle ground, and have rapidly perused several of these newspapers and read closely parts of four others, *Le Journal de Paris* and *Le Mercure de France* from the moderate right and *Le Patriote Français* and *La Chronique de Paris* from the moderate left. Any conclusions about this

press must remain tentative until further intensive research has been done. While it is tempting to quantify these centrist papers as I have done the radical press, the selection of an appropriate sample would require a complete compilation and evaluation of the centrist journals. Nonetheless, the impressionistic survey that I was able to make revealed that this center did accept the Revolution. One side wished to limit the Revolution, the other wished to extend it, but both restricted their efforts to a struggle for power within the constituted bodies. My investigation reveals that it is upon this theme of capturing power through legal means that most of these journals' articles are based.

14. See tables 2 and 3 of appendix B. These two tables will be the source of the data cited throughout the rest of this section of chapter 4.

15. *Journal Universel*, no. 301, September 19, 1790, p. 2405. District activities are included as informal political activity because at this point in the Revolution the districts were granted no such powers. For more information on the role of the districts, see Georges Garrigues, *Les Districts parisiens pendant la Révolution française* (Paris: Editions Spès, n.d.).

16. *Orateur du Peuple*, vol. 2, no. 24, n.d., pp. 190–91.

17. Ibid., vol. 1, no. 57, n.d., pp. 460–62.

18. *Mercure National*, no. 4, August 1, 1790, pp. 278–81.

19. *Journal Universel*, no. 254, September 3, 1790, pp. 2031–32.

20. For an example, see ibid., no. 237, July 17, 1790, pp. 1891–92.

21. *Orateur du Peuple*, vol. 1, no. 59, n.d., pp. 479–80.

22. For more detail, see Jacques Godechot, *The Taking of the Bastille*, trans. Jean Stewart (New York: Charles Scribner and Sons, 1970).

23. For an example, see *Orateur du Peuple*, vol. 1, no. 61, n.d., pp. 495–96.

24. *Journal Universel*, no. 298, September 16, 1790, pp. 2383–84.

25. Ibid., no. 297, September 15, 1790, pp. 2375–77.

26. *Orateur du Peuple*, vol. 1, no. 43, n.d., pp. 340–42.

27. Ibid., vol. 1, no. 43, n.d., pp. 342–43.

28. *Révolutions de Paris*, no. 53, July 16, 1790, pp. 30–32.

29. *Révolutions de France et de Brabant*, no. 34, August 18, 1790, pp. 488–97.

30. *Journal Universel*, no. 254, August 3, 1790, pp. 2025–27.

31. *Orateur du Peuple*, vol. 1, no. 40, n.d., pp. 316–17.

32. *Révolutions de Paris*, no. 57, August 13, 1790, pp. 239–42.

33. In this section of the analysis, the percentages referred to are those that indicate the amount of newsprint, not the number of articles, devoted to any single category. The volume of data forces this limitation, and I have selected what I believe are the most representative statistics. Also, for the sake of simplicity, I have chosen in this study to deal with only those categories or category groups that comprise at least ten percent of the press. Using the score sheet numbers of pages 132–33, one can ascertain that these categories are numbers 6, 7–9, 10–11, 12–15, 19, 20, and 21.

34. See note 33.

35. The reason for calling an event that occupies one-quarter of the news and is carried in five papers a "dominant event" is obvious when examining tables 5 and 6 of appendix B, as only four occurrences of more than 600 conform to this standard, and the vast majority of these lesser events occupy very little space. Moreover, this concept will be more fully discussed below.

36. It may be argued that this sample includes too few events and too short a period to conclude that events do not change the pattern of attention. I agree that this objection is accurate in the long term, and events, over time, do shape the radicals' ideas. Nevertheless, the pattern of attention remains, with variations, roughly the same in the ten weeks in mid-1790 and is virtually unchanged in the spring of 1791 as the corroborative study (table 7, appendix B) shows.

37. This week, under consideration here, is not typical of all weeks; and, given the disparity among weeks, it could not be. It is, however, average in its distribution of attention among various kinds of events (see table 1, appendix B) and should serve as a good survey of the variety of newspaper stories.

38. See table 1, appendix B.
39. These percentages may seem high to the modern reader, but it must be stated that the total production of these journals was only very slight compared to a twentieth-century newspaper. Because of this severe space limitation a fairly complete explanation of an event might consume ten percent of a journal without any extraordinary desire on the journalist's part to emphasize especially this story. To devote ten percent of one's journal to an issue was not unusual or significant at this time.
40. See table 5, appendix B.
41. They worked with the Cordeliers and with each other, as chapter 1 indicates.
42. Table 5, appendix B, shows that for the four weeks where one event is covered by at least five papers and occupies over twenty-five percent of the newsprint, the average newsprint devoted to events covered in only a single journal is thirty-four percent compared to an average (in other weeks) of forty-eight percent.
43. I have demonstrated earlier in this chapter and recalled here that the pattern of interest differed little among journalists, but nonetheless, they did report on different activities within this general rubric. I have tried, in chapter 2, to indicate the direction of these private and semiprivate sectors, but these individual orientations to the news deserve a separate study of each paper and cannot be accounted for in this collective study. Some efforts have already been made among the biographers of the journalists; for an example, see Gérard Walter, *Marat* (Paris: Editions Albin Michel, 1933).
44. The trends described here are also found in the *Journal Universel* of February through April, 1791. As table 7 of appendix B reveals, the pattern of attention between the two periods in question is strikingly similar. Furthermore, the tendency to report on a wide number of incidents without any lasting special emphasis appears here. There is some concentration (of varying degrees) on the weekly activities of the National Assembly, the flight of the king's aunts, the *Journée des Poignards*, National Assembly debate on the organization of the National Guard, some ambassadorial appointments by Montmorin, and the story of popular reaction to Mirabeau's death. However, these events are covered along with 300 others. Consequently, I believe it is fair to assume, until contrary evidence can be produced, that the trends evident in mid-1790 continue throughout the entire two-year period in question here.

# CHAPTER 5

1. *Orateur du Peuple,* vol. 2, no. 55, n.d., p. 435.
2. *Révolutions de Paris,* no. 39, April 12, 1790, pp. 57–59.
3. For an example, see *Orateur du Peuple,* vol. 2, no. 55, n.d., pp. 435–37.
4. *Révolutions de France et de Brabant,* no. 26, May 24, 1790, pp. 569–77.
5. *Journal Universel,* no. 269, August 18, 1790, pp. 2148–51.
6. *Ami du Peuple,* no. 124, June 5, 1790, pp. 1–2.
7. *Orateur du Peuple,* vol. 1, no. 26, n.d., p. 202.
8. *Ami du Peuple,* no. 26, October 6, 1789, pp. 224–25.
9. *Révolutions de France et de Brabant,* no. 21, April 19, 1790, pp. 329–33 and *Journal Universel,* no. 161, May 2, 1790, p. 1284.
10. *Révolutions de Paris,* no. 14, October 17, 1789, pp. 7–9, and *Révolutions de France et de Brabant,* no. 38, April 7, 1790, p. 6.
11. *Ami du Peuple,* no. 157, July 8, 1790, pp. 7–8.
12. *Révolutions de Paris,* no. 44, May 15, 1790, pp. 320–23.
13. *Orateur du Peuple,* vol. 2, no. 22, n.d., pp. 172–73, and *Révolutions de Paris,* no. 63, September 25, 1790, pp. 533–38.
14. *Révolutions de France et de Brabant,* no. 26, May 24, 1790, pp. 569–77. For another example of Desmoulins's hostility to the ministers, see ibid., no. 29, June 14, 1790, pp. 209–10.

15. *Mercure National,* no. 30, October 15, 1790, pp. 1059–66.
16. Almost all general histories and many monographs as well detail the problems and occasional successes of the Necker ministry and its successors. While any attempt to write a complete bibliography of works that treat ministerial action and difficulties from 1789 to 1791 must be voluminous, a few books should be mentioned. In particular, one might consult: R. K. Gooch, *Parliamentary Government in France: Revolutionary Origins, 1789–91* (Ithaca: Cornell University Press, 1960), passim; Jacques Godechot, *The Counter-Revolution: Doctrine and Action, 1789–1804,* trans. Salvator Attanasio (New York: Howard Fertis, 1971), passim; and Marquise de la Tour du Pin, *Journal d'une femme de cinquante ans,* 2 vols. (Paris: Librairie Chapelot, 1919), vol. 1, pp. 199–290.
17. For an example of the popularity of Lameth in mid-1790, see *Mercure National,* no. 40, September 14, 1790, pp. 698–702.
18. See *Révolutions de Paris,* no. 72, November 27, 1790, pp. 359–61, for a sample of the initial reaction to this new ministry.
19. *Ami du Peuple,* no. 296, November 30, 1790, pp. 6–7.
20. *Révolutions de Paris,* no. 91, April 9, 1791, pp. 674–82, and *Révolutions de France et de Brabant,* no. 73, April 18, 1791, pp. 335–36.
21. *Orateur du Peuple,* vol. 3, no. 45, n.d., pp. 547–48.
22. *Mercure National,* no. 42, November 26, 1790, p. 1639.
23. *Ami du Peuple,* no. 296, November 30, 1790, pp. 6–7.
24. *Orateur du Peuple,* vol. 1, no. 54, n.d., pp. 432–36.
25. *Ami du Peuple,* no. 206, August 30, 1790, pp. 4–6.
26. Robert Darnton, "The High Enlightenment and the Low-Life of Literature in Pre-Revolutionary France," *Past and Present,* no. 51 (1971), pp. 81–115. Several studies of the events preceding the Revolution attest even more than Darnton to the importance of the queen in antiestablishment propaganda. See Alfred Cobban, *A History of Modern France,* vol. 1 (New York: George Brazillier, 1965), pp. 119–21.
27. *Révolutions de France et de Brabant,* no. 3, December 12, 1789, pp. 97–99.
28. *Révolutions de Paris,* no. 13, October 10, 1789, pp. 29–34. The king and the queen had come to Paris because they feared violent repercussions among, and the reprisals of, the crowd that had marched to Versailles to demand food. Nonetheless, all the revolutionaries, even the radicals, perceived that the royal family had come to Paris to show their good will for the Revolution.
29. *Ami du Peuple,* no. 385, February 28, 1791, pp. 4–5.
30. For examples of both spellings of the Austrian Committee, see *Révolutions de France et de Brabant,* no. 61, January 24, 1791, p. 428, and *Journal Universel,* no. 578, June 23, 1791, p. 10018. The characterization of the queen as an Austrian reveals a certain degree of French nationalism among the radicals. However, the national sentiment of the radicals was a very complex concept, and one must resist facile generalization and await a more detailed study.
31. See chapter 3, p. 52.
32. See chapter 3, p. 52.
33. *Révolutions de Paris,* no. 73, December 4, 1790, p. 390.
34. *Journal Universel,* no. 242, July 22, 1790, pp. 2932–33.
35. For examples, see ibid., no. 368, November 25, 1790, p. 2938, and *Révolutions de Paris,* no. 74, January 15, 1790, pp. 8–17.
36. *Révolutions de France et de Brabant,* no. 1, November 28, 1789, p. 9.
37. *Orateur du Peuple,* vol. 2, no. 29, n.d., pp. 153–55.
38. *Mercure National,* no. 30, October 15, 1790, pp. 1066–70. For more information on the Jacobins, see Crane Brinton, *The Jacobins: An Essay in the New History* (New York: Macmillan, 1930), passim.
39. *Orateur du Peuple,* vol. 2, no. 29, n.d., pp. 153–55.
40. *Révolutions de Paris,* no. 29, January 30, 1790, pp. 1–16.
41. *Journal Universel,* no. 536, May 12, 1791, pp. 6085–88.
42. For example, see *Mercure National,* no. 51, December 28, 1790, pp. 1973–81.
43. *Journal Universel,* no. 576, June 21, 1791, p. 10005.

44. *Révolutions de France et de Brabant,* no. 67, March 7, 1791, pp. 51–52. The *Journée des Poignards* was an episode that occurred in February 1791. While the complexity of the event precludes a detailed explanation here, on this day a large number of the Paris poor, against Cordelier advice, marched on Vincennes, where they clashed with Lafayette. Simultaneously, a group of nobles (approximately 400) were admitted to the Tuileries to defend the monarch, who was presumably threatened by this confrontation at Vincennes. The Jacobins' role on this day had been to work against the march, then defend the *peuple,* and finally to lead the attack on the admission of nobles to the royal palace.

45. The history of these developments has never been systematically compiled but is available through a number of sources, the most important of which are: Georges Garrigues, *Les Districts parisiennes pendant la Révolution française* (Paris: Editions Spès, n.d.), passim; Louis R. Gottschalk and Margaret Maddox, *Lafayette in the French Revolution through the October Days* (Chicago: University of Chicago Press, 1969), passim; L. Foubert, "L'Idée autonomiste dans les districts de Paris en 1789 et en 1790," *Révolution Française,* no. 28 (1885), pp. 141–60; Grace M. Jaffé, *Le Mouvement ouvrier à Paris pendant la Révolution française, 1789–1791* (Paris: Librairie Felix Alcan, n.d.), passim; Georges Lenôtre, *Paris in the Revolution,* trans. H. Noel Williams (London: Hutchinson and Co., n.d.), passim; and Ernest Mellié, *Les Sections de Paris pendant la Révolution française, 21 Mai 90–19 Vendemaire An IV* (Paris: Société de l'histoire de la Révolution française 1898), passim.

46. See *Ami du Peuple,* no. 18, September 28, 1789, pp. 154–55.

47. *Révolutions de Paris,* no. 11, September 25, 1789, pp. 30–34; ibid., no. 14, October 17, 1789, pp. 15–21; and ibid., no. 15, October 24, 1789, pp. 3–6.

48. *Ami du Peuple,* no. 14, September 24, 1789, pp. 121–22.

49. *Révolutions de France et de Brabant,* no. 48, October 25, 1790, pp. 390–91.

50. *Journal Universel,* no. 406, January 2, 1791, p. 3246. See also *Orateur du Peuple,* vol. 3, no. 35, n.d., pp. 275–82.

51. *Ami du Peuple,* no. 223, September 17, 1790, p. 6.

52. *Orateur du Peuple,* vol. 5, no. 19, n.d., p. 95.

53. *Journal Universel,* no. 454, February 19, 1791, p. 3632.

54. *Ami du Peuple,* no. 127, December 25, 1789, p. 5.

55. *Révolutions de France et de Brabant,* no. 83, January 2, 1790, pp. 254–57.

56. For example, see *Révolutions de Paris,* no. 12, October 2, 1789, pp. 34–39.

57. *Ami du Peuple,* no. 115, May 27, 1790, p. 4.

58. *Révolutions de France et de Brabant,* no. 32, July 5, 1790, pp. 387–88.

59. *Orateur du Peuple,* vol. 1, no. 62, n.d., pp. 497–501.

60. *Mercure National,* no. 25, September 29, 1790, pp. 895–99.

61. *Journal Universel,* no. 334, October 22, 1790, pp. 2670–72, and ibid., no. 370, November 27, 1790, p. 2956.

62. *Révolutions de Paris,* no. 70, November 13, 1790, pp. 235–38.

63. *Orateur du Peuple,* vol. 3, no. 25, n.d., p. 197.

64. *Ami du Peuple,* no. 423, April 8, 1791, p. 2.

65. *Révolutions de France et de Brabant,* no. 82, July 2, 1791, pp. 180–86.

66. *Ami du Peuple,* no. 71, December 19, 1789, p. 4.

67. *Révolutions de France et de Brabant,* no. 19, April 5, 1790, pp. 278–79.

68. Ibid., no. 8, January 16, 1790, p. 350.

69. See *Journal Universel,* no. 175, May 16, 1790, p. 1400.

70. Ibid., no. 45, January 6, 1790, p. 356.

71. *Révolutions de France et de Brabant,* no. 12, February 13, 1790, passim, and *Révolutions de Paris,* no. 29, January 30, 1790, pp. 14–16.

72. *Ami du Peuple,* no. 95, January 12, 1790, p. 5.

73. Ibid., no. 141, June 22, 1790, p. 6, is an example of this frequent attack.

74. Ibid., no. 147, June 28, 1790, pp. 1–2.

75. *Révolutions de France et de Brabant,* no. 34, August 9, 1790, pp. 616–17. As their hostility grew toward Lafayette, whose full name was Marie Joseph Motier Lafayette, the radicals increasingly referred to him as M. Motier, or M. Mottié, or several other

similar spellings. They did this partially because they believed that the abolition of noble titles should be accompanied by an abolition of the noble family name. The journalists also refused to use the name Lafayette, not for their own ideological purity, but to remind their readers of the general's background.

76. *Révolutions de Paris*, no. 56, August 7, 1790, pp. 173–85.
77. Of the many important events of the Revolution, Nancy and its aftermath have been among the most neglected. A thorough search uncovered no especial focus on these incidents. Nonetheless, an outline of the details can be found in J. M. Thompson, *The French Revolution* (Oxford: Basil Blackwell, 1943), p. 138.
78. *Orateur du Peuple*, vol. 2, no. 11, n.d., pp. 85–86, and ibid., vol. 2, no. 24, n.d., pp. 185–88.
79. *Mercure National*, no. 21, September 14, 1790, pp. 690–98.
80. *Journal Universel*, no. 334, October 22, 1790, pp. 2670–72.
81. Ibid., no. 356, November 13, 1790, p. 2848, and ibid., no. 459, February 24, 1791, pp. 3669–70.
82. *Mercure National*, no. 9, April 24, 1791, pp. 129–35.
83. *Orateur du Peuple*, vol. 5, no. 51, n.d., p. 425, and *Révolutions de France et de Brabant*, no. 74, April 25, 1791, pp. 411–42.
84. *Ami du Peuple*, no. 365, February 8, 1791, p. 3.
85. *Révolutions de Paris*, no. 51, July 3, 1790, pp. 685–93.
86. *Orateur du Peuple*, vol. 2, no. 26, n.d., pp. 201–4.
87. *Mercure National*, no. 50, December 24, 1790, pp. 1940–44.
88. For example, see *Révolutions de France et de Brabant*, no. 20, April 12, 1790, pp. 296–307, and *Ami du Peuple*, no. 165, July 16, 1790, pp. 5–7.
89. *Journal Universel*, no. 412, January 8, 1791, pp. 3291–96.
90. *Ami du Peuple*, no. 39, March 6, 1791, p. 728, and ibid., no. 428, April 13, 1791, pp. 1–8.
91. *Journal Universel*, no. 522, April 28, 1791, p. 5064.
92. For an example, see *Orateur de Peuple*, vol. 3, no. 33, n.d., pp. 252–55.
93. Unfortunately, it proved impossible to chart radical opinion of the National Guard because such opinion was composed both of the view of the general staff and of the view of the guard as a whole. To calculate, and thus chart, the meshing of these two factors proved to be fallacious, so I have consequently omitted such a graph.
94. For the general rise in the prestige of the king in 1788, one should consult Jean Egret, *La Pré-révolution française 1787-88* (Paris: Presses Universitaires de France, 1962), passim.
95. It is important to note here that this change of opinion actually occurred, with one exception, prior to the flight to Varennes, the event usually cited for the king's loss of popularity.
96. *Révolutions de Paris*, no. 13, October 10, 1789, p. 29, and ibid., no. 30, February 6, 1790, pp. 26–31.
97. *Journal Universel*, no. 78, February 8, 1790, p. 641, and *Révolutions de France et de Brabant*, no. 12, February 13, 1790, p. 560.
98. *Ami de Peuple*, no. 120, June 1, 1790, pp. 6–7.
99. *Mercure National*, no. 35, November 2, 1790, pp. 1275 and 1281.
100. *Révolutions de Paris*, no. 21, December 5, 1789, pp. 17–18.
101. *Journal Universel*, no. 75, February 5, 1790, pp. 613–14.
102. *Révolutions de Paris*, no. 30, February 6, 1790, p. 31.
103. For an example of this criticism, see *Révolutions de Paris*, no. 52, July 10, 1790, pp. 739–40.
104. This type of critique may be found in *Ami du Peuple*, no. 200, August 24, 1790, pp. 1–2.
105. Ibid., no. 180, August 3, 1790, pp. 11–12, and ibid., no. 305, December 9, 1790, pp. 5–8.
106. *Orateur du Peuple*, vol. 3, no. 66 (second issue with same number), n.d., p. 449.
107. Ibid., vol. 5, no. 44, n.d., pp. 365–68. Tarquin was a king of Rome who gained power by murdering his predecessor. After that, he instituted an absolute despotism, reinforced with a reign of terror.

108. *Mercure National,* no. 68, June 24, 1791, pp. 1070-82.
109. *Ami du Peuple,* no. 180, August 3, 1790, pp. 11-12, and ibid., no. 438, April 24, 1791, pp. 1-2.
110. Ibid., no. 497, June 22, 1791, p. 4.
111. *Journal Universel,* no. 591, July 6, 1791, pp. 11026-27, and *Révolutions de France et de Brabant,* no. 84, July 16, 1791, pp. 271-73.
112. For the reverence given to the National Assembly early in the Revolution, see Cornwell B. Rogers, *The Spirit of Revolution in 1789: A Study of Public Opinion as Revealed in Political Songs and Other Popular Literature at the Beginning of the French Revolution* (Princeton: Princeton University Press, 1949), passim.
113. For some samples of this ambiguous treatment, compare *Journal Universel,* no. 612, July 27, 1791, pp. 12089-96, with ibid., no. 649, September 2, 1791, pp. 14185-92.
114. See figure 5.5.
115. It would be useful to describe the radical opinion of the factions of the National Assembly; however, the available data far exceeds the limits of this study. A separate study is planned on Cordelier opinion of Mirabeau, Lameth and his followers, Maury, Malouet, and Robespierre and his clique.
116. *Journal Universel,* no. 161, May 2, 1790, p. 262.
117. Ibid., no. 113, March 15, 1790, p. 922.
118. *Révolutions de Paris,* no. 7, August 28, 1789, pp. 37-38.
119. A sample of this attitude may be found by checking *Orateur du Peuple,* vol. 2, no. 33, n.d., pp. 177-81; ibid., vol. 2, no. 51, n.d., pp. 401-2; and ibid., vol. 2, no. 58, n.d., pp. 457-61. These three passages strikingly reveal Fréron's wavering in his view of the National Assembly.
120. *Ami du Peuple,* no. 80, December 28, 1789, pp. 5-8; ibid., no. 91, January 7, 1790, pp. 1-8; and ibid., no. 192, August 15, 1790, pp. 5-6.
121. *Ami du Peuple,* no. 217, September 10, 1790, pp. 3-5, and ibid., no. 376, February 19, 1791, pp. 1-8.
122. Ibid., no. 513, July 7, 1791, pp. 4-5.
123. Here I shall be concerned only with those institutions and individuals where there was a shift in radical opinion. These are the Paris Municipality, Bailly, Lafayette, Louis XVI, and the National Assembly. The reason for imposing such a limit is, simply, that I am seeking to isolate the period when opinions did change. Thus, it is necessary to focus on those subjects where there was an opinion shift. Furthermore, although the radical opinion of the National Guard did alter, the guard must be excluded at this juncture because of the difficulty in placing these views in a precise time period. See also note 93.
124. The coverage given to those events and developments that must have caused this disillusionment is practically nil. While much has been written on the political history of 1789 and 1791, 1790 is usually omitted or thought of as a fairly stable period. A good example to support this statement is George Lefebvre's *The French Revolution from Its Origins to 1793,* trans. Elizabeth Evanson, vol. 1 (London: Routledge and Kegan Paul, 1962). Here, this eminent historian devotes only 9 pages out of a total 300 to the developments and the events of 1790.

# CHAPTER 6

1. There are, of course, other sources for the mentality of the radicals. One can consult, in order to modify or confirm my findings, the records of the municipality, the districts, the sections, and the clubs. Also, there are important observers, such as Hardy, who can illuminate the discussions of the cafes and the streets.
2. Robert Darnton, "The High Enlightenment and the Low-Life of Literature in Pre-Revolutionary France," *Past and Present,* no. 51 (1971), pp. 81-115.
3. Only Lebrun-Tondu, Hugou de Bassville, and Carra, all of the *Mercure National,* were not avid supporters of Robespierre. Further, while I asserted this large degree of

continuity between the Cordeliers, I have not advanced a precise statistical analysis. An accurate tabulation of this data must await a later study.

4. Albert Soboul, *The Sans-Culottes*, trans. Rémy Inglis Hall (New York: Anchor Books, 1972), passim.

5. Michael J. Sydenham, *The Girondins* (London: Athlone Press, 1960), passim.

6. Richard Cobb, *The Police and the People* (Oxford: Clarendon Press, 1970), passim.

7. George Rudé, *The Crowd in the French Revolution* (Oxford: Clarendon Press, 1959), passim. For a comparative view of the relationship between the written word and crowd action, see E. P. Thompson, "The Moral Economy of the English Crowd in the Eighteenth Century," *Past and Present* no. 50 (1971), pp. 76–136.

8. Most twentieth-century historians have interpreted the actions of the revolutionaries and of the counterrevolutionaries to be a response to certain concrete circumstances and contingencies. Of these, one should note Alphonse Aulard, *The French Revolution: A Political History,* trans. Bernard Miall, 4 vols. (New York: Scribner's and Brothers, 1910), passim; Rudé, *The Crowd in the French Revolution*, passim; Albert Soboul, *Précis d'histoire de la Révolution française* (Paris: Editions Sociales, 1962), passim; Crane Brinton, *A Decade of Revolution, 1789–99* (New York and London: Harper and Brothers, 1934), passim; Cobb, *The Police and the People,* passim; Albert Mathiez, *The French Revolution,* trans. Catherine Alison Phillips (New York: A. A. Knopf, 1928), passim; and Michael J. Sydenham, *The French Revolution* (New York: Capricorn Books, 1966), passim.

9. For two notable historians who have concentrated on the role of ideas, see Jacques Godechot, *The Counterrevolution: Doctrine and Action, 1789–1804,* trans. Salvator Attanasio (New York: Howard Fertis, 1971), passim, and Robert R. Palmer, *The Age of the Democratic Revolution: A Political History of Europe and America, 1760–1800,* 2 vols. (Princeton: Princeton University Press, 1969), passim.

10. For an outline of the endurance of the ideology of popular sovereignty, see Isser Woloch, *Jacobin Legacy: The Democratic Movement under the Directory* (Princeton: Princeton University Press, 1970), passim.

## NOTES TO APPENDIX A

1. In fact, the amount of newsprint was so great that it proved impossible to apply even this quantitative technique to the entire run of the left-wing press. Below I shall justify the sample I did take.

2. The following is a full statement of my hypotheses.

   a. In most papers published during the French Revolution, actions of the National Assembly, in particular, and those of the constituted legal bodies dominate the news; but in the radical press there is less focus on such institutions and more interest in informal political bodies.

   b. The radical revolutionaries believed that the king was manipulated by the ministers, and they focused more attention on the latter's activities than those of the monarch.

   c. The extreme left reported the plots of the *aristocrates* more than they reported their own activities.

   d. They reported the activities of the arts and of foreign governments, not because of any interest in these affairs, but only when these bodies also conformed to particular interests of the journalists.

   e. Although fiscal affairs, economics of dearth, social services, the arts, foreign affairs, ecclesiastical affairs, and peasants' interests were either important issues within the state or traditional sources of reporting, the emphasis on political affairs left these areas with very scarce coverage. Only fiscal affairs were at all closely followed and this was a function of their close relationship to the political process.

   f. The journalists' span of attention was very short although a single event might mobilize the media for short periods of time.

g.  No matter whether one event was dominant or not, the pattern of attention did not greatly shift.

h.  The *aristocrates* came, in general, from the former privileged groups and also from the "fourth" estate—the so-called dregs of society.

3.  Here I wish to define political to mean those institutions and those activities that focus on power relations within a society.

4.  Because of the differences in total page production among journals, an article of ten pages in the *Ami du Peuple*'s forty-eight sheets is clearly more important than an equivalent news account in the more voluminous (seventy-two page) *Mercure National*. Hence to simply count pages would make the interests of the larger journals more important than those of their less productive (or concise) counterparts. To compensate for these differences and place all the papers on a par, I counted the number of pages of an account as a percentage of the weekly output of their particular journal. This method of quantifying assumes equal importance for all journals. This equality is a necessary and useful assumption because of the difficulties involved in weighing the role of one journal against another. Moreover, to ensure this equality I made certain adjustments throughout this essay to compensate for the fact that some journals were weeklies and others dailies. Whatever minor distortions in understanding result from this methodological technique are more than compensated for by the benefits of generalizing about this important collection of journals.

5.  *Orateur du Peuple*, vol. 2, no. 14, n.d., pp. 111–12.

6.  *Révolutions de Paris*, no. 62, September 18, 1790, pp. 461–78.

7.  *Mercure National*, no. 4, August 1, 1790, pp. 269–72.

8.  True, more sophisticated statistical techniques could be employed to substantiate this sample; however, for the purposes of a single chapter, this moderate control appears to be a sufficient check.

# Selected Bibliography

I. Primary—Newspapers
  A. The major sources for this book were six Parisian newspapers. Of these journals I read all of every issue between the dates indicated below:

*Ami du Peuple* September 12, 1789–November 1, 1791

*Journal Universel* November 23, 1789–October 1, 1791

*Mercure National*
    *Journal d'Etat et du Citoyen* August 13, 1789–December 27, 1789
    *Mercure National ou Journal d'Etat et du Citoyen* December 31, 1789–August 30, 1790
    *Mercure National et Révolutions de l'Europe* September, 1790–March 29, 1791
    *Mercure National ou Journal Politique de l'Europe* April 17, 1791–June 30, 1791

*Orateur du Peuple* May, 1790–October, 1791

*Révolutions de France et de Brabant* November 28, 1789–December 12, 1791

*Révolutions de Paris* July 17, 1789–October 10, 1791

  B. I also read in depth the pages of the following newspapers within the following periods:

*La Chronique de Paris* August, 1789–August, 1791

*Le Journal de Paris* July, 1789–June, 1790

*Le Mercure de France* September, 1789–October, 1791

*Le Patriote Français* January, 1790–January, 1791

*Père Duchesne* August, 1790–August, 1791

*Le Point du Jour* October, 1789–August, 1791

*Révolutions de Paris* (Tournon) October 24, 1789–April, 1790

  C. I also consulted random issues of forty-two other revolutionary journals that lasted more than eighteen months from 1789 to 1791. Three were read in somewhat greater depth:

*Annales de Chimie*

*Feuille du Jour*

*Questions sur la Physique, sur l'Histoire Naturelle, et sur les Arts*

II. Primary—Printed Sources
*Archives Parlementaires.* Edited by M. J. Mavidal and M. E. Laurent, vols. 1–31. Paris: Librairie Administrative de Paul Dupont, 1879–1888.

Chaumette, Pierre Gaspard. *Papiers publiés avec une introduction par F. Braesch.* Paris: Société de l'histoire de la Révolution française, 1908.

Desmoulins, Camille. *Oeuvres, précédés d'une étude biographique et littéraire.* Edited by Jules Clarétie. 2 vols. Paris: Charpentier, 1874.

*Dictionnaire de l'Académie française.* 2 vols. Paris: Chez J. J. Smits et Cie., 1798.

Fabre d'Eglantine, Philippe. *Oeuvres choisies.* Paris: Babo-Butschert, 1824.

Lacroix, Sigismond. *Actes de la Commune de Paris pendant la Révolution.* Paris: Société Française d'Editions d'Art, 1895–1909.

La Tour du Pin, Marquise de. *Journal d'une femme de cinquante ans.* 2 vols. Paris: Librairie Chapelot, 1919.

Marat, Jean-Paul. *The Chains of Slavery.* London: 1774.

Maréchal, Sylvain. *Apologues, ré-édites.* Edited by M. Dommanget. Paris: Librairie du Travail, 1922.

Prudhomme, Louis-Marie. *Histoire générale et impartiale des erreurs, des fautes, et des crimes commis pendant la Révolution française.* Paris: 1796–97.

Robert, François. *Le Républicanisme adapté à la France.* Paris: L'Auteur, 1790.

Robert, Louise Félicité. *Collection des meilleurs ouvrages français, composés par des femmes, dédiés aux femmes françaises.* Paris: L'Auteur, 1786–9.

Sieyès, Emmanuel Joseph. *What is the Third Estate?* Translated by M. Blondel and S. E. Finer. London: Pall Mall Press, 1963.

Tournon, Antoine. *Etat historique et critique des petits abus, des grandes pensions, et des jolies erreurs de Mm. les administrateurs de l'Hôtel des Invalides.* Paris: Desenne, 1790.

III.  Secondary Sources—Three sources are central to any study of the revolutionary press. For an exhaustive bibliography one should consult Claude Bellanger, et al., *L'Histoire générale de la presse française,* vol. 1. Paris: Presses Universitaires de France, 1969. Further, a complete list of the revolutionary press, including the vital statistics (number of pages, frequency, and dates of publication, editors, and the like) of each newspaper is available by combining André Martin and Gérard Walter, *Catalogue de l'histoire de la Révolution française,* vol. 5, Paris: Editions des Bibliothèques Nationales, 1940, with *Catalogue collectif des périodiques conservés dans les bibliothèques de Paris et les bibliothèques universitaires,* 43 vols., Paris: Bibliothèque Nationale, 1940–62.

Antheunis, L. *Le Conventionnel Belge François Robert (1763–1826) et sa femme Louise de Kéralio (1758–1822).* Belgium: Editions Bracke Wetteren, 1955.

Arnaud, Raoul. *Journaliste, sans-culotte et thermidorien, le fils de Fréron, 1754–1802.* Paris: Librairie Académique Perrin et Cie., 1909.

———. *La Vie turbulente de Camille Desmoulins.* Paris: Plon, 1928.

Aspinall, Arthur. *Politics and the Press, c. 1780–1850.* London: Home and Van Thal, Ltd., 1949.

Aulard, Alphonse. "Bailly et l'affaire du Champ de Mars." *Révolution Française* 13 (1887):289–96.

———. "Danton au Club des Cordeliers et au département de Paris." *Révolution Française* 24 (1893):226–46.

———. "Danton au district des Cordeliers et à la Commune de Paris." *Révolution Française* 24 (1893):113–44.

———. "Danton en 1791 et en 1792." *Révolution Française* 24 (1893):304–44.

———. "Figures oubliées de la Révolution. Fabre d'Eglantine." *Nouvelle Revue* 35 (1885):59–86.

———. *The French Revolution: A Political History.* Translated by Bernard Miall. 4 vols. New York: Scribner's and Brothers, 1910.

———. *Histoire politique de la Révolution française.* 4 vols. Paris: Librairie Armand Colin, 1901.

———. "La Législation des clubs pendant la Révolution." *Révolution Française* 17 (1889):255–67.

———. "Le Tutoiement pendant la Révolution." *Révolution Française* 34 (1898):481–89.

Aussy, Denys d'. "Elisée Loustallot." *Revue de la Révolution* 11 (1888):113–42.

Avenel, Henri. *Histoire de la presse française depuis 1789 jusqu'à nos jours*. Paris: E. Flammarion, 1900.

Babut, E. "Une Journée au district des Cordeliers." *Revue Historique* 81 (1903):279–300.

Barthe, Claude-Michel. "Recherches sur l'opinion parisienne à la veille de la Révolution." Dissertation, Faculté des Lettres de Paris, 1955.

Bax, Ernest Belfort. *Jean-Paul Marat, the People's Friend*. London: Grant Richards, 1900.

Bellanger, Claude; Godechot, Jacques; Guiral, Pierre; Terrou, Fernand. *L'Histoire générale de la presse française*, vol. 1. Paris: Presses Universitaires de France, 1969.

Benétruy, J. "L'Atelier de Mirabeau." Dissertation, Université de Paris, 1962.

Berlanstein, Lenard R. *The Barristers of Toulouse in the Eighteenth Century (1740–1793)*. Baltimore: Johns Hopkins University Press, 1975.

*Biographie générale*. Edited by De. M. Le Hoefer. 46 vols. Paris: Firmin Didot Frères, Fils et Cie., 1862–1870.

*Biographie universelle, ancienne et moderne*. Edited by M. Michaud. 45 vols. Paris: Chez Madame L. Desplaces, 1854.

Bosher, John. *French Finances, 1770–1795: From Business to Bureaucracy*. Cambridge: Cambridge University Press, 1970.

Bougeart, Alfred. *Les Cordeliers, documents pour servir à l'histoire de la Révolution française*. Caen: Henri Delesques, 1891.

———. *Marat, l'ami du peuple*. 2 vols. Paris: A. Lacroix, Verbaeckhouen, 1865.

Bouloiseau, Marc. "Les débats parlementaires pendant la Terreur et leur diffusion." *Annales historiques de la Révolution française* 35 (1963):337–45.

———. "Aux origines des légendes contre-révolutionnaires: Robespierre vu par les journaux satiriques (1789–1791)." *Annales historiques de la Révolution française* 30 (1958):28–49.

Bourdin, Isabelle. *Les Sociétés populaires à Paris pendant la Révolution*. Paris: Recueil Sirey, 1937.

Braesch, Frédéric. "Chaumette et les *Révolutions de Paris*." *Révolution Française* 76 (1923):157–59.

———. "Nouveaux documents sur les sections et sur le Club des Cordeliers." *Révolution Française* 51 (1906):481–505.

Brinton, Crane. *A Decade of Revolution, 1789–99*. New York and London: Harper and Brothers, 1934.

———. *The Jacobins: An Essay in the New History*. New York: The MacMillan Company, 1930.

Brunet, Charles. *Marat, dit l'ami du peuple. Notice sur sa vie et ses ouvrages*. Paris: Librairie Poulet-Malassis, 1862.

Buchez, P.-J.-B. and Roux, P.-C. *Histoire parlementaire de la Révolution française ou Journal des Assemblées Nationales depuis 1789 jusqu'à 1815*. 40 vols. Paris: Parlin Librairie, 1835.

Cabanès, Augustin. *Marat inconnu. L'Homme privé*. Paris: Genonceaux, 1891.

Cardenal, L. de. "La Liberté de la presse sous la Constituante." *Cahiers de la Presse* 1 (1939): 52–80.

Carré, H. "La Presse clandestine à la fin de l'ancien régime." *Révolution Française* 26 (1894):102–127.

Cassirer, Ernst. *The Philosophy of the Enlightenment*. Translated by Fritz Koelln and James P. Pettegrove. Princeton: Princeton University Press, 1951.

Castelnau, Jacques-Thomas de. *Marat, l'ami du peuple, 1744–1793*. Paris: Hachette, 1939.

*Catalogue collectif des périodiques conservés dans les bibliothèques de Paris et les bibliothèques universitaires*. 43 vols. Paris: Bibliothèque Nationale, 1940–62.

Catterall, Ralph. "The Credibility of Marat." *American Historical Review* 16 (1910):24–35.

Charrier, Jules. *Claude Fauchet, Evêque constitutionnel du Calvados*. 2 vols. Paris: Champion, 1909.

Chevremont, François. *Jean-Paul Marat, orné de son portrait.* 2 vols. Paris: Chez L'Auteur, 1880.

———. *Marat, index du bibliophile et de l'amateur de peintures, gravures, etc.* Paris: L'Auteur, 1880.

Chomsky, Noam. *Language and Mind.* New York: Harcourt Brace and World, Inc., 1968.

Chuquet, A. "La Jeunesse de Camille Desmoulins." *Annales Révolutionnaires* 1 (1908):1–26.

———. "La Jeunesse de Chaumette." *Revue critique d'histoire et de littérature* (1909), 1–26.

Clarétie, Jules. *Camille Desmoulins, Lucile Desmoulins, étude sur les Dantonistes d'après des documents nouveaux et inédits.* Paris: Plon, 1875.

———. "Fabre d'Eglantine à la Comédie Française." *Révolution Française* 33 (1897):385–404.

Clouse, Georges. "La Presse de la Marne pendant la Révolution." Dissertation, Université de Paris, 1971.

Cobb, Richard. *Les Armées révolutionnaires: Instrument de la Terreur dans les Départements.* 2 vols. Paris: Mouton, 1961–63.

———. *The Police and the People.* Oxford: Clarendon Press, 1970.

Cobban, Alfred. *A History of Modern France,* vol. 1. New York: George Brazillier, 1965.

———. *The Social Interpretation of the French Revolution.* Cambridge: Cambridge University Press, 1965.

Compton, Piers. *Camille Desmoulins: a Revolutionary Study.* London: E. Partridge, 1933.

Cordier, Stéphane. *Jean-Paul Marat.* Brussels: A. de Roche, 1967.

Daline, V. M. "Babeuf et Marat en 1789–1790." *Annales historiques de la Révolution française* 30, no. 150 (1958):16–17.

Darnton, Robert. "The High Enlightenment and the Low-Life of Literature in Pre-Revolutionary France." *Past and Present,* no. 51 (1971), pp. 81–115.

———. *Mesmerism and the End of the Enlightenment in France.* Cambridge: Harvard University Press, 1968.

———. "Reading, Writing, and Publishing in Eighteenth Century France: A Case Study in the Sociology of Literature." *Daedalus* 100 (1970):214–56.

———. "In Search of the Enlightenment. Recent Attempts to Create a Social History of Ideas." *Journal of Modern History* 43 (1971):113–32.

Deschiens, F. *Collection des materiaux pour l'histoire de la Révolution de France depuis 1789 jusqu'à ce jour: Bibliographie des journaux.* Paris: Barrois, L'Aîné, 1829.

*Dictionnaire de biographie française.* Edited by J. Balteau, M. Barroux, and M. Prévost. 13 vols. Paris: Librairie Letouzey et Ané, 1933–73.

Dommanget, Maurice. *Sylvain Maréchal, l'egalitaire, "l'homme-sans-Dieu," 1750–1803. Vie et oeuvre de l'auteur du "Manifeste des Egaux."* Paris: R. Lefeuvre, 1950.

Dowd, David. "Art as National Propaganda in the French Revolution." *Public Opinion Quarterly* 15 (1951):532–46.

Edelstein, Melvin A. "'La Feuille Villageoise,' Communication and Rural Modernization in the French Revolution." Dissertation, Princeton University, 1965.

———. "'La Feuille Villageoise.' The Revolutionary Press, and the Question of Rural Political Participation." *French Historical Studies* 7 (1971):175–204.

Egret, Jean. *La Pré-révolution française, 1787–88.* Paris: Presses Universitaires de France, 1962.

Espezel, Pierre d'. *Le Palais-Royal.* Paris: Calmann-Lévy, 1936.

Fajn, Max. "Le Journal des Hommes Libres." Dissertation, University of Chicago, 1971.

Farge, René. "Le Local du Club des Cordeliers et le coeur de Marat." *Annales historiques de la Révolution française* 4 (1927):320–47.

Fleury, Edouard. *Etudes révolutionnaires; Camille Desmoulins et Roch Marcandier. La presse révolutionnaire.* 2 vols. Paris: Didier, 1851.

Fleury, Jules. *Histoire de la caricature sous la République, L'Empire, et la Restauration.* Paris: E. Dentu, 1877.

Forster, Robert. *The House of Saulx-Tavanes.* Baltimore: Johns Hopkins, 1971.

Foubert, L. "L'Idée autonomiste dans les districts de Paris en 1789 et en 1790." *Révolution Française* 28 (1885):141–60.

Fournel, Victor. "Fabre d'Eglantine, le comédien, l'auteur dramatique et le révolutionnaire." *Revue des questions historiques* 54 (1893):145–215.

Furet, François et al. *Livre et société dans la France du XVIIIe siècle.* 2 vols. Paris: Mouton et Cie., 1965–1971.

Fusil, C.-A. *Sylvain Maréchal ou l'homme sans Dieu.* Paris: Plon, 1936.

Gabriel-Robinet, Louis. *Histoire de la presse.* Paris: Hachette, 1960.

———. *Journaux et journalistes hier et aujourd'hui.* Paris: Hachette, 1962.

Gaffarel, P. *François Robert, ses travaux scientifiques, son rôle politique, son rôle artistique.* Dijon: Darantière, 1889.

Galambos, Louis. "Research Technique: Content Analysis Described and Debated." In *Public Image of Big Business in America, 1880–1940: A Quantitative Study in Social Change.* Baltimore: Johns Hopkins University Press, 1975.

Gallois, Léonard. *Histoire des journaux et des journalistes de la Révolution française, 1789–1796.* 2 vols. Paris: Au Bureau de la Société de l'industrie fraternelle, 1845–46.

Ganiage, J. "Etude de quatre journaux contrerévolutionnaires." Dissertation, Université de Paris, 1944.

Garrigues, Georges. *Les Districts parisiens pendant la Révolution française.* Paris: Editions Spès, n.d.

Gauthier, Pierre. "Maitre Sonthonax 'anticoloniste.'" *Visages de l'Ain* 80 (1965):38–43.

Gershoy, Leo. *The French Revolution and Napoleon.* New York: Appleton, Century, Crofts, 1964.

Gilchrist, John T. and Murray, William J. *The Press in the French Revolution.* New York: St. Martins Press, 1971.

Gillispie, Charles. "The Encyclopédie and the Jacobin Philosophy of Science." In *Critical Problems in the History of Science.* Edited by Marshall Clogett. Madison: University of Wisconsin, 1959.

Godart, F. *Camille Desmoulins, d'après ses oeuvres.* Paris: 1889.

Godechot, Jacques. *The Counter-Revolution: Doctrine and Action, 1789–1804.* Translated by Salvator Attanasio. New York: Howard Fertis, 1971.

———. "Index bibliographique, 1956–1958." *Etudes de Presse* 10 (1958):248–303.

———. *The Taking of the Bastille, July 14, 1789.* Translated by Jean Stewart. New York: Charles Scribner and Sons, 1970.

Gooch, R. K. *Parliamentary Government in France: Revolutionary Origins, 1789–91.* Ithaca: Cornell University Press, 1960.

Gossman, Lionel. *French Society and Culture: Background for 18th Century Literature.* Englewood Cliffs: Prentice Hall, 1972.

Gottschalk, Louis R. *Jean-Paul Marat: A Study in Radicalism.* New York: Greenberg, 1927 and Chicago: University of Chicago Press, 1967.

———. "Marat dans la journée du 14 juillet 1789," *Révolution Française* 76 (1923):13–18.

———, and Maddox, Margaret. *Lafayette in the French Revolution through the October Days.* Chicago: University of Chicago Press, 1969.

Goubert, Pierre. "The French Peasantry of the Seventeenth Century: A Regional Example." In *Crisis in Europe, 1500–1660.* Edited by Trevor Aston. New York: Basic Books, 1965.

Graham, Hugh Davis. *Crisis in Print.* Nashville: Vanderbilt Univerity Press, 1967.

*Grande encyclopédie, La.* 31 vols. Paris: H. Lamiraut et Cie., n.d. (c. 1890).

Greenlaw, Ralph. "Pamphlet Literature in France during the Period of the Aristocratic Revolt (1787–1788)." *Journal of Modern History* 29 (1957):349–54.

Greppo, Francisque. "Un Lyonnais, imprimeur et journaliste. Le journal: *Les Révolutions de Paris.*" *Revue Lyonnais,* fifth series, 29 (1900):42–59.

Guillaune, James. "Le Vandalisme de Chaumette." *Révolution Française* 32 (1897):385-402.

Hampson, Norman. *A Social History of the French Revolution.* London: Routledge and Kegan Paul, 1953, and Toronto: University of Toronto Press, 1963.

Hartcup, John. *Love is Revolution: the Story of Camille Desmoulins.* New York: Staples Press, 1950.

Hatin, Eugène. *Bibliographie historique et critique de la presse périodique française.* Paris: Librairie de Firmin Didot Frères, Fils et Cie., 1866.

————. *Histoire du journal en France.* Paris: Havard, 1846.

————. *Histoire politique et littéraire de la presse en France.* 8 vols. Paris: Poulet-Malassis et de Broise, 1859-61.

Héritier, Louis. "Jean-Paul Marat avant 1789." *Revue Socialiste* 22 (1895):436-50.

Hughon, Marius. *Journals and Periodicals published in France and Other Countries during the Revolution and Napoleonic Period.* Versailles: M. A. Hughon and Co., n.d.

Hyslop, Beatrice. *French Nationalism in 1789 According to the General Cahiers.* New York: Columbia University Press, 1934.

Isambert, Gustave. *La Vie à Paris pendant une année de la Révolution (1791-1792).* Paris: F. Alcan, 1896.

Jacob, Louis. *Fabre d'Eglantine, chef des fripons.* Paris: Librarie Hachette, 1946.

Jaffé, Grace M. *Le Mouvement ouvrier à Paris pendant la Révolution française, 1789-91.* Paris: Librairie Felix Alcan, n.d.

Jaurès, Jean. *Histoire socialiste de la Révolution française.* 6 vols. Paris: Editions Sociales, 1968.

Kennedy, Michael. "The Development of a Political Radical, Jean-Louis Carra, 1742-87." In *Proceedings: Western Society for French History.* Edited by Brison Gooch. Dallas: WSFH, forthcoming.

Kulstein, David I. "The Ideas of Charles-Joseph Pankoucke, Publisher of the *Moniteur Universel* in the French Revolution." *French Historical Studies* 4 (1966):304-19.

Laborie, P. "Le Patriote Français." Dissertation, Université de Toulouse, 1961.

Labracherie, Pierre. *Camille Desmoulins, grandeur et misère d'une âme ardente.* Paris: Librairie Hachette, 1948.

————. "A Travers l'histoire de la presse aux Archives Nationales." *Etudes de Presse* 5, no. 6 (1953):41-45.

La Farge, Anatole de. "La Liberté de la presse pendant la Révolution française." *Révolution Française* 1 (1881):41-52.

Lalain, P. de. *L'Imprimerie et la librairie à Paris de 1789 à 1813.* Paris, 1899.

Lanfranchi, M. "Le Régime de la presse sous la Révolution." Dissertation, Université de Paris, 1908.

Laurens, A. "*Les Actes des Apôtres,* journal contre-révolutionnaire." Dissertation, Université de Toulouse, 1963.

Laurent, Gérard M. *Le Commissaire Sonthonax à Saint-Domingue.* Port-au-Prince: Imprimerie la Phalange, 1965.

Laurent, Jules. *La Liberté de la presse.* Paris: Editions Nouvelles, 1955.

Ledré, Charles. *Histoire de la presse.* Paris: Fayard, 1958.

Lefebvre, Georges. *The Coming of the French Revolution.* Translated by Robert R. Palmer. New York: Vintage Books, 1947.

————. *The French Revolution from its Origins to 1793.* Translated by Elizabeth Evanson. Vol. 1. London: Routledge and Kegan Paul, 1962.

————. *La Grande Peur de 1789.* Paris: Librairie Armand Colin, 1932.

Legg, L. G. W. *Documents Illustrative of the History of the French Revolution: The Constituent Assembly.* Oxford: Clarendon Press, 1905.

Leith, James A. *Media and Revolution: Moulding A New Citizenry in France during the Terror.* Toronto: Canadian Broadcasting Corporation Publications, 1968.

Lenôtre, Georges. *Paris in the Revolution.* Translated by H. Noel Williams. London: Hutchinson and Co., n.d.

Le Poitevin, G. *La Liberté de la presse depuis la Révolution (1789-1815).* Paris: A. Rousseau, 1901.

Lescure, Mathurin. *Correspondance secrète inédite sur Louis XVI, Marie Antoinette, la cour et la ville, 1777–92*. Paris: H. Plon, 1866.

"Liste des D. E. S. d'histoire concernant l'histoire de la presse, 1941–1957." *Etudes de Presse* 11 (1959):190–193.

Livois, René de. *Histoire de la presse française*. 2 vols. Paris: Librairie Arthème Fayard, 1965.

McDonald, Joan. *Rousseau and the French Revolution, 1762–91*. London: Anthlone Press, 1965.

McLuhan, Marshall, and Fiore, Quentin. *The Medium is the Massage*. New York: Bantam Books, 1967.

McManners, John J. *French Ecclesiastical Society under the Ancien Regime*. Manchester: Manchester University Press, 1960.

Madelin, Louis. *Danton*. Translated by Mary Loyd. London: William Heinemann, 1921.

Manevy, Raymond. *La Presse française, de Renaudot à Rochefort*. Paris: Foret, 1958.

———. *La Révolution et la liberté de la presse*. Paris: Editions Estienne, 1964.

Martin, Gaston. *J.-P. Marat, l'oeil et l'ami du peuple*. Paris: Rieder, 1938.

Martin, Gérard. *L'Imprimerie*. Paris: Presses Universitaires de France, 1963.

Massin, Jean. "Marat, un intellectuel de gauche du XVIII siècle." *Nouvelle Critique*, n.s., 1, no. 182 (1967):13–16.

Mathiez, Albert. "Chaumette et les fabrications de guerre." *Annales Révolutionnaires* 14 (1922):511.

———. "Chaumette, franc-maçon." *Révolution Française* 43 (1902):121–41.

———. *Le Club des Cordeliers pendant la crise de Varennes et le massacre du Champ de Mars*. Paris: Librairie Ancienne H. Champion, 1910.

———. *The French Revolution*. Translated by Catherine Alison Phillips. New York: A. A. Knopf, 1928.

———. "Marat, père des sociétés fraternelles." *Annales revolutionnaires* 1 (1908):661–64.

Matrat, Jean. *Camille Desmoulins*. Paris: Editions J. A. R., 1956.

Mazédier, R. *Histoire de la presse parisienne, de Théophraste Renaudot à la IVe République, 1631–1941*. Paris: Editions du Pavois, 1945.

Mellié, Ernest. *Les Sections de Paris pendant la Révolution française, 21 mai 90–19 Vendemaire An IV* Paris: Société de l'histoire de la Révolution française, 1898.

Mermet, A. *La Presse, l'affichage et la colportage*. Paris: Marpon et Flammarion, 1881.

Merrill, John C. *The Elite Press, Great Newspapers of the World*. New York: Pitman Publishing Corp., 1968.

Methley, Violet. *Camille Desmoulins*. London: Martin Secker, 1914.

Michelet, Jules. *History of the French Revolution*. Vol. 4. Translated by Keith Botsford. Wynnewood: Livingston Publishing Co., 1972.

Michon, G. *Le Rôle de la presse en 1791–1792, la Déclaration de Pillnitz et la guerre*. Paris: TEPA, 1941.

Monseignat, Charles de. *Un Chapitre de la Révolution française, ou histoire des journaux en France de 1789 à 1799*. Paris: Librairie Hachette, 1853.

Morton, J. B. *Camille Desmoulins and Other Studies of the French Revolution*. London: Weiner Laurie, 1950.

Muffraggi, François. "'Les Annales monarchiques.' Contributions à l'histoire de la presse de la Révolution." Dissertation, Universite de Paris, 1949.

Murray, William J. "The Right-Wing Press in the French Revolution, 1789–1792." Dissertation, Australian National University, 1971.

Nigay, Gilbert. "Les Inventaires, répertoires, et catalogues des périodiques." *Revue Historique* 239 (1968):123–32

Palmer, Robert R. *The Age of the Democratic Revolution: A Political History of Europe and America, 1760–1800*. 2 vols. Princeton: Princeton University Press, 1969.

Parker, Harold T. *The Cult of Antiquity and the French Revolutionaries*. Chicago: University of Chicago Press, 1937.

Patrick, Alison. "Political Divisions in the French National Convention, 1792–93." *Journal of Modern History* 41 (1967):421–74.

Pegg, Carl Hamilton. "Sentiments républicains dans la presse parisienne à partir du retour de Louis XVI jusqu'au rapport des sept comités." *Annales historiques de la Révolution française* 13 (1936):342–56.

Pellet, Marcellin. *Elisée Loustallot et les "Révolutions de Paris."* Paris: Armand Le Chevalier, 1872.

Pilon, Edmund. "Fabre d'Eglantine." *Revue d'Art dramatique* (1903), 141–57.

Rader, Daniel L. "The Breton Association and the Press: Propaganda for Legal Resistance before the July Revolution." *French Historical Studies* 2 (1961):64–82.

Raphael, Paul. "Panckoucke et son programme de journal officiel." *Révolution Française* 64 (1913):216–19.

Reber, Charles. *Un Homme cherche la liberté.* Boudry-Neuchâtel: Baconnière, 1949.

Regnard, A. "Chaumette et la Commune de 93." *Revue Socialiste* 11 (1890), 68–86.

Robinet, Jean. "Danton et le Club des Cordeliers en 1791." *Révolution Française* 17 (1889):130–59.

Robiquet, Jean. *Daily Life in the French Revolution.* Translated by James Kirkup. London: Weidenfield and Nicholson, 1964.

Rogers, Cornwell, B. *The Spirit of Revolution in 1789: A Study of Public Opinon as Revealed in Political Songs and Other Popular Literature at the Beginning of the French Revolution.* Princeton: Princeton University Press, 1949.

Rouff, Marcel. "Le personnel des premières émeutes de 1789." *Révolution Française* 57 (1909):212–59.

———. "Le peuple ouvrier de Paris aux journées du 30 juin et du 30 août 1789." *Révolution Française* 63 (1912): 430–54 and 481–505.

Rudé, George. *The Crowd in the French Revolution.* Oxford: Clarendon Press, 1959.

———. *Paris and London in the Eighteenth Century: Studies in Popular Protest.* New York: The Viking Press, 1971.

Rufas, Marcel. "Les Origines sociales de Fabre d'Eglantine." *Annales historiques de la Révolution française* 32, no. 161 (1960):294–300.

Sabatier, François. "Etude de la 'Feuille Villageoise.'" Dissertation, Université de Montpellier, 1963.

Sainte-Vinebault, M. *La Presse sous l'Assemblée constituante: un procès de Marat.* Paris: 1898.

Salmon, Lucy Maynard. *The Newspaper and Historian.* New York: Oxford University Press, 1923.

Sciout, M. "La Révolution à Saint-Domingue. Les Commissaires Sonthonax et Polveral." *Revue des questions historiques* 64 (1898):399–470.

Scott, Samuel. "Problems of Law and Order during 1790, the Peaceful Year." *American Historical Review* 80 (1975):859–88.

Shafer, Boyd C. "Bourgeois Nationalism in the Pamphlets on the Eve of the French Revolution." *Journal of Modern History* 10 (1938):31–50.

———. "Pamphlet Literature on the Eve of the Revolution." Dissertation, University of Iowa, 1932.

Soboul, Albert. *The Parisian Sans-Culottes and the French Revolution.* Translated by Gwynne Lewis. London: Oxford University Press, 1964.

———. *Précis d'histoire de la Révolution française.* Paris: Editions Sociales, 1962.

———. "Problems of Work in the Year II." In *New Perspectives on the French Revolution.* Edited by Jeffry Kaplow. New York: John Wiley and Sons, 1965.

———. *The Sans Culottes.* Translated by Rémy Inglis Hall. New York: Anchor Books, 1972.

———. *Les Sans-culottes parisiens en l'an II.* La Roche-sur-Yon: Henri Patier, 1958.

Söderhjelm, Alma. *Le Régime de la presse pendant la Révolution française.* 2 vols. Helsingfors and Paris: Hufvudstadsbladet, 1900–1901.

Stewart, John Hall. *A Documentary Survey of the French Revolution.* New York: MacMillan Co., 1951.

Sydenham, Michael J. *The French Revolution.* New York: Capricorn Books, 1966.

———: *The Girondins.* New York: Athlone Press, 1960.

———: "The Montagnards and Their Opponents: Some Considerations on a Recent Reassessment of the Conflicts in the French National Convention, 1792–93." *Journal of Modern History* 43 (1971):287–93.

Tarlé, E. "La Classe ouvrière et le parti contre-révolutionnaire sous la Constituante." *Révolution Française* 57 (1909):304–26.

Terroine, A. "L'Oeuvre bibliographique de M. G. Walter." *Annales historiques de la Révolution française* 20 (1948):1–26.

Thiers, M. A. *History of the French Revolution.* 4 vols. Translated by Frederick Shoberl. Philadelphia: Carey and Hart, 1842.

Thompson, E. P. "The Moral Economy of the English Crowd in the Eighteenth Century." *Past and Present,* no. 50 (1971), pp. 76–136.

Thompson, Eric. *Popular Sovereignty and the French Constituent Assembly, 1789–91.* Manchester: Manchester University Press, 1952.

Thompson, J. M. *The French Revolution.* London: Hazell, Watson, and Viney, Ltd., 1943 (paperback edition, Oxford: Basil Blackwell).

Tourneux, Maurice. *Bibliographie de l'histoire de Paris pendant la Révolution.* 5 vols. Paris: Ville de Paris, 1890–1913.

———. "Le Régime de la presse de 1789 à l'an VIII." *Révolution Française* 28 (1893):193–214.

Trévedy, J. *Fréron et sa famille.* Saint-Brieuc: 1889.

Vandershueren, Bernadette. "Les premières années du *Journal Général de l'Europe.*" *La Vie Wallonne* 34 (1960):245–82.

Varin d'Ainvelle, Madeleine. *La Presse en France, genèse et évolution de ses fonctions psychosociales.* Paris: Presses Universitaires de France, 1965.

Villacèque, Georges. "*Les Révolutions de Paris.*" Dissertation, Université de Toulouse, 1961.

Voyenne, Bernard. *Guide bibliographique de la presse.* Paris: Centre de Formation des Journalistes, 1958.

Walter, Gérard. *Marat.* Paris: Editions Albin Michel, 1933.

———. *Répertoire de l'histoire de la Révolution française.* 2 vols. Paris: Bibliothèque Nationale, 1941.

———. *La Révolution française vue par ses journaux.* Paris: Flammarion, 1948.

Walter, Gérard, and Martin, André. *Catalogue de l'histoire de la Révolution française.* 5 vols. Paris: Editions des Bibliothèques Nationales, 1940.

Weill, Georges. *Le Journal: origines, évolution, et rôle de la presse periodique.* Paris: Renaissance du Livre, 1934.

———. "Les Récents Travaux sur l'histoire de la presse." *Revue historique, économique, et sociale* (1932), 241–51.

Woloch, Isser. *Jacobin Legacy: The Democratic Movement under the Directory.* Princeton: Princeton University Press, 1970.

# Index

179

*THE JOHNS HOPKINS UNIVERSITY PRESS*

*This book was composed in Times Roman text and
display type by Jones Composition Company, Inc. from a design
by Patrick Turner. It was printed on 50 lb. Cream White Bookmark
paper and bound by Thomson-Shore, Inc.*

**Library of Congress Cataloging in Publication Data**

Censer, Jack Richard.
   Prelude to power.

   Bibliography: p. 169
   Includes index.
   1. France—History—Revolution, 1789-1799—
Journalists. 2. France—History—Revolution, 1791-1792.
3. Press—France. I. Title.
DC 158.8.C4      074'.36      76-7968
ISBN 0-8018-1816-8